THE COMPLETE STEP-BY-STEP GUIDE TO MAKING
SWEETS, CANDY & CHOCOLATES

THE COMPLETE STEP-BY-STEP GUIDE TO MAKING
SWEETS, CANDY & CHOCOLATES

150 irresistible confectionery recipes shown in over 750 exquisite photographs

sweets, candies, toffees, caramels, fudges, candied fruits, nut brittles, nougats, marzipan, marshmallows, taffies, lollipops, truffles and chocolate confections

CLAIRE PTAK

LORENZ BOOKS

This edition is published by Lorenz Books,
an imprint of Anness Publishing Ltd,
Blaby Road, Wigston, Leicestershire LE18 4SE

info@anness.com

www.lorenzbooks.com;
www.annesspublishing.com

If you like the images in this book and would like to investigate
using them for publishing, promotions or advertising,
please visit our website www.practicalpictures.com for
more information.

A CIP catalogue record for this book is available from the
British Library.

Publisher: Joanna Lorenz
Senior Editor: Lucy Doncaster
Editor: Kate Eddison
Copy Editor: Catherine Best
Photographer: Nicki Dowey
Food Stylist: Claire Ptak
Food Stylist's Assistants: Kate McCullough and
    Adriana Nascimento
Prop Stylists: Wei Tang and Marianne de Vries
Designer: Nigel Partridge
Production Controller: Pirong Wang

PUBLISHER'S NOTE
Although the advice and information in this book are believed
to be accurate and true at the time of going to press, neither
the authors nor the publisher can accept any legal
responsibility or liability for any errors or omissions that may
have been made nor for any inaccuracies nor for any loss,
harm or injury that comes about from following instructions
or advice in this book.

NOTES
Bracketed terms are intended for American readers.
For all recipes, quantities are given in both metric and imperial
measures and, where appropriate, in standard cups and
spoons. Follow one set of measures, but not a mixture,
because they are not interchangeable.
• Standard spoon and cup measures are level. 1 tsp = 5ml,
1 tbsp = 15ml, 1 cup = 250ml/8fl oz.
• Australian standard tablespoons are 20ml. Australian readers
should use 3 tsp in place of 1 tbsp for measuring small quantities.
• American pints are 16fl oz/2 cups. American readers should
use 20fl oz/2.5 cups in place of 1 pint when measuring liquids.
• Electric oven temperatures in this book are for conventional
ovens. When using a fan oven, the temperature will probably
need to be reduced by about 10–20°C/20–40°F. Since ovens
vary, you should check with your manufacturer's instruction
book for guidance.
• The nutritional analysis given for each recipe is calculated per
portion (i.e. serving or item), unless otherwise stated. If the
recipe gives a range, such as Serves 4–6, then the nutritional
analysis will be for the smaller portion size, i.e. 6 servings.
The analysis does not include optional ingredients, such as salt
added to taste.
• Medium (US large) eggs are used unless otherwise stated.

Some of the recipes in this book previously appeared in
The Home-Made Sweet Shop (published by Aquamarine).

CONTENTS

THE STORY OF SWEETS AND CHOCOLATES

CONFECTIONERY HAS A SURPRISINGLY LONG HISTORY, DATING BACK THOUSANDS OF YEARS. FROM THE EARLIEST USE OF HONEY TO THE DISCOVERY OF SUGAR CANE, AND FROM THE ANCIENT PREPARATION OF THE CACAO SEED INTO A BITTER CHOCOLATE DRINK, THROUGH TO THE STUNNING CREATIONS OF ARTISAN CHOCOLATIERS, THIS CHAPTER TRACES THE LANDMARKS IN SWEET- AND CHOCOLATE-MAKING THAT HAVE SHAPED THE WORLD'S LOVE FOR ALL THINGS SWEET.

THE HISTORY OF SUGAR AND SWEETS

In every corner of the world, people delight in buying, making and sharing sweet treats – both for special occasions and as more everyday indulgences. Offered as small tokens of appreciation to old friends or used as an introduction to new ones, sweets can put smiles on tearful faces, reward children and soothe broken hearts. In every case, the offerings clearly demonstrate the power of sweets to transform situations and bring pleasure.

Sugar is the central ingredient in sweet-making (candy-making), and it is available in a multitude of forms: from honey to malted grains, from fruit juices to dried fruits, and from cane sugar to syrup tapped from trees.

Honey: the first sweetener

Sweeteners have been used throughout human history to enhance the flavour of foods and, in some cases, for medicinal purposes. The first of these was honey, a natural sugar that is the product of wild bees. The practice of honey-harvesting can be traced back many thousands of years, as is demonstrated by a cave painting in Spain that dates from at least 10,000 years ago. This painting shows a determined man collecting honeycombs from a hole in a cliff wall, as wild bees circle round his head.

One of honey's first uses was probably in mead, a fermented drink of honey and water, which is said to have inspired poets, politicians and priests, among others. This drink was offered to the gods in ancient Egypt; they believed

Below: This 14th-century Italian vellum from the Tacuinum Sanitatis *shows beehives as part of medieval life.*

Above: Honey appears in texts as old as the Bible as a sweet offering. This oil on canvas painting, Samson Offering His Parents a Honeycomb, *by Guercino (Giovanni Francesco Barbieri) (1591–1666) depicts Samson sharing honeycomb with his parents.*

that bees were formed from the teardrops of Ra, the Sun God, and honey was his gift to mankind. Used as currency to pay taxes, honey clearly had commercial value; pots of the precious golden liquid were found buried with the pharaohs, and hives were found in the Sun Temple. Bees made an appearance in hieroglyphs during the 3rd and 4th centuries BC, which is around the time people first began to domesticate them. We know that by 2500BC, Egyptians were making moulded confections using honey.

The ancient cultures of Babylon, Assyria, Persia, India, Greece and Rome all domesticated bees, but not every landscape provided the floral banquet the bees needed to thrive. In order to overcome this, hives were moved by camel, mule or cart to better locations. An alternative mode of transport was also used by the Greeks, Romans, and even 19th-century English beekeepers, who created floating beehives. Loading the hives on to rafts or schooners, they drifted with them

upstream or downriver, allowing the bees to take advantage of more verdant pastures during the day, then return to the hives at night.

Other evidence of the uses of honey includes earthenware colanders from the Neolithic period, which have been discovered in what is now Switzerland. These are similar to utensils employed by present-day inhabitants of the Alps to strain honey, forging a link between past and present.

Today, honey remains extremely popular around the world, although with bees under threat from Colony Collapse Disorder it is becoming increasingly precious. Bee-keeping has seen a resurgence in recent years, and honey is frequently used as a natural remedy for all kinds of minor ailments, from easing sore throats and tickly coughs to soothing burns and cuts. It is also widely used in cooking, adding both sweetness and flavour to all manner of dishes, from cakes and confections to savoury food.

Besides honey, other unrefined sugar sources include maple syrup and maple sugar, palm sugar, birch syrup, gur, panela date sugar, agave nectar, fresh fruit and berries, and malted grains. These are most commonly used in the countries where the ingredients grow, but with the globalization of different cuisines they are becoming increasingly popular throughout the world.

BIBLICAL IMPORTANCE

There are frequent mentions of honey in the Bible, such as the Promised Land being described as 'flowing with milk and honey', which gives some indication of honey's value. Luke also reported that Christ was fed a honeycomb on the day he rose from the dead.

Sugar: sweetest of all

Despite honey's widespread appeal and value, it was sugar that would become one of the world's most prized ingredients. Originating in Polynesia around 5,000 years ago, sugar cane was transported to the coastal regions of India, but remained a well-kept secret for many thousands of years. In 510BC, however, Emperor Darius of Persia invaded India and discovered that the people there were harvesting an even sweeter crop than honey, one he would call 'the reed which gives honey without bees.' Local people had, like the Polynesians, developed a method for extracting the sweet sap from the cane. They had been using it for centuries in food preparation, including the making of confections similar to nougat and marzipan. The emperor returned to Persia bearing his sweet spoils, and sugar replaced honey there as the sweetener of choice.

The spread of sugar continued in the 4th century AD, when Alexander the Great encountered the canes in western Asia. Having awakened a hunger for the product in ancient Greece and then Rome, trading routes were established and sugar was imported as both a luxury and a medicinal commodity. The invasion of Persia by

Below: This oil painting, Sellers of Sugar Cane, Egypt *(1892), by David Bates shows the sugar cane trade in North Africa.*

the Arabs in the 8th century AD further increased the spread of the sweetener, when the Arabs established sugar cane production along the route of their conquests, which included North Africa, Sicily, Spain and the south of France.

Despite its appearance in so many regions of the world, sugar production remained limited, and during the Middle Ages it was extremely expensive and hard to obtain. Determined to increase the production of such a prized crop, the Spanish and Portuguese in particular determined to find new places in which to cultivate it. With such a goal in mind, Christopher Columbus brought sugar cane cuttings with him to San Domingo in 1493, on his second voyage to the New World. This tropical island in the Caribbean Sea proved to have the perfect climate and soil conditions in which to grow the crop.

Reports of this success soon spread and the West Indies were rapidly colonized by Europeans, becoming the centre of sugar production in the world. Determined to cash in on the industry, British, French and Dutch farmers started growing the canes in Brazil, Cuba, Mexico and the West Indies. They relied initially on local labour, but later, on slaves from Africa. By the late 18th century, refined cane sugar had superseded honey as the sweetener of choice and, with the popularization

Above: This early 20th-century sepia photograph captures barrels of molasses, a by-product of the sugar-making process, being loaded in the West India Docks in London. By this time, sugar-making was a hugely profitable industry and slavery had been abolished.

of the confections that could now be made, it grew into such a lucrative industry that the product was dubbed 'white gold.'

Sugar made from cane continued to hold sway in Europe until the Napoleonic wars in 1793–1815. During this period, blockades prevented imports from the plantations, and farmers turned instead to sugar beet, an indigenous crop from which a German scientist called Andreas Marggraf had succeeded in extracting sugar in 1747. Being very well suited to the cooler European climate, sugar beet was easy to grow and this, coupled with the abolition of slavery on the plantations (pushing the cost of labour up considerably), led to the dominance of sugar derived from beet by 1880. The difficulties of importing cane sugar during World War I further enhanced the viability of sugar from home-grown sugar beet, and its production and refinement soon became major industries. Today, about 20 per cent of the world's sugar supply comes from sugar beets.

Above: Sugar cane grows in hot, tropical climates and accounts for about 80 per cent of the world's sugar supplies.

From cane or beet to sugar

Refining sugar cane is a complicated, multi-step process. The tough, fibrous canes are first crushed to extract the raw syrup, which is then boiled. After the syrup crystallizes, it goes through a centrifuge, where it separates into dark brown raw sugar and molasses. The raw sugar is then either further refined to produce white granulated, caster (superfine) or icing (confectioners') sugar, or flavoured with added molasses and sold as light muscovado (brown), soft brown or demerara (raw) sugar. All of these have distinctive textures and flavours, and are used to make a range of different foods. Sugar beets are refined in a similar manner, although they only produce white sugar.

Confections made with sugar

The earliest confections were probably honey-coated nuts, seeds or berries. A halva-like snack made with sesame seeds was eaten as long ago as 3000BC, and versions made with semolina, nuts and dried fruits were made by the ancient cultures of China, the Middle East and the Mediterranean. Eventually, sugar replaced the honey, and egg whites were added to the concoction, resulting in nougats. There were many variations of nougat, but in most cases

they were available only to the wealthy and served only for special occasions. Today, nearly every region of the world has its own version of nougat. In Iran, *gaz nougaz* contains pistachios and is flavoured with rose water. A Chinese version contains peanuts and may come wrapped in edible rice paper. Nougat is called *torrone* in Italy and *turrón* in Spain. Both are usually made with almonds. The Australian version of *turrón* contains macadamias.

By the first century AD, sweets may also have been used as digestifs at the end of a large meal or banquet, and by AD700, disguising the unpleasant taste of medicines with a sweet flavouring or coating was common practice. Whether shaped into lozenges or fashioned into sticks, over time these digestive aids owed much of their potency to sugar. As Mary Poppins famously said, 'A spoonful of sugar helps the medicine go down in a most delightful way', and tablets are still coated in a sugary shell today.

Marzipan, a mouldable sugar-and-almond paste confection first made in Egypt, came to prominence in Europe in the 13th century. An ornamental 'sotelty' scene, sculpted from coloured almond paste, was often served at medieval feasts to honour the accomplishments of the host or commemorate a special occasion. Now frequently hand-crafted into fruit and vegetable shapes, marzipan still fulfils a decorative function as well as being a tasty treat.

By the Renaissance, sugar was more accessible and sweet-making had become an art form. Centrepieces were crafted in the design of churches and castles, sometimes gilded with real gold leaf. Candied fruit peel and even whole candied fruit delighted both courtiers and the common man. Fresh citrus peel cooked in a sugar syrup then smothered in sugar remains a popular treat today. The French glaze their freshest fruits in a process that can take a week, but the results are so good, they are known as *les fruits nobles*.

Another type of confectionery found in many cultures is a jelly made from fruit juices or purées, or flavoured with

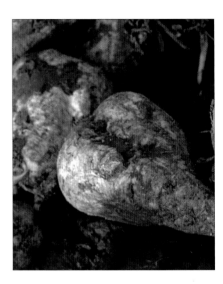

Above: Sugar beet is a tuber that thrives in cooler climates. It accounts for about 20 per cent of sugar produced.

fruit and flower essences. Turkish Delights were first made in Turkey in the 15th century, and were popularized in Britain in the 19th century. An Eastern European version made with quince is called *kotonjata*. In Spain, *membrillo* is the quince paste commonly served with cheese. Today, along with jelly beans, gum drops and other similar concoctions, these light treats are the essence of sweetness.

Home-made confections

Before sweet shops, cinema candy counters and the commercially produced confections available today, people made sweets at home.

Perhaps as a reaction to the highly commercialized world of the 21st century, more and more people are increasingly intrigued by do-it-yourself possibilities, and this extends to making sweets (and other foods) at home. These can either be devoured with relish or given as a gift that is infinitely more thoughtful than anything made in a factory. There are few greater pleasures in life than receiving a selection of confections artfully presented in a box or decorative container tied with satiny ribbon or strips of fabric, and the effort required to make them is a great expression of love and affection.

New traditions from old

Anyone craving childhood sweets that no longer appear in stores can find satisfaction in home-made confections that reproduce old favourites. With a few basic tools and some practice, every cook can produce a surprising range of delectable treats, reviving traditions and hopefully instilling the next generation with a sense of heritage. In fairy tales it takes a conjurer to change one substance into another one, but in the kitchen, that alchemy occurs every time sugar and water are put on to boil, and a syrupy-sweet transformation takes place. Although making confections at home can be challenging, it can also be one of the most magical and satisfying of activities.

The science of candymaking

Sweet-making is both a science and an art. It can be approached as an exciting chemical experiment, or it can be indulged in simply with a love for traditional methods and products. When making a recipe for the first time, it is important to allow adequate time, as the processes involved often require patience and cannot be rushed. Like baking, it is a great Sunday afternoon project to do with family or friends (provided they are not too distracting) or a good hobby to tackle when you have two or three uninterrupted hours at your disposal.

Below: Sugar can be coloured and shaped into an endless variety of products, such as traditional striped British rock.

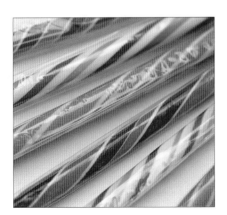

SWEETS AND THE ARTS

Sugary treats have appeared in literature, music, song and dance for many centuries. George Herbert (1593–1633) provides an early written reference to sugar cane: 'Lovely enchanting language, sugar-cane, Honey of roses, wither wilt thou fly?', and the word 'sweets' is used by both John Milton and Shakespeare. On the stage, one of the most famous manifestations of confectionery is *The Nutcracker* ballet. The music, written in Russia in 1891 by Tchaikovsky from a story by E. T. A. Hoffmann, describes young Clara's dream visit to the Kingdom of Sweets. She and her prince (transformed into a man from a toy nutcracker) encounter the Sugar Plum Fairy, who wears a crown of sugar and a skirt of candy floss. Her retinue includes dancers delectably costumed as candy canes, bonbons, taffy clowns, marzipan shepherds and shepherdesses, ribbon candy and chocolate. For any child with a tutu and a sweet tooth, the experience is irresistible.

More recently, both the book and film of *Charlie and the Chocolate Factory* elevated author Roald Dahl's much-loved story to iconic stature, with its depiction of gum-chewing bad girls and cocky little cowboys. Set in a whimsical confectionery cosmos where the river flows with chocolate and everything is edible, the tale of Charlie Bucket and the golden ticket is both a tempting and a cautionary one for sweet- and chocolate-lovers. The Oompa Loompas' anthems encourage moderation ('If you're not greedy, you will go far'), but everything else about Willy Wonka's world is lusciously extravagant.

Sweets and sweet shops play a similarly memorable role in the Harry Potter books and films, with 'Honeydukes' selling a spectacular range of magical treats, including 'Fizzing Whizbees', which make the consumer float, and 'Bertie Bott's Every Flavour Beans', whose flavours range from apple and raspberry to salt, sand and sardine.

Crystal sugar is solid at room temperature. To make sweets, the sugar is heated and dissolved. As the water evaporates, a chemical reaction takes place, while the heat breaks the

Below: Different varieties of sugar will all yield different results in sweet-making – certain types are suited to specific recipes.

crystals apart. Continued cooking brings them back together as a syrup. The texture changes as the mixture is cooked for longer, and the sugar syrup becomes further reduced.

The result of the process depends on the length of time the syrup is cooked for and on how much water evaporates in the process. Sugar can be combined with a large quantity of water to make a simple syrup that can be flavoured with fruit zest and drizzled on a cake; it can be cooked down to a chewy, soft caramel; or cooked further to produce a hard toffee. Further cooking will result in a hard-boiled sweet, such as rock, hard candy, lollipops or lemon drops. A sugar thermometer, essential for sweet-making, is clipped to the inside of the cooking pan to indicate when the syrup has reached the exact temperature required for the particular confection being made.

Left: A candy store in a historically preserved US gold-rush town sells traditional treats.

The art of sweet-making

Although it sounds obvious, the key to successful sweet-making lies in following a recipe properly. Recipes should be read through completely from beginning to end, before you even consider buying any ingredients. Having ensured you have everything you need, including the right tools, the basic directions should be followed exactly.

FAIRTRADE AND ORGANIC

As people become increasingly aware of the plight of farmers around the world, and as concern about climate change increases, organic and fairtrade ingredients are gaining in popularity. First appearing in the mid-1990s, fairtrade supports farmers in developing countries and helps them to access better terms of trading in global markets. The additional money gained can be used for schools, infrastructure and community development. Organic farming practices mean better welfare for the workers, less damage to the environment, and a healthier product for the consumer. Organic sugar is less refined than conventional sugar and therefore retains slightly more nutrients.

Having mastered the simplest version of a confection, you can then get creative and experiment with flavourings.

The old saying, 'A watched pot never boils', suggests that time will pass more quickly if you take your mind off your work by doing something else. This folk wisdom should not be applied to sweet-making, where watchfulness at every phase of the process is a necessity.

All tools should be to hand, spotlessly clean and dry, and ready for use at a moment's notice. All ingredients should be measured out in advance so they can be added as soon as the syrup reaches the appropriate stage. Tins (pans) and moulds should be oiled or buttered and lined as required by the recipe, so that confections can be transferred to them at precisely the right moment.

Allow the sugar to dissolve in the water slowly at a moderate temperature. Once it has dissolved, the temperature can be raised until the mixture comes to a boil and reaches the desired stage. In the process, sugar crystals may form on the sides of the pan. These should never be scraped back into the mixture, as they may cause the syrup to crystallize. Instead, dampen a clean pastry brush (used only for this purpose) with hot water and brush the sides of the pan where the crystals have formed. The crystals will melt, at which point they can be mixed back into the syrup.

Expect a disappointment or two along the line. Even professional chefs have disasters, but failures are as important as successes, since they provide learning opportunities. Ingredients are expensive, so discovering what works and what does not is vital. Learning what not to do is part of becoming a good sweet-maker.

If a recipe just is not working, it is worth checking that you are using the correct tools. Heavy copper pans really are best for cooking with sugar, and if the pan you are using is too thin, or heat is unevenly distributed, then this will affect the chemistry of the sugar and not produce the exact result required. It is also important to use the correct form of sugar, as the crystalline structures of each type do vary.

From penny sweets to prestigious confectioneries

Sweet shops have a special place in the hearts and minds of people the world over, and the words 'penny sweet' or 'penny candy' (though they are no longer quite so inexpensive) still bring to mind a delightful picture. From old-fashioned stores selling salt-water taffy, candy floss or rock in seaside villages, to modern urban outlets such as Dylan's Candy Bar in New York City, which claims to offer 5,000 kinds of candy, the sights and smells can tempt even the most disciplined dieter.

When you are young and enter a sweet shop glimmering with lollipops, jelly babies, humbugs and toffees, the possibilities seem awe-inspiring, and this experience can be as exciting for adults as it is for children. Succumbing to nostalgia, you may choose a timeless classic, such as a Sherbet Fountain, or you may decide to please your adult palate with nougat or candied fruit.

Sweets remain popular today and, in addition to the big manufacturers, there are now many retro stores, both on-line and in cities and towns. At home, sweet-making is seeing a comeback, with people wanting to relearn age-old skills.

SWEETS FOR FESTIVALS AND CELEBRATIONS

All around the world, holidays and confections go hand-in-hand. Often these sweet treats are only made and eaten during the specific festival, which makes them extra special.

Independence Day, 4th July (USA)

Marshmallows: A traditional summertime treat in the United States, especially on July 4, Independence Day, plump marshmallows are pierced with a long stick and roasted over an open fire until they are golden-brown.

Halloween, 31st October (USA & UK)

Caramel apples/toffee apples: Though some fruits were dipped in sugar syrups or honey to preserve them, caramel- or toffee-enrobed apples appear to have developed as a mid-20th century treat. They are eaten most often in the autumn, when the sugary coatings enhance the taste of freshly harvested apples, and they are served on a stick for easier eating.

Dias de los Muertos (Days of the Dead), 1st and 2nd November (Mexico)

Sugar skulls: The tradition of honouring family members who have passed away remains an important cultural holiday for Mexican families. *Dias de los Muertos* is celebrated on 1st and 2nd November with many special foods, including skull-shaped candies made in moulds then festooned with icing (frosting), feathers, and coloured foil. The skulls are placed on home or public altars with photos and other memorabilia of lost loved ones.

Bonfire Night, 5th November (UK)

Bonfire toffee/treacle toffee: Each year on 5th November, the UK celebrates the foiling of a 1603 plot to blow up the Houses of Parliament and overthrow King James I. That night, bonfires were lit throughout London to honour the king, and the tradition continues to this day with fireworks – and toffee! Bonfire toffee is made with black treacle (molasses) and has a rich flavour. It is especially popular in northern England.

Christmas, 25th December

Candy canes: The origin of these colourful treats dates back four hundred years to white sugar sticks. A century later, they began to be distributed at Christmastime in Germany, and other countries, as they still are today. Red and white stripes and mint flavouring were added around 1900.
Fudge: Invented in the USA, fudge is especially popular at Christmas. Sugar syrup is combined with milk or cream and butter, which can also be flavoured.
Panforte: Originating in 13th-century Siena, this spicy treat was historically made only at Christmas, but is now enjoyed all year. It is made from fruits, nuts, spices, honey, golden (light corn) syrup and a little flour.

Easter, March or April

For centuries eggs have been associated with this Christian holiday. The egg symolizes new life and rebirth. The modern custom of giving chocolate eggs has joined an old tradition of decorating hen's eggs. Easter egg hunts are a popular activity.

Above: American families get together to toast marshmallows over campfires during Independence Day celebrations.

Above: Halloween traditions include coating seasonal apples in delicious, sticky, toffee or caramel – a firm favourite with children.

Above: A Christmas tree would not be complete without festive red-and-white-striped candy canes adorning its branches.

THE HISTORY OF CHOCOLATE

First used in ancient sacred rituals, chocolate has undergone several transitions over the centuries and remains an important part of many celebrations today. Believed by the Mesoamericans to be a gift from the gods, chocolate has always been held in high regard, being used as a currency, an elixir, a nutritional aid and in love potions, and there is little doubt about its ability to lift the spirits. It remains one of the world's favourite confections.

There are many different types of chocolate available on the market today, from bitter couverture and bars with a high cocoa percentage to creamier, mellower versions. These have various flavouring qualities and melting properties that govern how each particular type should be used.

The origin of chocolate in Mesoamerica

The earliest evidence of the existence of the cacao seed, the primary ingredient in chocolate, has been traced back thousands of years to the Amazon region, where it was part of the diet of successive Mesoamerican civilizations, including the Olmec, Mayan, Toltec and Aztec peoples who lived in what is now the area between central Mexico and Nicaragua. The low-growing cacao trees flourished as wild plants in the rain forest, but may have been cultivated as

Below: This velum, Mexican Indian Preparing Chocolate, *from the Codex Tuleda, 1553, shows cocoa's long history.*

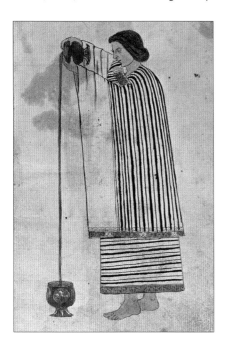

early as 600BC. Myth has it that the seeds of *quachahuatl*, which produce the cacao tree, were a gift to the Toltec people from Quetzalcoatl, the feathered serpent creator god also known as the 'good god of the garden'.

The sweet pulp may have been the first part of the plant to be eaten, then when wild yeasts in the air converted the sugars in the pulp to alcohol, this fermented version of cacao was drunk with water as a kind of chocolate beer. The pods themselves served as cups.

The seeds, too, changed in the fermenting process, developing a deep, dark, bitter flavour. When they were roasted, they gave off an appealing scent that provided inspiration once again. Ground in a mortar (*metate*), the roasted seeds were mixed with vanilla, pepper and spices to make *xocotlatl* or 'bitter water', the cold and frothy forerunner of the modern drink, hot chocolate.

Whatever its genesis, the cacao plant was an important talisman. It signified power and rank, and was available to only the loftiest members of the tribes. It was used in religious ceremonies as a divine offering. Drawings on pottery from the period show chocolate being drunk by kings and gods. It was said to have medicinal and aphrodisiacal benefits. The Aztecs levied a cacao tax on conquered people, and used the humble bean as currency.

Europeans discover chocolate

Cacao beans also exchanged hands along the extensive Mesoamerican trade routes. However, the pleasures and benefits of the plant were unknown in Europe until Christopher Columbus brought some of the New World beans to the Spanish Court in 1502 as souvenirs of his expedition to the territory near Honduras.

The beans paled in comparison to the other treasures he had plundered, and were for the most part ignored.

*Above: The Encounter Between Hernando Cortés and Montezuma II (*Le Costume Ancien et Moderne, *by Jules Ferrario).*

This changed in 1512, when the Aztec king Montezuma II offered a chocolate drink to the Spanish conquistador Hernan Cortés, whom Montezuma believed to be the reincarnation of Quetzalcoatl. Cortés' subsequent treatment of the Indians was anything but godly, however, as he conquered them and claimed their treasured cacao beans for himself and for Spain. Intrigued by the bracing effect the cacao drink had on his soldiers, Cortés commented that it was a "divine drink which builds up resistance and fights fatigue. A cup of this precious drink permits a man to walk for a whole day without food".

Having returned to Spain with corn, chilli peppers, vanilla, tomatoes, potatoes and a store of cacao seeds, however, Cortés discovered that the Spanish court found the fortifying chocolate drink too astringent. The addition of sugar and vanilla to the ground roasted beans soon resolved this problem and it became very popular, although its consumption was limited to royalty because of its scarcity and the complicated techniques required to process it. In fact, the Spanish nobility kept the bounty to themselves for some one hundred years, until a 17th-century Italian trader brought cacao beans home from his travels to Spain and the West Indies. A chocolate drink called 'bavaresia' was created, and the tradition of Italian chocolate-making was born with its centre in Turin.

From Italy, chocolate fever spread to England, France, Germany, Austria, Switzerland and the Netherlands. A new European passion for the flavourful hot drink – one that intensified the already strong craving for sugar – took hold, and the first cocoa-growing colonies were established in Ceylon (British; now Sri Lanka), the West Indies (French), and Venezuela, Java and Sumatra (Dutch).

The chocolate revolution

Until the Industrial Revolution began in 1765, chocolate was produced by hand and enjoyed only as a beverage. The introduction of new machinery and improved techniques, however, made mass production of chocolate possible in Britain and then across the rest of Europe. This lowered costs, and meant that the general public could finally afford a delicacy that previously had been reserved for only the very wealthy.

Many of the names of the men who transformed the chocolate industry and started prominent businesses are still familiar today. Among them was Conrad Van Houten, a Dutch chemist, who

created the first cocoa press in 1815, and who patented a process and a machine that improved the way cocoa butter was separated from chocolate liquor. Not stopping there, he added alkali to the resulting cocoa so that it would mix more easily, creating a method called 'Dutching', which produces darker, milder-flavoured cocoa, and cocoa butter as a by-product. This discovery was to prove vital to the genesis of the solid chocolate bar, and in 1847 Joseph Fry, an English Quaker, discovered a way to blend cocoa butter with sugar into a paste

Above: Bournville, depicted here in 1931, was built by John Cadbury in the UK as somewhere for his workers to live.

and form it into a bar that could be eaten without being cooked or mixed with water. This astounding invention led to great success for his business and Fry's company was one of the major manufacturers of chocolate until it merged with Cadbury in the early 20th century.

Meanwhile in Birmingham, John Cadbury, another Quaker and grocer, also started to experiment with roasting and grinding beans to produce chocolate. In 1868, the company became the first to sell boxed chocolates, which were presented in packages decorated with sentimental Victorian illustrations. The company grew and prospered, and in 1879 it moved to the Birmingham suburb of Bournville, where it built a factory and a model village for its workers. "The idea," according to Cadbury's great-great-granddaughter Felicity Loudon, "was nobody should ever work or live where a rose cannot grow." Today, Cadbury (now owned by the American company Kraft) is the world's biggest confectionery producer.

CHOCOLATE AS LOVE MEDICINE

Why did Montezuma drink chocolate before visiting his harem? What made Casanova sip cocoa every day? Why do sweet shops sell millions and millions of chocolate hearts every year on Valentine's Day? Why, for so many men, women and children all around the world, does chocolate mean love?

The vaguely heart-shaped cacao bean may have been the original inspiration. Pre-Columbian Indians ground it and used it as an elixir to cure everything from scorpion bites to bronchitis, and when the love bug bit, chocolate would have been the natural remedy. In modern times, among the many recognized benefits of cocoa is its ability to reduce heart disease.

Artfully decorated boxes of chocolate bonbons appeared in the late 19th century, and their appeal was immediate. Once the confection had been eaten, the boxes were often saved for storing love letters.

The other major British maker of the time was Rowntree, another family of Quaker grocers, whose products competed with those of Fry and Cadbury until they were bought by Nestlé in 1988.

Despite the existence of these major British producers, it was Switzerland that dominated the chocolate industry throughout the 19th century. The Swiss reputation as premier chocolatiers owes a debt to a trio of its inventive citizens. These were Henri Nestlé, who found a way to condense milk in 1867; Daniel Peter, with whom Nestlé worked to combine the sweetened condensed milk with chocolate and make the first milk chocolate bar; and Rudolf Lindt, who in 1879 invented the conching machine, which grinds and smooths the chocolate liquor, sugar and milk.

In the United States, Milton Hershey was a caramel manufacturer who had already had two failed candy businesses. On an 1893 visit to the World's Columbian Exhibition in Chicago, he was so impressed with German chocolate-making machinery on display that he decided then and there to change

Above: Cacao pods are fruits that contain cocoa beans, which must be extracted and dried out.

Above: Once processed, cocoa beans produce cocoa butter, chocolate mass and cocoa powder.

course once again. "Caramels are only a fad," he is reported to have said. "Chocolate is a permanent thing." He located his Pennsylvania factory close to the dairies that would supply milk for his milk chocolate confection. Like John

Cadbury, he built a model town nearby for his employees. During both world wars, Hershey's produced chocolate ration bars for American soldiers, making more than a billion of them during WWII. The Hershey Company is today the leading North American manufacturer of chocolate confectionery.

The process of making chocolate

Making chocolate is labour-intensive. Cacao trees produce their first crops three to five years after being planted. Harvested twice a year, ripe cacao pods range in colour from red to green, yellow and purple. Harvesters use machetes or sharp knives to hack the pods from the trees and cut them open, revealing the seeds encased in a sweet white pulp. Both seeds and pulp are scooped out and are usually left to ferment for a period of about a week, generally at or near the cacao farm.

Wild yeasts in the air convert the sugars in the pulp to alcohol, breaking the seeds down, activating enzymes and helping to develop the flavour. The highest quality chocolate is always made from properly fermented beans. The seeds must then be dried, usually on racks in the sun. Cacao brokers or, increasingly, artisan chocolate

FAIRTRADE-CERTIFIED CHOCOLATE

Cacao is time-consuming to produce and difficult to process and, early on in the chocolate rush, unscrupulous cost-cutters resorted to slave labour to produce this profitable crop for export. Chocolate pioneers Joseph Fry, John Cadbury, Joseph Rowntree and Milton Hershey in the United States strove to end the practice, but with limited success.

The vexing truth is that, even today, the tradition of coerced labour for chocolate production has not totally disappeared. Most cacao is grown and harvested by hand on small farms operated by farming families in traditional ways, some of them accessible only by donkey or other pack animal. Often, the farms are part of a larger farming estate, and several middlemen may be involved in the operation. Growers often receive low prices for their crops,

and some worrying reports show that children are still being used to work on the plantations.

Fairtrade-certified chocolate tries to address these issues by helping farming families improve the quality of their lives. Certification demands humane practices and prohibits slave labour. The price paid for cacao is guaranteed to be sufficient to meet basic human needs and to allow farmers to invest in their communities, and production methods on the farms must be environmentally sustainable.

A handful of artisan chocolatiers are now Fairtrade-certified and the number is expected to continue to grow as demand increases. In 2009, Cadbury's Dairy Milk, the company's largest and most popular brand, became Fairtrade-certified – the first mass-market chocolate to do so.

company buyers, select and purchase single-estate beans or mixes of beans, which are bagged and shipped to chocolate companies throughout the world.

Having reached the factories, seeds are roasted, then shelled and winnowed to separate out the nibs, which are the essence of chocolate. The nibs are crushed into chocolate mass or liquor (a paste that contains no alcohol), and additional pressure is applied to separate out the cocoa butter. The remaining solids are pulverized into cocoa powder.

Manufacturers combine chocolate liquor, cocoa butter and cocoa powder in various ways along with sugar and/or milk to create different kinds of chocolate. The mixture is then smoothed by rotating blades in a process called conching, which removes moisture and volatile acids. The last step is to temper the chocolate to the desired consistency, texture and glossiness.

Artisan chocolates

Despite the huge range of mass-market, commercially produced chocolate bars available there is a growing interest in artisan products, made by an innovative generation of chocolatiers who treat chocolate production as an art form. Of course, this is really nothing new. Before chocolate companies became international conglomerates, chocolate was always made by hand in small quantities. Today, artisan chocolate manufacturers are once again creating unique types of chocolate and chocolate confections in small batches, often using antique equipment found discarded in warehouses. They craft chocolate in the same way that a knowledgeable vintner crafts a fine wine, or a passionate coffee roaster creates a unique blend – with attention to detail, respect for the ingredients and a search for something special.

Bean-to-bar artisan chocolatiers are alert to cacao's sensitivities and possibilities, and create their product guided by taste and talent and, in some cases, by a heightened dedication to the sustainability of the land and forests where the cacao is farmed, and concern for the people who grow and harvest it. These chocolate makers select the highest quality cacao beans themselves, often from a single region, estate or co-operative to guarantee the consistency and flavour. They roast their own beans, refine their own chocolate liquor, conch and temper their own chocolate and make their own chocolate bars.

The popularity of this type of chocolate has grown in recent years, and artisan companies selling high-quality chocolate at premium prices now exist throughout the world. From the Chocolate Valley of Tuscany (such as Amadei) to the Rogue River Valley of Oregon (such as Dagoba Organic), dedicated chocolate makers are building on the traditions of old to create new ones of their own. This success has not escaped the attention of large international producers who are branching into artisan-like production themselves or buying up small artisan companies and adding them to their own roster of businesses.

Below: Chocolatiers today produce vast arrays of high-quality confections, some of which can be extremely expensive.

Home-made chocolates

With so many chocolate companies and so many unique and delicious chocolate products being made today, why make chocolates at home? Admittedly, it is a bit of a challenge. Attention to timing and temperature can mean the difference between a successful confection and a failure. Good-quality (and sometimes expensive) ingredients are also essential, and it is vital that recipes are followed very carefully.

The primary motivating factor is the satisfaction that is to be gained from creating perfect chocolate confections that taste infinitely better than any store-bought variety. A home-made plate of chocolate truffles flavoured with praline filling or scented with jasmine tea makes a statement that even the fanciest box of store-bought chocolate confections cannot.

Filling your kitchen with the irresistible smell of cooking chocolate, learning what works and what does not work, beginning to notice the chemistry of change, and, finally, tasting the fruits of your labour is definitely worth the time and money. In the words of Milton Hershey, "Chocolate is a permanent thing", and goes on giving pleasure to people of all ages around the world.

MAKING SWEETS AND CHOCOLATES

THIS CHAPTER GIVES ALL THE TECHNICAL INFORMATION
EVERY SWEET-MAKER NEEDS UP HIS OR HER SLEEVE.
MAKING CONFECTIONERY SUCCESSFULLY REQUIRES
ATTENTION TO EXACT (OFTEN TINY) QUANTITIES OF
SPECIFIC INGREDIENTS, AS WELL AS USING THE RIGHT
EQUIPMENT FOR PERFECT RESULTS. IN THIS SECTION
YOU WILL FIND ADVICE ON TOOLS AND EQUIPMENT,
A DETAILED GUIDE TO INGREDIENTS AND A COMPREHENSIVE
DIRECTORY OF TECHNIQUES, WITH STEP-BY-STEP SEQUENCES
TO DEMONSTRATE EVERY SKILL YOU WILL NEED.

Tools and Equipment

It is an undeniable fact that a few essential pieces of cooking equipment will make sweet-making at home much easier and more rewarding. Many people will have most of these items in the kitchen already, and may only need to invest in a couple of extra utensils, such as a copper pan and a sugar thermometer, to get started. Read through your recipe before starting to make sure you have all the equipment necessary.

The following pages give descriptions of the most useful tools for sweet-making. Cooks can use this list to check whether they have all they need to whip up the most delicious confections.

Large equipment

A good quality, unlined, solid copper pan with a heavy base is always worth the money. There is no better container in which to boil sugar. The copper conducts heat more efficiently than other metals, and also looks most attractive hanging in the kitchen.

Cake tins (pans) are indispensable in sweet-making. Square and rectangular tins (pans) are good for setting fudge, ganache, fruit paste and jellies, whereas round tins (pans) are useful for some nougats and panforte. Square or rectangular straight-sided baking sheets or Swiss roll tins (jelly roll pans) can be used for making taffies

Below: Copper pan

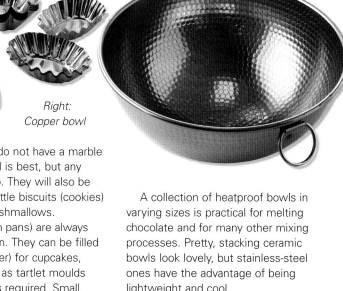

Above:
Tartlet tins

Right:
Copper bowl

and toffees, if you do not have a marble slab; stainless steel is best, but any heavy metal will do. They will also be perfect for baking little biscuits (cookies) and for setting marshmallows.

Patty tins (muffin pans) are always useful in the kitchen. They can be filled with cake mix (batter) for cupcakes, and are also useful as tartlet moulds if a deeper tartlet is required. Small individual decorative metal moulds can be very useful for petits fours or for making patterned impressions in liquorice or other sweets.

A collection of heatproof bowls in varying sizes is practical for melting chocolate and for many other mixing processes. Pretty, stacking ceramic bowls look lovely, but stainless-steel ones have the advantage of being lightweight and cool.

A wire rack has many uses in the kitchen. It is especially handy when sugaring delicate flower petals or cooling chocolate moulds. The best racks have a cross-hatch pattern, making them perfect for supporting miniature confections.

Left: Square and round cake tins (pans), and patty tins (muffin pans)

Left: Marble slab

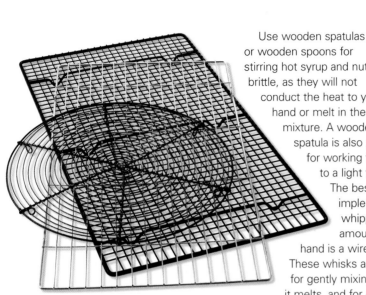

Above: Zesters

Right: Mandolin

Use wooden spatulas or wooden spoons for stirring hot syrup and nut brittle, as they will not conduct the heat to your hand or melt in the mixture. A wooden spatula is also perfect for working fondant to a light texture. The best implement for whipping small amounts of cream by hand is a wire balloon whisk. These whisks are also useful for gently mixing chocolate as it melts, and for combining chocolate and cream in a ganache.

A fine-mesh sieve (strainer) is vital for straining flavourings out of steeping creams and seeds out of preserves, or for sifting dry ingredients such as icing (confectioners') sugar or unsweetened cocoa powder over finished truffles.

Cutting tools

Good knives are vital for sweet-makers. A heavy, solid, sharp chef's knife is the most practical implement for chopping hard ingredients such as chocolate and nuts, while a long, narrow-bladed knife will make slicing fudge, jellies and fruit paste easier. A small, sharp paring knife is essential for peeling and coring fruit or for cutting up small pieces of candied citrus peel.

A mandolin or V-slicer yields a paper-thin slice. This is a good way to slice the pears in the recipe for Baked Pear Crisps, for example. Sturdy, sharp kitchen scissors are vital for

Left: Mortar and pestle

cutting toffees and taffies, as well as snipping baking parchment to size. A fine zester is ideal for grating citrus rind, and ordinary box graters work well for grating blocks of chocolate into fine pieces.

Decorating tools

Specialist chocolate dipping forks can be used to dip prepared ganache into tempered chocolate, or to mark a pattern on the top of each coated chocolate truffle. The small rasp side of a box grater or nutmeg grater is also perfect for making markings on sweets, particularly marzipan fruits. A new nailbrush is another unusual way to make an interesting texture when decorating chocolate truffles.

Paintbrushes can be useful for fine decoration. They do not need to be expensive, but beware of the cheapest ones, which can shed bristles. Cocktail sticks (toothpicks) are perfect for lifting paste or gel food colourings out of the jar (these colours are very concentrated, so a little goes a long way).

It is possible to make your own piping (pastry) bags out of paper, but a good quality cloth bag (preferably with a plastic coating) or disposable plastic ones are very useful. There is a great choice of nozzles (tips), couplers and bags at cookware stores.

Above: Paintbrushes

Above: Wire racks

Small equipment

Ladles, spatulas and spoons are vital pieces of equipment for sweet-making. A ladle will help with delicate operations such as pouring chocolate into moulds or transferring liquids into jars. A funnel with a catch mechanism is another wonderfully useful pouring tool that allows a specific amount of liquid to be measured out. A good rubber spatula is essential for mixing and scraping bowls; the best ones are heat-resistant. Thin metal spatulas are ideal for lifting confections from baking sheets or coaxing sweets out of baking tins (pans). The smaller ones are ideally suited for icing cupcakes or smoothing the top of ganache.

Below: Metal spatulas

Above: Funnel

Above: Scraper

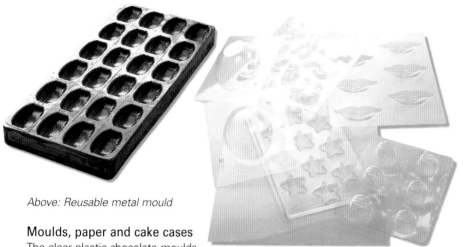

Above: Reusable metal mould

Moulds, paper and cake cases

The clear plastic chocolate moulds sold in most cake-decorating stores are generally considered to be disposable. Once used, they can be very carefully washed with soapy water and a soft cloth, but any scrapes and scratches that remain will appear on the surface of the next batch of chocolates. Serious chocolate-makers should invest in some professional reusable chocolate moulds.

There are several different kinds of baking paper available. Waxed and greaseproof paper are best used as a wrapper for finished sweets. Baking parchment is usually the most appropriate for oven use; silicone paper is more expensive and even more non-stick than parchment. There are also reusable liners on the market. These should be kept flat or rolled; to clean them, wash gently with warm soapy water and dry well. Disposable paper cake and sweet cases are readily available in all sorts of exciting colours and patterns, and also come in tiny versions that are perfect for truffles.

Above: Plastic chocolate moulds

Measuring tools

The most important tool in sweet-making, at the heart of many of the recipes in this book, is a sugar thermometer. Thermometers should be clearly marked with the temperature in Celsius and/or Fahrenheit, plus the main stages for sweet-making, for example 'thread', 'soft-ball', 'firm-ball' and 'hard-ball'. They are very fragile and should be wrapped for storage. Special chocolate thermometers measure the lower melting point of chocolate, and they are helpful in achieving a glossy finish.

Glass and plastic measuring jugs (cups) for liquid are essential, while sturdy metal, ceramic or plastic

Far right: Chocolate thermometer

Right: Sugar thermometer

Below: Paper cake cases

The most common tin (pan) used for the recipes in this book is a square one. They are very simple to line.

1 Use a pastry brush to brush a little oil or melted butter inside your cake tin, being sure to get the oil well into the corners.

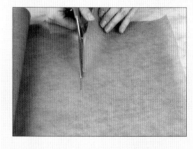

2 Cut a sheet of baking parchment just slightly narrower than the width of the tin (pan) and long enough to come up the sides at each end, allowing a little overhang on both sides. Cut another piece of paper to cross the length and come up the sides.

3 Press the first sheet into the tin, then press the second sheet on top so that all four sides are covered. There should be a little overhang on all sides to allow you to remove the contents when cooked or set.

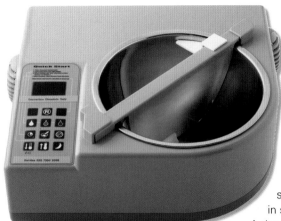

Left: Chocolate-tempering machine

measuring spoons are vital for adding small quantities of ingredients. A ruler helps the home cook to mark the size of truffles, pastes and fudges accurately before cutting them for a beautiful, professional-looking result.

Electric appliances

A good, strong mixer on a stand is a great help in the sweet-making kitchen. It should come with whisk, paddle and hook attachments. Always start with a spotlessly clean, dry mixing bowl, as any residue in the bowl will affect the volume of the mixture.

If a stand mixer is unavailable, the next best thing is an electric hand mixer or whisk, but it should have a strong motor, as some are too weak to beat a large batch of meringue or marshmallow. Hand blenders also

have their place, for instance when trying to rescue a ganache that has started to separate. Small coffee or spice grinders have powerful motors and will pulverize whole spices such as cinnamon sticks, star anise and liquorice root in seconds.

A domestic chocolate-tempering machine is fairly expensive, but if you plan on making a lot of truffles, such a machine might be a good investment for you. Tempering gives chocolate a smooth, glossy, professional-looking finish, perfect for making your home-made confectionery even more attractive.

Finally, digital scales are a must for the sweet-maker's kitchen. They give very accurate readings and will ensure absolute precision when measuring the tiny quantities that are required of certain ingredients in these recipes.

Storage containers

Most sweets and chocolates should be stored in an airtight container, but always check the instructions on the individual recipe for how to store each confection.

TYING A PERFECT BOW

Tied with skill, a bow can create a simple but professional finish for a home-made gift.

1 Hold one end of the ribbon in the centre of the top of the gift box, with enough remaining at the end for one loop of the bow.

2 Wrap the ribbon around the box and, when it meets the centre, turn it 90° and wrap it the other way, bringing the ribbon back to the top. Secure it by wrapping it over and then back under the ribbon in the centre so you have a cross on top.

3 Tie the two ends of ribbon into a neat bow, loosely at first to make sure you make the loops the same size, then pull it tight once you are happy with the shape. Trim the ends of the ribbons, if necessary, to make them the same length.

GIFT-WRAPPING TIPS FOR HOME-MADE CONFECTIONERY

Presenting home-made treats in pretty packages adds to the fun. Here are some practical and decorative ideas for making the most of sweet gifts:
• Line a container with colourful tissue paper, then add a piece of waxed paper to stop the oils seeping through.
• Reuse gift boxes by covering them with new, colourful paper.
• Tin boxes make practical presentation containers – shiny solid-coloured ones for modern tastes, or favourite oldies for a nostalgic look.

• Antique plates or bowls are easy to use. Wrap the entire container in a big square of cellophane gathered together on top with a ribbon.
• Vintage plates are easy to find at charity shops (thrift stores) at great prices, and they become a reusable part of the gift.
• Add a bow in a matching colour. Satin and grosgrain ribbons make a beautiful package, but you can also use raffia, string or cord.
• Package the confectionery at the last minute to keep it at its best.

THE SWEET-MAKER'S STORE CUPBOARD

One of the best things about making sweets at home is that you, as the cook, have complete control over what goes into them. The ingredients should be pure, fresh and of the highest quality. The majority of the ingredients called for in this book can easily be purchased from a local store. A few select ingredients may be harder to come by, but are worth seeking out. If something proves difficult to find locally, it may be possible to order it on-line.

SUGAR AND OTHER SWEETENERS

The most important ingredient in sweet-making is, of course, sugar. There are many different kinds of sugar. They are all derived from sugar beets or sugar cane, but are processed in different ways, so it is important to use the correct one for the recipe.

Icing (confectioners') sugar is refined sugar that has been pulverized to a delicate, white powder. It is the best type to use when a very fine texture is needed, for example in an uncooked almond paste. It is also the sugar of choice for dusting the tops of cookies and cakes, giving an attractive finish.

Caster (superfine) sugar is used when sugar needs to dissolve quite quickly. It is not as fine as icing sugar, but not as coarse as granulated (white) sugar. It is ideal for baked confections and sponges, and can also be used in sugar syrups, which form the basis of many confectionery recipes.

Below (clockwise from top right): Icing (confectioners') sugar, caster (superfine) sugar, demerara (raw) sugar, soft light brown sugar and soft dark brown sugar

Granulated (white) sugar has a slightly coarser texture than caster (superfine) sugar and is also less expensive. It dissolves easily, but not so quickly that it could burn. It is the ideal sugar for melting into syrups and caramels.

Preserving sugar, sometimes known as lump sugar, is even coarser than granulated (white) sugar, with large irregular crystals. The large crystals allow water to percolate between them, and it will yield a beautiful clear syrup that is perfect for candying fruits or for making fruit pastes and jellies.

Organic sugar is always less refined, and although it has a similar texture to caster (superfine) or granulated (white) sugar, it has a pale brown colour and a slightly richer flavour. This is hardly noticeable once it is cooked.

Demerara (raw) sugar is named after the area in Guyana where it was originally processed. Its pale golden brown colour

Right: Black treacle (molasses)

lends a deeper tint and subtle flavour to sweets, and may appeal to those who prefer a less refined sugar.

Soft light or dark brown sugar is refined caster (superfine) or granulated (white) sugar with added black treacle (molasses). The moisture in the treacle keeps the sugar soft. Recipes will sometimes call for soft brown sugar to be 'packed' or pressed into a measuring cup, but if you want to be really precise about measurements, it is best to use digital scales.

Black treacle (molasses) is also known as dark or blackstrap molasses. It is extracted from sugar cane during the refining process, and then reduced and concentrated by heating. It is packed with iron and other minerals, and has a delicious, burnt caramel flavour. It is very dark in colour and is extremely thick and viscous. Black treacle is an essential ingredient in liquorice. If your local store does not stock it, it can usually be found in health food stores or from on-line retailers.

Golden syrup is a reduced by-product of sugar-cane refinement, like black treacle (molasses), but it is lighter in colour and flavour. It is an invert sugar, created by combining a small amount of acid, such as cream of tartar or lemon juice, with a sugar syrup and heating it. This inverts, or breaks down, the sucrose into glucose and fructose, thereby reducing the size of the sugar crystals, and this fine crystal structure produces a silky smooth golden syrup. A small amount can be added to sugar syrups in sweet-making to help keep a mixture from crystallizing. Its American equivalent is light corn syrup, which is an entirely different product but can be used in the same way, as it has the same properties.

Liquid glucose is also known as glucose syrup. It sometimes appears in the ingredients lists, for example when a bland-flavoured syrup is better suited to a recipe than the fuller-flavoured golden syrup, so that it does not interfere with other, more delicately flavoured, ingredients. Liquid glucose is normally made from wheat or potatoes. The US equivalent for this product is clear corn syrup, which is made from corn. It is not the same product, but can be used in the same way as liquid glucose. It is available in large supermarkets, specialist baking stores, and on-line.

Honey can range widely in flavour from light and sweet to dark and earthy, the flavour notes being dictated

Above: Preserving sugar

by the flowers that the bees feed on. Lavender and heather honeys are more delicate and mild, whereas mountain and chestnut honeys are intensely flavoured. It is important to taste the honey before you use it in a recipe so that it does not overpower your confection. A mild type such as lavender honey would be perfect in French nougat, for instance. It is also important not to overcook honey, as the character and flavour are altered with heat. For this reason, honey should be added at the last possible moment in the cooking process.

Above: Maple syrup

Maple syrup is made by collecting the sap of the maple tree and then removing the water, mostly by boiling, to reduce the sap into a syrup. Nothing is added, and nothing is removed except the water element of the syrup. It is traditionally produced in Canada and the USA, and is graded according to its density and translucency. The process is very time-consuming, and the concentration of the syrup means that there is a significant loss of volume, which is why maple syrup is an expensive ingredient. Used sparingly, however, it is worth the investment, as it has a flavour unlike anything else. Once opened, store it in the refrigerator.

Below (from left to right): Liquid glucose, honey and golden (light corn) syrup

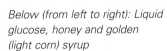

MEASURING STICKY SYRUPS, TREACLE AND HONEY
Viscous sweeteners such as black treacle (molasses), golden (light corn) syrup and honey can be difficult to measure accurately, as they stick to the measuring spoon. To prevent this, you can lightly grease the measuring spoon with a little flavourless oil, such as grapeseed oil or peanut (groundnut) oil, before use.

DAIRY PRODUCTS AND EGGS

Milk, cream, butter and eggs are essential ingredients in many sweets, particularly fudge, toffee and sponge mixtures. Most recipes will be quite specific about which kind of milk or cream to choose, as it will make a difference to the end result, so make sure you follow the recipe exactly.

Evaporated milk is a canned milk product made from milk that has had about 60 per cent of the water removed in an evaporation process which caramelizes it slightly, giving evaporated milk its distinctive beige colour. It has a unique flavour that is especially good in fudge recipes.

Sweetened condensed milk is found in many old recipes for fudge, and is also used in some liquorice recipes. It is made using the same process as is used for evaporated milk, with the addition of a substantial amount of sugar.

Cream comes in many varieties. Single (light) cream can be used in place of whole milk if a creamier result is desired, but cannot be a substitute for double (heavy) cream in sweet-making. This richer cream is a key ingredient in chewy caramel and fudge, and in the chocolate ganache for truffles. Ultra-pasteurized cream is exposed to a higher heat during processing, which makes it keep for a long time, but changes the flavour and behaviour. Crème fraîche is cream with an added bacteria culture that imparts a sour flavour and thickens the mixture. It is similar to sour cream, but with a denser texture.

Above: Sweetened condensed milk

Above: Eggs

Fresh milk will yield the best results for baking. Full-fat (whole) milk is always recommended for the recipes in this book, because the higher fat content will result in a smooth texture and rich taste. However, if you only have semi-skimmed (low-fat) milk, you can usually substitute that. Never use skimmed milk for sweet- and chocolate-making.

Yogurt is occasionally used instead of cream to create lighter, tangier results, for example in modern fudges.

Cream cheese is a soft cheese that is often used in baking. It can be swirled into mini brownies to create a complementary flavour combination.

Left: Double cream

Below: Butter

Butter should be of the unsalted variety for most sweet recipes. Choose butter with a high percentage of butterfat if you can. As with double (heavy) cream, the higher the fat content, the lower the water content, and the better it will perform in most of these recipes. If a recipe calls for oil instead of butter, it should be as bland as possible. Grapeseed is the best choice, followed by peanut (groundnut) or almond oil. Butter and oil can both be used for greasing equipment.

Eggs should be free range if possible – these will inevitably taste better. A really fresh egg will separate easily and whip successfully. Medium (US large) eggs are used unless otherwise stated.

USING EGGS
• Eggs for cooking should be at room temperature. If the eggs are chilled, warm them gently in a bowl of lukewarm water before using them in the recipe.
• When whisking egg whites, always make sure that the bowl is scrupulously clean and dry – any residue or grease will affect the end result.

FLOURS, RAISING AGENTS AND THICKENING AGENTS

The different types of flour and raising and setting agents all need to be reasonably fresh. Out-of-date ingredients from the back of the store cupboard will not perform as well as they should, and may affect the taste and texture of the recipe.

Plain (all-purpose) white flour is a finely milled flour made from soft wheat grain. It is used in making fragile pastry shells for delicate chocolate boats, as well as in recipes for chocolate brownies and tuiles.

Self-raising (self-rising) flour is plain flour with an added raising agent, usually bicarbonate of soda (baking soda) and cream of tartar. It is milled from a soft grain of wheat with little gluten content, which makes cakes and pastries light and delicate.

American cake flour is also made with a soft wheat and is sifted many times. Some manufacturers add cornflour (cornstarch) to cake flour. If you cannot buy cake flour, you can make your own: For every 115g/4oz/ 1 cup cake flour, substitute the same amount, minus 30ml/2 tbsp, of plain (all-purpose) flour, then add 15ml/ 1 tbsp cornflour (cornstarch) and sift thoroughly.

Raising agents such as bicarbonate of soda (baking soda) and baking powder behave differently when exposed to heat and other ingredients. These ingredients create carbon dioxide that will expand in the batter, giving greater height and volume. Baking powder consists of bicarbonate of soda (baking soda) with an acid added to it, usually cream of tartar.

Left: Tartaric acid

Below (left to right): Bicarbonate of soda (baking soda), baking powder and cream of tartar

Tartaric acid is a natural product found in grapes. It is used to add acidity to some confections.

Cream of tartar comes from tartaric acid and is a by-product of wine-making. It stabilizes and gives volume to beaten egg whites so they do not separate (break) while they are being whisked to stiff peaks. It is also used to produce a creamier texture in sweets because it inhibits the formation of crystals, and will help to stabilize a sugar syrup.

Citric acid comes from fruit and is both a natural preservative and a source of flavour. Like cream of tartar, it helps to prevent the formation of crystals in sugar. It can be more difficult to obtain, but is usually available in specialist stores or on-line.

Gelatine is a clear setting agent that helps give shape and brightness to jellies, marshmallows and gumdrops. Gelatine will allow the lovely, fruity texture of confections to shine, as well as giving them solidity. It comes in leaf and powdered form, and both are readily available in supermarkets and specialist stores. It is an animal product, but there are vegetarian alternatives available, which are derived from seaweed.

Pectin is a natural setting agent that is found in ripe fruit. It is used in recipes for fruit jellies and pastes. It is available in liquid or powdered form and either type can be used. The different quantities of each type of pectin will be specified in the recipe.

Below: Sheet gelatine

Below: Powdered gelatine

USING GELATINE
• Powdered gelatine must be softened with cool water or other liquid, which is then heated and stirred to dissolve the gelatine.
• Gelatine leaves should be softened in cool water until they are limp. Squeeze out any excess water and then heat with water or liquid as stated in the recipe until the leaf is completely dissolved.

FRUITS, NUTS, SEEDS, ROOTS AND FLOWERS

These natural ingredients play an important role in the making of sweets. Fresh fruits are wonderful when they are in season, and dried fruit and nuts from the store cupboard are sweet, crunchy and delicious. Nuts and seeds add taste and texture, and there are plenty of flowers that can be used to add an aromatic flavour.

Large orchard fruits such as apples, pears and quinces are perfect for cooking down into concentrated pastes. Their dense texture and high natural pectin content mean they set well with just the addition of a little sugar. Pears and apples can also be sliced paper-thin, poached in sugar syrup and dried out in a low oven for a crispy and almost translucent treat. Quinces are more difficult to find. They are akin to apples and pears, but with a tropical fragrance reminiscent of pineapples.

Smaller stone fruits such as apricots and cherries have very short seasons, so it is always exciting to see them when the fresh fruits arrive each year. Apricots are ideal for preserving as jellies or jams to be stored and used later in the year, while cherries are delicious served fresh and slightly chilled, stems and all, presented in a cup made of chocolate.

Citrus fruits, such as lemons, limes, mandarins, oranges and grapefruits, add brightness and sparkle to many sweets and chocolates. Grating a small amount of citrus rind into fondant or marzipan gives a really special flavour. Candied citrus peel is one of the most versatile ingredients in the sweet kitchen; the best types of fruit for this are organic oranges, mandarins or grapefruits.

Above: Clementines

Berries are ideal for puréeing and straining, then used as a flavouring and colouring. Raspberry purée makes dusky pink, tart marshmallows, blackberry purée can be transformed into a rich and intense paste, and strawberry purée makes a rich treat when folded into whipped cream and sandwiched between two meringues.

Fresh dates have tender flesh, encased in a papery skin, and are sweet and caramel-like in flavour. A little embellishment, such as stuffing with marzipan enlivened with grated orange rind, can make them very festive indeed.

Pineapples make some of the best candied fruits, as they are sweet and succulent but have enough acidity to handle prolonged soaking in sugar syrups. Stored properly, candied pineapple keeps for up to six months and makes a great decoration.

Above: Blackberries

Dried and candied fruits such as currants, sultanas (golden raisins), raisins, dried apricots, dried cranberries, sour cherries and figs make wonderful additions to divinity (a confection from the south of the US), lollipops, tablet or fudge. The Italian fruit cake, panforte, is packed with dried fruits and nuts that have been soaked in a sugar syrup. Candied fruits can be bought from supermarkets or, for a special flavour, made at home. Making them at home is time-consuming, but well worth the effort.

Ginger is an incredible root that soothes the stomach and satisfies the tongue. Stem ginger in syrup is easy to make at home, or buy a good quality version for making ginger gumdrops or sea foam.

Below (clockwise from top): Candied clementine, orange peel and chopped peel

Below: Dried currants, apricots and cranberries

Nuts have a short shelf life, and should be purchased in small batches and used immediately. It is better to toast nuts yourself, rather than buying them ready toasted, to bring out the best possible flavour.

Almonds are usually blanched (to remove the brown skin) and can be ground to a fine powder to form the base of a number of different recipes; alternatively, whole or flaked toasted almonds taste simply wonderful when chopped up and folded into meringues, pralines or chocolate bark. Pecans are slightly sweet, relatively soft nuts, and toasting gives them an appealing texture. Their flavour works well with molasses, brown sugar and caramel. Walnuts have a similar crinkly shape, and should always be warmed to awaken their fragrant oils, but should not be toasted, as they tend to become bitter.

Hazelnuts make the quintessential praline, and should be toasted and skinned to extract their true flavour. Pistachios, with their bright green colour, are often found in nougat and sprinkled as a decoration on other confections. Macadamia nuts have a waxy texture that is beautiful in fudge or buttery toffee.

Peanuts are not actually nuts, but are in fact legumes. They make a classic combination with chocolate or in peanut-flavoured popcorn.

Below (clockwise from top): Ground almonds, whole blanched and unblanched almonds, and flaked (sliced) almonds

Above: Shelled and unshelled pecan nuts

Flowers in the form of fresh petals, flower waters, essences and syrups can be a great taste experience. Rose petals can be crystallized to make beautiful sweets, and they are also used to produce rose syrup and rose water. Rose syrup is used in delectable rose creams, and rose water is used to give the famous perfumed flavour to Turkish delight. Violet, elderflower and lavender syrups are also available, and can be used in many recipes.

Right: Smooth peanut butter

Above: Rose petals

Seeds of many kinds add variety to sweet and chocolate recipes. Sesame seeds have great nutritional qualities and a lovely texture; they are a perfect match for honey and are delicious when toasted. Pine nuts are seeds with a lovely, delicate flavour. They add taste and texture to cookies and brittles.

Neither a fruit nor a nut, coconuts are huge seeds. They are filled with a liquid known as coconut water, which is full of nutrients. The flesh of the coconut has a lovely texture when grated fresh. However, coconut is more often used in its desiccated (dry unsweetened shredded) form, which is used to give texture and flavour to treats such as coconut ice and chocolate macaroons. Coconut oil has a very mild flavour that works well in place of butter in some recipes. It gives a silky texture to chocolate confections.

Nut Butters
Peanut butter is the most famous nut butter, and its smooth, creamy or crunchy consistency makes for indulgent confections. Other nuts, such as almonds and cashews, can also be made into nut butters.

FLAVOURINGS AND COLOURINGS

There are so many ways to make sweets look and taste wonderful, from extracts of spices and flowers to food colourings and even gold leaf. It is always worth tasting store-bought extracts before use, as they vary greatly in concentration.

Vanilla pods (beans) come from a climbing orchid native to Mexico. Each flower produces a single pod. There is a great deal of labour involved in the growing and curing of vanilla pods, which is reflected in the price as they are very expensive. Each pod contains thousands of tiny seeds that lend both taste and texture to recipes. You could also use vanilla extract, but be sure to buy good quality extract in order to get the full flavour. Never use vanilla essence, as it has a synthetic taste.

SPLITTING A VANILLA POD

1 Lay the vanilla pod (bean) flat on a chopping board. Slice the pod lengthways using a small sharp knife, keeping the pod flat to the surface.

2 Run the knife along the inside of the pod to scrape out the sticky black seeds.

Rose water and orange blossom water are created through a distillation process. They should both be used sparingly, as they can overwhelm a delicate confection. Flower syrups, such as rose and violet syrup, are more concentrated and are sweetened with sugar syrup. Well-flavoured flower syrups from France, Italy and the Middle East can be found in speciality stores and delicatessens.

Alcohol used for cooking should always be good enough to drink on its own. For example, Grand Marnier truffles really should be made with Grand Marnier, not a generic orange liqueur. Kirsch and maraschino are both cherry-flavoured liqueurs, but they are a million miles apart in taste – kirsch has a pure, fruity flavour, while maraschino uses the cherry stones (pits) and stems in the production, giving it an earthy and almond-like flavour. Sparkling wines all taste different, too. Champagne is wonderful, but if you want to use a less expensive option, Italian prosecco, Spanish cava and some New World sparkling wines are delicious.

Coffee beans should always be bought freshly roasted and whole, if possible. It is better to grind your own beans as needed, unless you are going to use the coffee in a recipe immediately.

Left: Grand Marnier

Right: Brandy

Above: Aniseeds

Dried spices do not keep for ever. Think twice before digging to the back of the cupboard for a packet of aniseeds you bought years ago – it will only spoil the quality of the finished product. Buy some fresh ones and you will notice the difference from their aroma.

Salt is now available in many different forms. A fine cooking or table salt is essential for mixing into recipes in which it needs to dissolve quickly. However, when it comes to decorating sweets, or when a more complex salty taste and a coarser texture is desired, there are many varieties to choose from. Salt can be in shades of red, pink, white and grey, and can be fine, flaky or coarse. A good salt complements liquorice, caramel and chocolate.

Below: A selection of extracts and syrups

Below: Liquid, gel and paste food colourings

Below: Lustre dusts

1 Using a clean, dry paintbrush (or pastry brush), carefully remove a little gold or silver leaf from the paper.

2 Carefully lift it gently from the paper and lower it on to the surface you wish to decorate.

Food colouring comes in paste, gel, liquid and powder form. Colourings can be found in dizzying variations at cake-decorating stores. Use a cocktail stick (toothpick) to remove a tiny amount of paste or gel from the jar to colour marzipan or fondant. Remember, you can always add more colour, but you cannot take it away once it has been added. Liquid colours are lower in concentration than pastes or gels, and you will have to use a lot more to get the desired shade; however, using too much liquid colour can taint the flavour of your sweets.

Powders and lustre dusts are wonderful for creating texture and highlights. Use a soft paintbrush to collect some dust from the tub, then tap the brush against your hand while holding it over the sweets. Sparkly sprinkles will float down and stick to the tops. Powdered colours can be mixed with vodka or another bland drinking alcohol to make the consistency liquid, and this can then be painted on to marzipan, chocolates, fondants and more with a fine brush.

Candy sprinkles and decorations come in many shapes and sizes, including hundreds and thousands (tiny rainbow-coloured sprinkles), large sugar shapes and silver and gold balls or dragées. Use colourful sprinkles for festive decorations or on treats for children (or for the child in you). For a more sophisticated look, you could opt for monochromatic or metallic sprinkles. For the largest selections, try on-line baking and cake-decorating stores.

Edible gold and silver dust are found in cake-decorating stores and art stores. They are edible in small amounts, but be sure to read the label. Like other dusts, gold or silver dust can also be mixed with clear unflavoured vodka and then painted on top of chocolates for a decadent adult finish.

Edible gold and silver leaf comes in sheets from cake-decorating stores and from specialist on-line retailers. Be sure to check it is an edible variety that is suitable for food use. The sheets are available loose, between sheets of paper, or pressed on to sheets of paper. The loose type must be applied with a paintbrush and is best for recipes that call for a piece to be delicately placed on to a soft confection. The type that is fixed to paper must be rubbed on, so it could damage a soft sweet.

Below: Sugar flowers

Below: Multi-coloured sprinkles

CHOCOLATE AND COCOA

Chocolate and its powdered version, cocoa, come in so many different varieties that the choice may seem bewildering at first. However, there is one simple rule to remember: always choose the best quality you can find when buying chocolate for your recipes. It will make a huge difference to the end result.

Forms of chocolate vary and the different shapes and sizes fulfil every sweet-maker's requirements. Large blocks of chocolate for cooking are available at fine food stores and on-line, and some stores are also beginning to stock good chocolate, such as Valrhona and Callebaut, in large blocks. These large blocks are ideal for grating or chopping up finely, as they are easy to manipulate.

In addition to large blocks or bars, chocolate for sweet-making comes in the form of beans, lozenges, pastilles or drops (chips). Chocolate beans (not to be confused with cacao beans) are small individual pieces of chocolate that make measuring and melting easy. These small pieces need to be chopped even more finely with a large cook's knife for tempering.

Chocolate varieties depend on the percentage of pure chocolate in the mix. The recipes in this book suggest a specific percentage of chocolate, and while these are helpful guides,

Above: Melted milk chocolate, with its luxuriously smooth consistency

the best way to appreciate a particular chocolate's idiosyncrasies is to taste it for yourself. If a recipe calls for dark (bittersweet) chocolate, for example, decide whether you prefer a 64-per-cent or a 70-per-cent variety. Understanding the percentage of the different ingredients in each type of chocolate will also help in deciding which kind to select for particular recipes in this book. General guidelines are given below to help you achieve success. If a recipe calls for milk chocolate, it is never advisable to substitute dark (bittersweet) chocolate, as the two types are extremely dissimilar and they will perform very differently in the recipe.

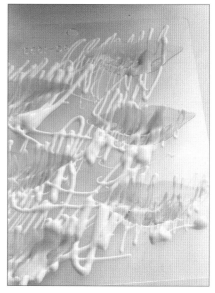

Above: Melted white chocolate, drizzled into a plastic mould

Cooking (unsweetened) chocolate is simple, unadulterated chocolate mass or liquor formed into a bar, with no other ingredients added. It is sometimes known as baking chocolate. It is very bitter in taste, and is not suitable for eating on its own. It works well in certain cake, brownie and confectionery recipes when it is used with sugar, as it imparts a deep and rich chocolate flavour. If wrapped well and stored in a cool, dry place, it will last a few years.

STORING CHOCOLATE
Chocolate can be stored for up to a year, if conditions are favourable. This means a cool, dry place, away from strong-smelling foods. If stored at higher temperatures, the chocolate may develop white streaks as the fat comes to the surface. Although this will not spoil the flavour (and it is fine to eat), it will mar the appearance of the chocolate, making it unsuitable for use in confectionery. Always check the 'best before' date on the pack to ensure you are using the chocolate when it is at its best.

Left: Lozenges of plain (semisweet), white and milk chocolate

Dark (bittersweet) chocolate is a combination of cocoa solids, cocoa butter and sugar. The amount of cocoa solids should be at least 55 per cent, but the finest ones are around 64–70 per cent. This is the best range to work with for the full-flavoured chocolate sweets and confections in this book.

Plain (semisweet) chocolate, like dark (bittersweet) chocolate, is a combination of cocoa solids, cocoa butter and sugar. In this case, the cocoa solids should be at least 15 per cent, but generally they contain 35–55 per cent cocoa solids. Using anything below 35 per cent is not recommended for the recipes in this book, unless a milk or white chocolate is required.

Milk chocolate is a combination of cocoa solids, cocoa butter and sugar, plus at least 12 per cent added milk or cream. In this case, the cocoa solids should be at least 10 per cent and can be as high as 45 per cent. Milk chocolates have improved greatly in recent years, and it is worth trying some of the new ones on the market, which contain higher percentages of cocoa solids. Again it is largely a matter of personal taste.

Above: Block of good quality French milk chocolate

White chocolate does not contain any cocoa solids at all, and therefore is often not classed as chocolate in a true sense. It consists of a combination of at least 20 per cent cocoa butter, sugar and milk, with no cocoa mass. The milk element should be at least 14 per cent. Today, there are some very flavourful white chocolates on the market, with which it is definitely worth experimenting.

Unsweetened cocoa powder has a distinctively bitter taste on its own, but mixed into cakes, biscuits (cookies) and sweets with added sugar, it is transformed. It also makes a delicious and attractive topping when dusted lightly over cakes, cookies and truffles as an alternative to, or in addition to, icing (confectioners') sugar.

VARIETIES OF UNSWEETENED COCOA POWDER

There are two types of unsweetened cocoa powder available: natural cocoa powder and Dutch-processed cocoa powder. It is best to use the type specified in any recipe, as the raising agents will also vary. The recipes in this book call for Dutch-processed cocoa powder as this is the best kind for making confectionery. This type is readily available in supermarkets.

• Natural cocoa powder is acidic and needs to be paired with bicarbonate of soda (baking soda) in order to help it to rise in the mixture.

• Dutch-processed cocoa powder is alkali and will require a non-acidic raising agent, such as baking powder, to be used with it in order for it to react and rise properly. It is slightly less bitter as a result of the alkalization, and has a reddish-brown colour. The Dutch process darkens the cocoa, so using this kind of cocoa powder results in confections with a lovely rich brown colour.

Below: White chocolate Easter egg

Below: Dark (bittersweet) chocolate cups

Below: Unsweetened cocoa powder

Basic Sweet-making Techniques

These pages provide a guide to working with the individual ingredients used in sweet- and chocolate-making. Learn how to prepare sugar and chocolate, and how to make the most of fruit and nuts by toasting, chopping, peeling or zesting them. Once the basic techniques have been mastered, the creative possibilities are endless – from fudge made with a simple sugar syrup to outrageous truffles and tuiles enhanced by grating, melting and tempering.

Preparing Sugar

Sugar is the very foundation stone of confectionery. Fancy sugar-work goes back centuries, and we have proof that spun sugar threads were made into nests and dishes to decorate banqueting tables in China at least 500 years ago. If sugar is cooked at a high temperature, it begins to caramelize. This caramelized sugar can be spun into beautiful lacy shapes by drizzling it when melted over something (such as a wooden spoon handle or rolling pin) to shape it, or it can be drizzled directly on to a confection to decorate it.

More intricate sugar work is done by transforming a cooled, pliable mass of sugar syrup into shapes (such as candy canes or aniseed twists) by stretching and pulling. Master confectioners can even blow bubbles in the mixture and make delicate, elaborate shapes from the sugar that resemble glass figures.

A sugar syrup is quite simply sugar that is dissolved in water and then heated. From the resultant solution, these two simple ingredients can form the basis of many things, from a light caramel sauce for drizzling over ice cream, chewy taffees, and soft fondant to a firm slab of nut brittle, boiled sweets and hard toffees.

The proportion of sugar to water is a factor in the finished product, but the result has more to do with how much water is boiled away in the cooking process. During cooking the syrup reaches various stages, from a delicate translucent thread to a dark, rich caramel. Each stage is suited for particular types of confection, and understanding these stages is the key to success. How to recognize and understand these stages is detailed on pages 36–37, but the first stage is to learn how to make a perfect sugar syrup.

Making a basic sugar syrup

To make a simple sugar syrup you will need a clean, dry, heavy pan that is large enough to accommodate three to four times the volume of ingredients. Using an unlined copper pan will always yield the best results, but if you do not have one, you can use a large, heavy stainless-steel pan instead. It is best to read through the recipe and get all the ingredients and equipment needed together before you start. You need to keep a close eye on sugar syrup, so you cannot leave the kitchen or start preparing something else while it is cooking. Prepare an ice-water bath and set it aside. You will need a long-handled wooden spoon, a sugar thermometer and a clean pastry brush to hand.

The ingredient quantities here will make a basic sugar syrup (for making fondant, for example), but you should use the quantities specified in the recipe you are making.

INGREDIENTS

400g/14oz/2 cups caster (superfine) sugar

150ml/¼ pint/⅔ cup water

1 Place the amount of sugar specified in the recipe in the pan. If the recipe calls for any additional ingredient to sugar and water, add that to the sugar at this stage (*see* box on page 35).

Using and Checking Your Sugar Thermometer

• Before making your syrup, you should check the accuracy of your thermometer by putting it in a pan of water and bringing the water to a boil. Water boils at 100°C/212°F. If the temperature on your thermometer varies from this, be sure to make the same adjustment when preparing your sugar syrup.

• Sugar thermometers are very delicate pieces of equipment, and should be stored and used carefully. A sugar thermometer can crack if it is immersed into boiling temperatures straight from cold. To avoid this, always let it sit in in a jug (pitcher) of hot water before immersing it in a boiling sugar syrup, just to warm it up a little.

2 Add the quantity of water specified in the recipe to the pan. Using a large wooden spoon, which will withstand the heat better than a metal or plastic spoon, slowly stir the sugar and water together over a moderate heat so as to avoid burning the mixture. Stirring is fine while the sugar is dissolving, but never stir the syrup once it is dissolved – this can cause the formation of sugar crystals, which will spoil the smooth texture and transparent quality of the sugar syrup.

3 Once the sugar is thoroughly dissolved, insert a sugar thermometer, increase the temperature and bring the syrup to a boil. Do not let the thermometer touch the bottom or sides of the pan, as this will affect the temperature reading. Most sugar thermometers come with a clip that can be attached to the side of the pan, suspending the bulb of the sugar thermometer in the sugar syrup. If you do not have a sugar thermometer, you can test the stage of your syrup in a bowl of cold water instead (using the chart on page 36), but using both techniques together – a thermometer and the cold-water test – will give the most accurate and reliable results of all.

4 If any small crystals have formed along the edge of the pan at this stage, they can be gently coaxed back into the sugar syrup with a clean, dampened pastry brush.

5 Let the mixture continue to cook until it reaches the desired stage and temperature as described in the recipe (*see* the chart on page 36 for a description of each stage). At that point, stop the cooking by removing the pan from the stove and dipping the bottom of the pan quickly into the ice water bath. Set the thermometer aside in a glass of hot water (to avoid breaking it) while you assess the syrup using the cold-water tests. If the syrup is ready, proceed to the next step in the recipe. If the syrup is not quite ready, clean the thermometer in hot water (any hardened syrup left on the thermometer could ruin the final result by causing crystallization) and place it back in the mixture before you continue cooking it. Return the pan to the heat and continue to test for the setting point required for the recipe.

ADDING INGREDIENTS TO THE SYRUP
Some recipes call for an additive such as golden (light corn) syrup, lemon juice or cream of tartar. These ingredients should be added to the sugar before it is heated. They help to prevent sugar crystals from forming in the syrup. Milk, cream, butter and other fats can also be used to stop sugar molecules from crystallizing in certain confections.

HOW TO PREPARE AN ICE-WATER BATH
Many recipes in this book will require an ice-water bath. An ice-water bath is a large bowl filled with cold water and some ice cubes to keep it very cold. Alternatively, you can fill a sink up with cold water. Once your sugar syrup has reached the required temperature, dipping the base of the pan into the ice-water bath will arrest the cooking. You should always make the ice-water bath before you start cooking your sugar syrup, as you need to be able to arrest the cooking immediately. You will be prompted at the start of the recipe to make your ice-water bath, if required.

Understanding the stages of sugar syrup

The chart on page 36 provides a comprehensive guide to recognizing the correct stage with your sugar syrup. There are six stages: thread, soft-ball, firm-ball, hard-ball, soft-crack and hard-crack. Learning the differences between these stages will help you create hundreds of different types of confectionery. The general rule is that the higher the temperature, the harder or more brittle the sweet will be.

There are two further stages in heating a sugar syrup, and these are for caramel. Caramel has all the water boiled out, so it can be easy to burn. A detailed explanation of caramel stages is provided on page 37.

Why there is a range for each stage

The stages in sugar syrup cover a range of temperatures because of the assorted additional ingredients called for in various recipes – these can affect how long it takes the mixture to reach the right stage. Use the temperatures listed in the chart for reference, but remember that the differences between the stages are very slight. Watch both the syrup and the thermometer carefully, so as not to overcook the mixture.

Testing for a Set

To test for the set indicated in the recipe, drop a teaspoonful of the sugar syrup into a cup of very cold water and test as indicated below. This chart is best used in conjunction with a sugar thermometer for the most accurate results.

Stage	Temperature	Cooking instructions	Ideal for	
Thread	106–112°C; 223–234°F	Lift the sugar solution lightly from the water with your fingers or a spoon – it should form a short thread. If not, continue cooking it until the syrup is a few degrees hotter.	A binding agent for nut pastes.	
Soft-ball	112–116°C; 234–240°F	While the syrup is still submerged in the water, form it into a small ball with your fingers. Remove the ball from the water – if it feels sticky, loses its shape and flattens out, it is at the soft-ball stage.	Turkish Delight, marzipan, fudge and fondant.	
Firm-ball	118–120°C; 244–248°F	While the syrup is still submerged in the water, form it into a small ball. Remove the ball from the water and hold it between your fingers. It should feel sticky, but hold its shape while still being malleable.	Caramel and divinity.	
Hard-ball	121–130°C; 250–266°F	While the syrup is still submerged in the water, it should easily form into a ball. Remove the ball from the water and hold it between your fingers. If it is sticky, but holds its shape and is rather rigid, it is at the hard-ball stage.	Marshmallows and salt-water taffy.	
Soft-crack	132–143°C; 270–290°F	Remove the syrup from the water and stretch it between your fingers – it should be slightly sticky and form a brittle thread that is bendable at first, but then cracks.	Taffy, toffee and Edinburgh rock.	
Hard-crack	149–154°C; 300–310°F	Remove the solidified syrup from the water. It should no longer feel sticky and will break easily. It should also have a slightly yellow colour.	Barley sugar, pralines and lollipops.	

Making caramel

For caramel, all the water in the sugar syrup needs to evaporate. Prepare an ice-water bath. You will need a long-handled wooden spoon, a sugar thermometer and a clean pastry brush.

INGREDIENTS

400g/14oz/2 cups caster (superfine) sugar

150ml/½ pint/⅔ cup water

1 Place the water and sugar in the pan and stir over a low heat to dissolve the sugar. Use a clean, wet pastry brush to brush any sugar crystals from the edge of the pan into the mixture.

2 Once the sugar has dissolved, increase the heat and bring the mixture to the boil. You can swirl the pan occasionally, but do not stir at this stage. Keep a close eye on the colour of the caramel, and use a sugar thermometer to measure its temperature. The mixture can be taken to the light or dark stage – see the temperature chart below.

3 As soon as the caramel reaches the desired temperature and colour, immerse the bottom of the pan in the ice-water bath to stop the cooking. The caramel is now ready to be used as required. You will need to work quickly before the caramel sets. (If it does set too firm, heat it gently until it melts.)

CARAMEL SAFETY

As it gets extremely hot, making caramel can be dangerous, if you are not careful.

• Never leave the pan unattended – caramel can burn very quickly.

• Beware of the caramel bubbling up and spattering you. It is best to wear long sleeves and gloves.

• Keep an ice-water bath nearby into which you can plunge your hand if it does get burnt by hot caramel.

Making caramel without water

Caramel can be made (by an experienced confectioner) out of melted sugar without any water. This is more difficult to do – making caramel with at least a little water gives the cook more control and there is less chance of burning the mixture. If you would like to try your hand at making caramel without water, melt the sugar slowly over a very low heat in a heavy pan, stirring gently as it begins to melt and adding more sugar, a little at at time, until you have the amount of caramel you need.

TESTING FOR CARAMEL

Caramel reaches higher temperatures than sugar syrups used for other confections. You will still need to rely on a sugar thermometer to give you accurate temperature readings, but can also use the appearance of the caramel to assess when it is ready. There are two stages: light caramel and dark caramel.

Stage	Temperature	Cooking instructions	Ideal for	
Light caramel	160–170°C; 320–335°F	When all the water has been cooked out of the sugar syrup and the colour has changed to a shade of light honey, it has reached the light caramel stage.	Praline.	
Dark caramel	Up to 177°C; Up to 350°F	When the sugar syrup has darkened to an amber colour, it has reached the dark caramel stage. Beware: sugar darkened beyond this stage will have an unpleasant, bitter taste.	Caramels that will be lightened by the addition of cream or butter.	

WORKING WITH FONDANT

The name 'fondant' comes from the French word *fondre*, which means 'to melt'. It is a smooth, rich, opaque sugarpaste, achieved from a simple sugar and water syrup. It can be made into a confection by cutting it into designs, shaping it into a menagerie of animals or a floral centrepiece, or simply rolling it into a smooth and delicious sheet to blanket a cake. Its sweet taste also blends beautifully with fruits, nuts and chocolate, which means it can form the basis of many confections. Start making this the day before you need to use it.

Making fondant

To make fondant, after heating sugar syrup to the soft-ball stage, you need to stop the cooking by standing the pan in an ice-water bath. You can then transform the syrup into fondant following this method. Firstly moisten a marble slab, a metal scraper and a wooden spatula with cold water.

1 Pour the syrup out on to the clean marble slab that has been moistened with cold water. Leave for 3 minutes.

2 Use the dampened metal scraper to fold the syrup over itself continuously as it cools and thickens.

3 Once it starts to thicken, switch to the dampened wooden spatula and work the fondant using a figure of eight motion, until it becomes white in colour as tiny sugar crystals are formed.

4 Once the fondant is firmer and has become white in colour, switch back to the metal scraper, moistened again with cold water, and continue to work the fondant. You should try to keep the fondant moving for about 10 minutes in total.

5 The fondant will soon start to become very firm, so, when it can no longer be worked with the scraper, gather it up into a ball. Moisten your hands with cold water and knead the fondant for a further 10 minutes to remove all the lumps, creating a smooth sugarpaste.

BASIC FONDANT RECIPE

Some recipes in this book will require a quantity of fondant, and will refer to the quantity made here. Start making this the day before you need to use it.

MAKES ABOUT 400G/14OZ

400g/14oz/2 cups caster (superfine) sugar

150ml/¼ pint/⅔ cup water

1 Make a basic sugar syrup with the sugar and water, following the steps on pages 34–35.

2 Cook the syrup until it reaches the soft-ball stage (114°C/238°F on a sugar thermometer – *see* page 36).

3 Follow the steps on this page for 'Making fondant' and 'Resting the mixture'. Your fondant is then ready to use in the recipe.

Resting the mixture

Allowing the fondant to rest gives it the chance to soften and become more workable after kneading. This resting or 'ripening' time is vital unless the fondant is to be melted for coating confections or pouring into sweet cases, in which case, the resting process is not necessary.

1 Place the fondant in a bowl lightly moistened with cold water. Cover with a damp, clean dish towel and leave to rest overnight (or for at least 12 hours) in the refrigerator.

Adding colouring

When it comes to food colouring, a little goes a long way, so always start with a very small amount – just a few drops of gel, paste or liquid can colour a very large quantity of fondant. Remember, you can always add more colouring, if you need to.

1 Place a lump of rested white fondant on a cool surface dusted with icing (confectioners') sugar. Using a cocktail stick (toothpick) or skewer, lift a drop of gel, paste or liquid food colouring out of the container. Dab it in the middle of the fondant then press it into the fondant.

2 Wearing rubber or latex gloves to protect your hands from staining, gently knead the colour into the fondant. Continue to knead until there are no coloured streaks – this may take some time.

3 When the colour is evenly distributed, assess the overall tone. If you want a deeper hue you can add a bit more colouring, but remember that you can never take the colour away, so add only a tiny amount at a time. The only way to reduce the colour strength is by adding more white fondant.

Adding flavouring

Citrus zest, a dash of freshly squeezed lemon juice or vanilla extract are good choices for flavouring fondant. Extracts of lime or orange work equally well, as does classic peppermint. Lightly dust a cool work surface or marble slab with icing (confectioners') sugar. Drop or dab the flavouring in the centre of the fondant and knead it in in the same way as with food colouring, making sure it is evenly distributed. It is a good idea to wear latex gloves.

Rolling and shaping

If you want to use fondant to cover a cake, you will need to roll it out to slightly larger than the size of the cake, to make sure it covers it properly.

1 Lightly dust a cool work surface or marble slab with icing (confectioners') sugar. Place the fondant on the surface and sift a little more sugar on top.

2 Using a sturdy rolling pin, roll the fondant out into a smooth, flat, round shape and cut as required. If it is going to cover a cake, roll it to the desired thickness, then, starting at one edge, wrap the fondant around the rolling pin until it is completely lifted from the work surface, and unroll it over the cake.

Melting and dipping

Transforming fondant into a smooth satiny liquid takes some care, but it can then be poured into moulds or used to coat fruit. A smooth coating of lemony fondant on a beautifully ripe strawberry is a fresh and summery alternative to a chocolate-covered berry.

1 Take a lump of prepared fondant that has been kneaded but not ripened, and place it in a heatproof bowl over a pan of simmering water that comes up the side of the bowl to the level of the fondant.

2 Stir until the fondant melts, then add colouring or flavouring as desired.

3 Add water a little at a time and stir until it is fluid and reaches 60°C (140°F). Do not overcook. It can now be poured into moulds or used to cover fruit.

WORKING WITH TAFFY AND TOFFEE

The words 'taffy' and 'toffee' sound very similar, but although they both refer to sweets made principally of sugar syrup, the end results look and taste rather different.

Taffy

Whereas simple hard-boiled sweets are made from a simple sugar syrup heated to the hard-crack stage and then allowed to set in shapes, pulled taffies are heated to the soft-crack stage and then manipulated by pulling and stretching. This gives dramatically different results, as hundreds of tiny air bubbles are incorporated into the syrup, giving it a lighter colour and texture. Softer, chewier taffies are taken to lower temperatures so that they do not set as hard sweets, but as soft and chewy delights.

Making taffy

The way the syrup is handled will dictate the texture of the finished taffy. Turning, pulling, stretching and manipulating the mixture between the hands incorporates tiny air bubbles. Depending on how firmly and for how long the mixture is turned and mixed, you can end up with hard, glossy candies such as bull's eyes and lemon drops or softer, chalky ones such as Edinburgh rock.

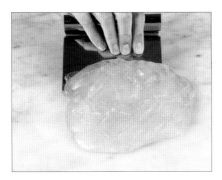

1 As soon as the syrup has reached the temperature specified in the recipe, it should be poured out on to a pre-oiled marble worktop or other clean, smooth, dry work surface. Using an oiled metal scraper, turn the edges of the pool of syrup in on itself. This helps the syrup to cool evenly and begins the process of incorporating air.

Colouring taffy

If the entire confection is to be one colour, fold a little colouring into the pool of syrup with the metal scraper. If the recipe calls for two contrasting colours, such as Rhubarb and Custards or Peppermint Humbugs, separate the syrup on the oiled marble slab or baking sheet. Place one piece in an oiled ovenproof dish in a warm oven while the first one is coloured, stretched and pulled. When the first piece is properly mixed, swap them over. Finally, remove the first piece from the oven (it may need a little more stretching to bring it back to life) and combine the two pieces of taffy according to the recipe.

Pulling and stretching taffy

Taffy starts out quite yellow, but the pulling and stretching incorporates thousands of tiny air bubbles that make it turn white. If the taffy goes too hard, place it into a warm oven for a few moments – that should melt it enough to make it pliable again. In extreme cases, the taffy mixture can crystallize. If this happens, put it back into the pan and add a little water, then bring the syrup back up to the original temperature and begin the process again. Taffy must be handled quickly, but be very careful that it does not burn your hands. Oil your hands, as well as the work surface, so that the sugar does not stick to them.

1 Coax the syrup into a cylinder shape, then take each end and stretch it out. It will be very soft at first and may break. Do not worry about this, simply gather up the pieces and push them together again.

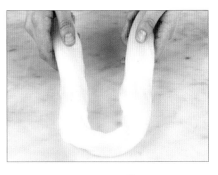

2 Stretch and pull the taffy into a long rope and then bring the ends towards you to create a horseshoe shape.

3 Now grab the top of the horseshoe with one hand, and the bottom (where the two ends meet) with the other hand. Twist the ends in opposite directions, bringing the two sides together into one rope.

4 Repeat the stretching and twisting process until the syrup begins to harden. Each individual recipe will give instructions as to the length of time for which you will need to work the taffy. For harder sweets, it will be 15–20 minutes, for chewier taffies, it may be only 10 minutes. The taffy is now ready to be cut and shaped, and this should be done immediately.

Cutting and shaping taffy

Taffy should be cut as soon as the pulling process is finished, or it will set too hard to shape. The best tool to use is a pair of oiled kitchen scissors. The pieces look like little pillows if left just as they are, such as in the Rose Water Edinburgh Rock recipe, or they can be quickly rolled into balls or into shapes, as in the traditional Lemon Drops recipe.

Toffee

A softer confection than taffy, toffee has substantial quantities of butter and cream added to the basic sugar syrup. A good example is the classic Butterscotch recipe. Other toffees, such as Peanut Brittle and Honeycomb, have bicarbonate of soda (baking soda) added to the syrup so that the dense mixture fills with tiny air bubbles.

Making toffee

There is not one simple method for making toffee, as each recipe requires different ingredients in different quantities. Some toffees, such as Bonfire Toffee, are thin and brittle, and are set in shallow baking trays. Others, such as Honeycomb Toffee, are set in a square cake tin (pan), giving chunky squares.

Pouring toffee

For toffees that are set in a cake tin (pan), you must prepare the tin first.

1 Grease the tin with butter or oil, as specified in the recipe, and line it with baking parchment so that the parchment comes up the sides of the tin.

2 Carefully pour the mixture into the prepared cake tin.

Scoring toffee

The toffee should then be set aside to cool for about 30 minutes, or until it is starting to set. At this point, it must be scored, which will allow you to break or cut it into squares when it has set completely.

1 While it is still warm, use a sharp knife to score the toffee into bitesize pieces. Set it aside to cool and set completely. Once cold, you can lift it out using the sides of the baking parchment and place the toffee on a chopping board, then break or cut it up along the scored lines.

STORING TAFFIES AND TOFFEES

If you are not serving them immediately (or you have some left over), the best way to keep toffees and taffies fresh is to wrap them individually in greaseproof (waxed) paper, baking parchment, cellophane or pretty foil wrappers. You can buy sweet wrappers from specialist stores or from on-line retailers. A candy dish or jar with a tight-fitting lid is ideal for storing the wrapped sweets, as they will soften in the open air.

Stretching toffee

Some toffee recipes, such as Peanut Brittle, require the toffee to be stretched. This introduces air bubbles to the toffee, giving it a different texture.

1 Prepare and cook the toffee mixture according to the recipe, and pour it out on to an oiled marble slab or baking sheet. Spread it out with an offset spatula as quickly as possible. Let it rest until cool enough to touch but still pliable.

2 Once the toffee is cool enough to touch, grasp the edges with oiled hands and gently pull it to stretch it out and make it lacy.

3 Once the toffee has been stretched, let it rest and cool completely before breaking it up into pieces. The back of a soup spoon is ideal for this task.

Working with Caramel and Fudge

As with most home-made confections, caramel and fudge take time and attention, but the result is definitely worth the effort. Fudge can be either smooth or grainy; both kinds are equally delicious, but are made slightly differently. Caramels, like fudge, contain plenty of cream and butter, which makes them soft and chewy at room temperature, rather than hard like most boiled sweets (hard candy).

The basic fudge technique
Fudge is very closely linked to caramel and fondant and is really only differentiated by the addition of varying amounts of cream or milk, fat and a flavouring. Fudge is cooked to the soft-ball stage (114°C/238°F) and then beaten to add air to the mixture. This causes the formation of sugar crystals, giving it its characteristic dense structure.

1 Full-fat (whole) milk, butter, sugar and any flavourings specified in the recipe (such as vanilla seeds) are heated together in a large pan until the sugar has dissolved and the butter has melted. Stir the mixture gently so that the syrup on the bottom does not burn. Cook the fudge until it reaches the soft-ball stage (114°C/238°F on a sugar thermometer).

Cook's Tip
Always keep a glass of warm water near the pan in which you are heating the sugar syrup. It will come in handy when the sugar thermometer needs to be taken out of the pan in a hurry.

2 Take the fudge off the stove, add any additional ingredients (such as chocolate, nuts, vanilla extract, etc) and dip the bottom of the pan into an ice-water bath to halt the cooking. Do not be tempted to stir it.

Grainy fudge
For grainy fudge, beating the mixture is very important.

1 As soon as the pan has been dipped in the ice-water bath, begin beating immediately and vigorously with a wooden spoon.

2 Continue beating until it has thickened slightly and starts to have a dull appearance. This is due to the formation of the sugar crystals. Do not overbeat – just work it until it starts to thicken, and then follow the next step of the recipe.

Smooth fudge
This type of fudge requires less beating than grainy fudge.

1 Once the pan has been dipped in the ice-water bath, place the pan in a cool area of the kitchen and allow it to cool to 50°C/122°F – it will become opaque and begin to thicken. Now, start to beat the fudge with a wooden spoon until it is thick but still pourable.

Smooth fudge without beating
Some smooth fudges can be made with no beating at all. They have a thickening agent, such as chocolate or nut butter, which solidifies at room temperature. They are silky smooth.

1 Gently stir in the additional ingredients before the pan goes into the ice-water bath. Do not beat the mixture.

Cook's Tip
Fudge and caramel bubble up while cooking, so it is vital to use a large pan. Boiled-over sugar syrup is very messy. If spills do happen, the best way to clean it is with lots of water – hardened sugar can be removed by gentle soaking.

Making caramel

Caramel is made by boiling sugar, milk, sweetened condensed milk, cream or water, butter and flavouring together in the same way as fudge. However, it is cooked to either the firm-ball stage (120°C/248°F) or the hard-ball stage (130°C/266°F), and is never stirred once cooked.

Pouring fudge and caramel

Line a cake tin (pan), preferably one with a removable bottom, with baking parchment. When the fudge or caramel has reached the desired thickness, you will be ready to pour it into the prepared tin.

1 Pour the fudge or caramel into the lined tin, using a spatula to help you get it all out of the pan. Make sure any scorched bits from the bottom of the pan are not added to the mixture, as they will spoil the flavour.

2 Smooth the top with an offset metal spatula or palette knife and tap the tin on the worktop to release any air bubbles and even out the surface. Remember to work quickly with fudge and caramel, as it starts to set very quickly. Leave the mixture to cool at room temperature for at least 3 hours.

Cutting fudge

For grainy fudge, it is a good idea to score the surface, marking the size of the pieces before it cools completely.

1 Once the fudge has set, lift the paper containing the set mixture out of the tin (pan), or remove the bottom of the tin, taking the slab with it.

2 Place the fudge face down on a board and peel the paper away.

3 Using a sharp knife, slice the fudge into bitesize pieces.

Cutting caramel

Use the same technique as for cutting fudge, but for softer caramel, a paper towel dipped in vegetable oil will come in handy. After each cut, wipe the blade on the oiled paper.

Wrapping caramel

Caramel has a higher moisture content than fudge, and the pieces will begin to droop slightly if left in the open air, so wrap them individually as soon as they are cut. Waxed and siliconized papers work well and show off the caramel's distinctive colour, but lovely little foil wrappers look wonderfully festive when piled high in a pretty dish.

FLAVOURINGS FOR FUDGE AND CARAMEL

There are plenty of ways to experiment with caramel and fudge. Salted caramel is wonderful. Here are a few more ideas.

Citrus juice and zest can be added for a fruity flavour.

Chopped nuts and/or chopped chocolate are lovely in fudge.

Smooth nut butters, such as peanut butter, give a rich finish.

WORKING WITH MARSHMALLOW AND NOUGAT

Aerated confections such as marshmallow and nougat are defined by their unique combination of sugar syrup, foamy egg whites and/or gelatine. Originally, marshmallows were made with a sticky substance from the root of the mallow plant, which is where they got their name, but today they are set with gelatine. The sugar syrup is made first, then dissolved gelatine is added to it. Meanwhile, egg whites are whipped in an electric stand mixer. The sugar syrup mixture is then slowly whisked into the whipped egg whites. This mixture sets and can then be cut into marshmallows.

Nougat contains egg whites but no gelatine, and has a very different texture. It ranges from chewy to brittle, depending on the cooking method. Iranian nougat is usually on the more brittle, chalky side, much like divinity from the southern United States. Chewy nougat from France, Spain and Italy contains honey, golden (light corn) syrup, glucose syrup or invert sugar to stop sugar crystals from forming, giving the nougat its delightfully soft texture.

ADDING FLAVOURINGS TO MARSHMALLOWS

Lots of different flavours can be added to marshmallow. Vanilla, fruit purées or flower extracts work well, and food colouring can give a fun aspect to marshmallow creations. A raspberry purée will lend a pretty bluey-pink colour, and peppermint marshmallows look great when tinted pale green.

If any flavour or colour is needed, add it to the syrup mixture just before it is whipped into the egg whites.

Basic marshmallows

The most important part of making marshmallows is the careful combination and aeration of egg whites, sugar syrup and gelatine.

MAKES ABOUT 900G/2LB

vegetable oil, for greasing

50g/2oz/½ cup icing (confectioners') sugar

50g/2oz/½ cup cornflour (cornstarch)

2 egg whites

400g/14oz/2 cups caster (superfine) sugar

15ml/1 tbsp glucose syrup

375ml/13fl oz/generous 1½ cups cold water

60ml/4 tbsp powdered gelatine

1 Grease a shallow tin (pan) with the oil, then dust it with equal parts icing sugar and cornflour. Set aside. Whisk the egg whites to soft peaks using an electric mixer (this is best done in an electric stand mixer, though it is possible to do this in a copper or stainless-steel bowl with an electric hand whisk).

2 Make a sugar syrup with the sugar, glucose syrup and half of the water. Take the syrup to the hard-ball stage (127°C/260°F). While it bubbles, combine the powdered gelatine with the rest of the cold water in a small pan. When the sugar syrup is ready, take it off the heat and whisk in the dissolved gelatine. The mixture will probably bubble up a little.

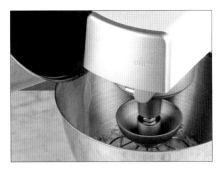

3 Turn the electric mixer on to medium speed and carefully drizzle in the syrup. The gelatine will begin to set immediately, so work quickly.

4 Once all the syrup is in the bowl, turn the mixer on to medium-high and whip the marshmallow until it is opaque. It should hold its shape on the end of the whisk when lifted out of the bowl – this will take about 7 minutes. Use a rubber spatula to scrape the sides and bottom of the bowl – at this point it may be necessary to whip the mixture a bit more. It should begin to stiffen but still be spreadable.

5 Pour into the prepared tin and smooth the top with a spatula. Dust a little more icing sugar and cornflour on top. Leave the marshmallows to set for at least 5 hours, or preferably overnight.

Cutting marshmallows

Marshmallow is very sticky, so you need to use a lightly oiled knife to cut it. It may be necessary to clean and re-oil the knife between cuttings so that it does not stick. Dust the surface with icing (confectioners') sugar and cornflour (cornstarch) before you start, and have some more of this mixture on hand with which to dust each piece as you cut it.

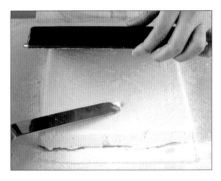

1 Use a small paring knife to neaten the edge of the marshmallows, then invert the tin (pan) on to the surface dusted with the icing sugar and cornflour mixture. Unmould the marshmallow mixture.

2 Using a lightly oiled knife, cut the slab into small cubes. Roll the sides of each cube of marshmallow in a little of the extra icing sugar and cornflour mixture. Leave to dry out for a few hours.

Storing marshmallows

Once the marshmallows have dried out, store them in an airtight container, with a little extra cornflour and icing sugar to prevent them sticking together. For gifts, package them into a cellophane bag or paper-lined box. The marshmallows should keep for about 2 weeks.

Making nougat

Nougat gets its distinctive texture from the mixture of sugar, water and glucose or corn syrup. It is slightly different in every country so no two recipes are exactly the same. Here is a basic recipe, to which you can add different nuts or fruits.

MAKES ABOUT 1KG/2¼LB

grapeseed or groundnut (peanut) oil, for greasing

rice paper

375g/13oz/scant 2 cups caster (superfine) sugar

15ml/1 tbsp glucose syrup

100ml/3½fl oz/scant ½ cup water

120ml/4fl oz/½ cup honey

2 egg whites

1 First line a cake tin (pan) with edible rice paper. Put the egg whites into the bowl of an electric mixer (preferably on a stand), whip them to stiff peaks and leave them to rest.

2 Combine the sugar, glucose syrup and water in a pan. Cook until the mixture reaches 138°C/280°F. Warm the honey in a separate pan until it is just boiling, then add it to the sugar syrup and bring the mixture up to 143°C/290°F.

3 Turn the electric stand mixer on, and drizzle the syrup into the whipped egg whites in a steady stream until the nougat thickens. Pour the mixture into the prepared tin. Cover with rice paper, then place a board and some weights on top. Leave it to set overnight.

ADDING FLAVOURINGS TO NOUGAT

Toasted nuts (such as hazelnuts, pistachios or almonds), orange blossom water and candied fruits make delicious additions to this basic nougat. Fold them into the mixture before spooning it into the prepared tin (pan).

Cutting nougat

It is important to use a very sharp knife, because you may be cutting through large pieces of fruit or nuts.

1 Remove the weights from the nougat.

2 Trim away any rough edges. Cut the slab into individual pieces, ready for wrapping or packing in a paper-lined box or tin. Nougat keeps well for 3 weeks.

PREPARING FRUITS

Perfectly ripe fruit at the height of its season really requires no embellishment to make it taste better. It can be the perfect finish to a meal or a lovely pick-me-up in the afternoon. However, turning fruit into a sweet is a dazzling transformation that everybody should try once. It heightens the intensity of the fruity sweetness to new levels.

Preparing citrus fruits

Citrus fruits can add colour, fragrance and flavour to many varieties of chocolates and sweets, or the fruits can stand on their own as simple and delicious candied treats. When candied and stored properly, they can be transformed into sugary jewels that will last for months. Candied fruits can be the main attraction on a sweet plate, or they can be diced and used in many other recipes for a bright burst of flavour. Careful preparation is vital, however, so the instructions must be followed exactly – a poorly prepared candied peel can be bitter and tough.

Removing citrus peel

Use a sharp paring knife to remove citrus peel, following these instructions.

1 First slice off the top and bottom of the fruit so that it can stand upright.

2 Use the paring knife to slice off the peel, from top to bottom.

Zesting citrus fruits

Most cooking and baking stores offer a variety of citrus zesters. They have different uses, so it is worth investing in two types.

If a fine zest is called for, use a rasp-type zester to give a thin, frilly zest that provides a delicate texture.

If a more intense flavour is needed (for example when flavouring the cream for ganache) then a canelle knife is perfect for creating curls of zest. These curls of zest infuse the cream with the essence of citrus flavour, but they should always be strained out of the cream using a sieve (strainer) before it is combined with the chocolate.

Juicing citrus fruits

For large quantities (when extracting juice prior to candying citrus peel, for example), the juicer attachment of a food processor is quick and easy. Be careful not to press down too hard on the fruit. If the juicer touches the white pith, the juice can become bitter. For smaller quantities, it is more practical to use a citrus juicer or reamer. For juicing, cut the citrus fruit across the centre in a horizontal way, so that you can see all of the segments.

A traditional juicer is quick and easy for juicing small quantites of fruit.

A citrus reamer also works well. Make sure you strain the juice through a sieve (strainer) before use.

Choosing fresh pineapple

Pineapple must be ripe when it is picked, otherwise the flavours will not be present. Pineapples should be heavy for their size, and neither rock hard nor soft; the fruit will soften a bit in the kitchen, but will not improve in taste. Sniff a pineapple – if it smells slightly fermented, it is past its prime. The colour does not have any bearing on its flavour. Fresh pineapple cannot be used with gelatine as it prevents it from solidifying.

Preparing a pineapple

It may be a good idea to wear rubber gloves for this process, as the leaves of the pineapple can be sharp and the skin prickly.

1 Top and tail the pineapple using a sharp knife on a chopping board set on a sturdy surface.

2 Use the knife to remove the skin carefully, cutting from the top to the bottom. The cut should go deep enough to get rid of all of the skin but still leave behind as much of the sweet flesh as possible. (The pineapple skin can be pulverized in a food processor with water and sugar and then strained to make a delicious and refreshing drink, if you like.)

3 The peeled pineapple can then be sliced into rounds.

4 Remove the fibrous core. The fruit is now ready for use in recipes.

CORING AN APPLE

The best way to core an apple neatly for sweet-making is with a small, curved, sickle-shaped knife called a bird's beak knife. If you do not have one, use a small paring knife. An apple corer is a useful tool, but it is more difficult to control where you are cutting around the core. Apples will turn brown once peeled – this can be avoided by dipping them in water mixed with a little lemon juice.

1 Place the apple on a chopping board. Using a sharp knife, cut the apple into quarters.

2 Take one quarter and hold it core side up in one hand. Take a paring knife and trim the peel or stem from the ends of the core. Be very careful not to cut your thumb with the sharp knife.

3 Peel the skin from each quarter using the paring knife. Work in single strokes, from top to bottom, until there is no peel remaining.

4 Scoop out the core. Run your thumb along the apple where the core has been removed to be sure there are no coarse fibres remaining. Trim away any coarse fibres that you find.

WORKING WITH FRUITS

The simplest combinations of fruit flavours are the most successful in sweet-making. The idea is to bring out the wonderful, individual flavours in fruits, then capture them, preserved in a glass-like sugar shell or set in a concentrated paste.

Making concentrated fruit paste

Many fruits can be transformed into a delicious paste that retains the intensely pure flavour of the fruit. However, this recipe does not work for juicy citrus fruits, which should be either combined with another fruit or made into gelatine-based sweets instead. The fruits that set best are those that are high in natural pectin, such as apples, blackberries and quince.

1 First, cook the fruit in a pan. This will take just a few minutes for blackberries, but up to an hour for quinces. Purée and strain cooked blackberries, or push cooked apples or quinces through a food mill.

2 Cook the strained and puréed fruit slowly with the specified amount of sugar – usually an amount equal to the weight of the fruit – until it becomes very thick. In some cases, additional pectin may be needed.

3 Test the mixture by putting a spoonful on a plate. It should firm up and, when it cools, it should be matte and not sticky. Pour the paste into a shallow tin (pan) lined with clear film (plastic wrap) and leave it to dry overnight, uncovered.

4 Remove it from the pan and cut the paste into shapes or strips. Coat them in caster (superfine) sugar or granulated (white) sugar. Fruit paste will keep for up to 3 weeks in an airtight container. It makes a fresh, nutritious and tasty treat, ideal for school lunchboxes or for packing in a picnic basket.

Making fruit jellies

Fresh fruit jelly sweets are set with gelatine. Soft fruits such as raspberries and strawberries are perfect for this type of mixture. First you will need to cook the berries in a pan for a few minutes, then strain them through a food mill or sieve (strainer) to remove the seeds. If you are using hard fruits such as apples or pears, you will need to peel, core and slice the fruit, then cook it in a covered pan with a small amount of water until it is very soft. Strain the fruit to remove any pulp.

1 Soften the gelatine in a small bowl of cold water according to the recipe. Cook the desired amount of sugar syrup to the soft-ball stage (114°C/238°F on a sugar thermometer).

> ### COOK'S TIP
> Preserving sugar has large sugar crystals so it dissolves more slowly and evenly. If you cannot find it, use granulated (white) sugar instead.

2 Add the softened gelatine and the fruit purée, and combine them with the syrup.

3 Pour the mixture though a sieve into a shallow tin (pan) sprinkled with a small amount of water, and leave it to set.

4 When the mixture is ready, turn it out of the tin and cut it into squares, triangles or decorative shapes using a tiny greased pastry (cookie) cutter or knife. Fruit jellies sparkle when rolled in caster (superfine) sugar.

5 Serve immediately or store them for 1–2 days in an airtight container in a cool, dry place. Do not refrigerate. If you do not serve them immediately, re-roll them in caster sugar just before serving.

Candy-coating soft fruits

Whole fruits, pieces of fruit and the sliced peel of citrus fruits such as oranges, clementines or grapefruit can all be candied. Always select fresh fruit that is just ripe, clean and dry – overripe, soft fruit will not stand up to this process.

Cook the desired quantity of sugar syrup to the hard-crack stage (154°C/310°F) or the caramel stage (160–177°C; 320–350°F). Remove the pan from the heat. To coat a piece of fruit, hold on to its stem, calyx or end and dip it into the hot syrup, being careful not to burn your fingers. Drag the bottom of the fruit across the edge of the pan to remove any excess syrup and rest the coated fruit in a sweet case to set. Repeat until you have used all your ingredients or until the syrup gets too hard. This technique requires quick, efficient movements because when the syrup is at the right temperature to set on the fruit, it can also set in the pan. Luckily, it is possible to reheat thickened syrup by returning the pan to the heat for a few minutes.

When candying soft fruits, eat them within a few hours or the fruit will start to weep and the candy shell will dissolve. Candied citrus peel, on the other hand, will keep in an airtight container for up to six months.

Candied citrus fruits

All types of citrus fruits can be sliced and candied.

1 Use a mandolin or a knife to slice the fruits into 3mm/⅛in slices. Place them in a large pan and cover with water. Bring the water to the boil, then drain the slices in a colander.

2 Return the fruit to the pan and cover again with cold water. Bring to the boil, then drain the fruit slices once more. Repeat this process a third time.

3 Put 2kg/4½lb/10 cups sugar and 2 litres/3½ pints/8 cups water in a clean pan. Bring to a boil over a medium heat, stirring occasionally, to dissolve the sugar.

4 Add the fruit and lower the heat so that the sugar syrup is at a very low simmer. Simmer for 45 minutes, then turn off the heat. Allow the fruit to cool in the liquid.

5 Remove the fruit from the syrup and lay it out on a wire rack positioned over some baking parchment to catch the drips. Discard the syrup. Leave to dry for 24 hours.

Candied citrus peel

Like candied citrus slices, you can also use any type of citrus fruit for this.

1 Wash the fruits. Cut them in half and juice them. Place the juiced shells in a pan and cover with cold water. Bring to the boil and cook for 10 minutes.

2 Drain, then return them to the pan and cover with fresh water. Bring to the boil again and drain. Repeat the blanching process until no resistance is felt when the peel is pierced with a knife.

3 Drain and allow to cool. Scrape away the pith using a spoon. Slice the peel into 1cm/½in strips with a sharp paring knife.

4 Place 800g/1¾lb/4 cups granulated (white) sugar in a clean pan with 400ml/14fl oz/1⅔ cups water. Stir over medium heat to dissolve the sugar.

5 Add the peel and bring to the boil. Boil for 45 minutes, until the syrup reduces and small bubbles form on top. Leave the peel to cool in the syrup overnight.

6 Transfer the peel to a wire rack placed over a piece of baking parchment to catch the drips. Leave to dry for 24 hours, then toss in caster (superfine) sugar.

PREPARING NUTS AND SEEDS

Walnuts, hazelnuts, almonds, brazils, pistachios, pecans, macadamias, pine nuts, peanuts, coconuts – nuts and seeds come in many varieties, with distinctive flavours and attributes. They provide countless opportunities for creative sweet- and chocolate-making, and can make masterpieces from ordinary ingredients. The most important thing to remember is that their proper preparation should never be neglected – it is essential to the success of the recipe.

Removing the skins

The first step in preparing nuts for use in sweet-making is to remove their skins. There are two main methods, blanching and roasting.

Blanching is the easiest way to remove the skins of thick-skinned nuts such as almonds, pistachios and chestnuts.

1 Drop whole shelled almonds or pistachios into a pan of boiling water, and boil them for a few minutes until the skins loosen.

2 Drain the blanched nuts in a sieve (strainer) and set them aside in a small bowl until they are just cool enough to handle.

3 Slip off the loosened skins using your fingers and discard them.

Roasting in a hot oven works well for removing the skins of hazelnuts, walnuts and brazil nuts. The skin will start to flake off and turn brittle as it heats.

1 Spread the nuts out on a baking tray lined with baking parchment. Place them in a hot oven and bake for 10–15 minutes.

2 Once the nuts are a lovely golden brown, remove them from the oven and transfer them to a generously sized clean dish towel.

3 Bring the sides of the dish towel up over the nuts and rub the nuts against one another until all the skins have fallen off.

Roasting nuts for flavour

The process of roasting nuts in the oven cooks the oils and enhances the taste. However, the oils are delicate, and roasting the nuts for too long can result in a burnt flavour – gentle warming is usually sufficient. All nuts require different roasting times. Watch them closely while roasting – the colour should be pale golden brown and they should begin to smell toasted.

Chopping nuts

Nuts should be chopped in small quantities – it makes the whole process easier and the pieces will be more uniform in size.

1 Use a large, heavy knife, with your non-dominant hand holding the tip of the knife down. Hold the handle of the knife with your dominant hand and chop the nuts by moving the handle up and down, keeping the tip steady. Repeat this motion, moving the knife around the board until all the nuts are chopped. Place the chopped nuts in a sieve (strainer) and shake it to remove any ultra-fine dust. (Any nut dust can be reused as a sprinkle topping or mixed into brownies and cookies.)

COOK'S TIP
Chestnuts are easier to deal with if you cut a small cross in the bottom of the nut with a sharp knife first. When they are cooked, drain the chestnuts and let them dry and cool down. Using a paring knife or a special chestnut knife (available in Italy), peel back the skins, starting from where the cut was made.

Grinding or pounding nuts

The act of grinding and pounding nuts is as old as civilization itself, and the mortar and pestle found in modern kitchens is not very different from the grinding rock used to pulverize seeds and nuts in ancient times. For cooks in a hurry, a food processor or clean coffee grinder makes quick work of this task.

1 Place the nuts in a food processor or coffee grinder and use the pulse setting to grind them finely.

2 Ground nuts can go from a floury powder to an oily mass in a matter of moments, so check them carefully as you grind them.

Roasting seeds

The flavour of seeds, such as sesame seeds, can be improved by 'roasting' them carefully in a dry frying pan for a few minutes.

1 Spread the seeds out in a thin layer in a large non-stick frying pan and place over a medium heat.

2 Cook the seeds for 2–3 minutes, tossing them frequently, until they are golden brown. Be careful not to scorch them.

PREPARING COCONUT

Coconuts are actually seeds, not nuts. The hard fibrous shell hides a sweet, watery juice and a unique-tasting white flesh. Breaking though the tough exterior takes determination, but the rewards are great.

1 If the coconut still has a tuft of hairy fibres at the end, use a heavy chef's knife to remove these and reveal the three black eyes beneath. Tap the eyes with a metal skewer or screwdriver to pierce them.

2 Strain the coconut water into a jug (pitcher) – it is full of antioxidants and makes a refreshing drink.

3 Use the heavy chef's knife or a hammer to tap the coconut forcefully about one-third of the way from the end opposite the eyes.

4 As you rotate and tap the coconut, a natural seam should form, allowing the seed to be broken open.

5 Use a paring knife to score the coconut meat into wedges within the shell, then take a spoon to coax the flesh out gently. The thin brown skin that remains on the white flesh is edible and can look very pretty as a contrasting edge on pieces of thinly sliced coconut. If you prefer the flesh to be pure white, the skin can be cut away.

6 Slice or grate the coconut flesh, according to the recipe. Grated coconut flesh can be used to make coconut milk – soak the grated coconut in hot water, then strain through muslin (cheesecloth).

WORKING WITH NUT PASTE

There are two kinds of nut mixture often used in sweet-making: uncooked and cooked. Cooked nut paste is also known as marzipan. Making a nut paste is easy. Simply grind shelled and skinned nuts into a fine powder with a mortar and pestle or pulverize them in a food processor, add sugar, then bind them with other ingredients according to the recipe. The uncooked method requires ground nuts, sugar, egg whites and nothing more. A cooked nut paste is made by heating the ground nuts with a sugar syrup and adding egg whites, yolks, or sometimes whole eggs.

Icing (confectioners') sugar will make the smoothest-textured nut paste, but caster (superfine) or granulated (white) sugars can also be used. Extra sugar can be added if desired, for an ultra-sweet variation. Almonds make the best-textured nut pastes, but they can be combined with other nuts, such as hazelnuts, for added flavour. It is always advisable to have some almonds forming the base of your nut paste, even when using other nuts for flavour.

SIMPLE ALMOND PASTE

MAKES ABOUT 500G/1¼LB

200g/7oz/2 cups ground almonds

300g/11oz/2¾ cups icing (confectioners') sugar

1 egg white

2 drops bitter almond oil (optional)

1 Mix the ground almonds and icing sugar together in a large mixing bowl.

2 In a small bowl, use a fork or small whisk to beat the egg white until slightly frothy.

3 Slowly add the white to the almond and sugar mixture, stirring until it just comes together. You may not need all of the egg white.

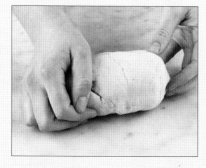

4 Add the bitter almond oil, if using, and knead through. Avoid over-kneading, however, as it will cause the mixture to become brittle.

5 Use the paste according to the recipe. If you do not want to use it immediately, wrap the almond paste tightly in two layers of clear film (plastic wrap) and store in an airtight container in the refrigerator for up to 2 weeks. You can also freeze it for up to 3 months.

Adding flavourings to marzipan

You can add all sorts of flavourings to marzipan. Liqueurs work well to give a sophisticated flavour, as do coffee, chopped nuts and citrus zest.

1 Break the marzipan into small pieces and place in a large mixing bowl.

2 Add all the flavouring ingredients and work them into the marzipan, using the back of a spoon or your hands.

Colouring marzipan

The technique for adding colour to cooked nut paste is similar to that used for fondant (see page 39). The resultant colours will be different because marzipan is a beige, while fondant is white. You can use liquid, gel or paste food colourings. Always start with a small amount of colouring – you can add more if needed.

1 Dust a cool work surface or marble slab with icing (confectioners') sugar. Place the nut paste on the work surface or marble slab, and use a cocktail stick (toothpick) or skewer to scoop a small quantity of food colouring from its container and add it to the nut paste.

2 Wearing rubber or latex gloves to protect your hands from staining, gently begin to knead the colour into the marzipan.

3 Continue to knead until the colour is an even shade throughout the nut paste. Assess the hue and add more colouring if desired. Be warned: it is always possible to add more colour, but it cannot be removed from the mixture. If you add too much, the only way to lighten the colour is by kneading in more uncoloured nut paste.

BOILED MARZIPAN

MAKES ABOUT 600G/1LB 6OZ

300g/11oz/1½ cups caster (superfine) sugar

150ml/¼ pint/⅔ cup water

200g/7oz/2 cups ground almonds

1 egg white, slightly beaten

icing (confectioners') sugar, for dusting

1 First, prepare an ice-water bath and set it aside. Place the sugar and water in a heavy pan. Heat over a medium heat until the sugar has dissolved, then increase the heat and cook until the mixture reaches the soft-ball stage (114°C/238°F on a sugar thermometer – see page 36).

2 As soon as the mixture reaches the soft-ball stage, immediately dip the base of the pan into the ice-water bath. Add the ground almonds and stir. Stir in the egg white and return to the heat.

3 Stir over a low heat until the marzipan thickens slightly, then remove from the heat and leave to cool a little.

4 Dust a clean, dry work surface with icing sugar and turn the almond mixture out on to it. Begin to knead.

5 Knead gently for 5–6 minutes until it is smooth and holds together.

6 Use according to the recipe. If you do not want to use it immediately, wrap it tightly in two layers of clear film (plastic wrap) and store in an airtight container in the refrigerator for 2 weeks or freezer for 3 months.

Working with Aniseed and Liquorice

Aniseed, liquorice and star anise are strong and wonderful spices. They can be found in four variations: in their seed form as whole spices; pulverized into a powder; in oil form; or as an extract. These all have their uses in different recipes, so check which one is called for before you start.

One of the most difficult things about using aniseed and liquorice is finding a good quality source. Not all manufacturers are created equal, and it is a very good idea to try a few different brands before making a recipe.

Tips for Spices

Many things can go wrong with spices, so there are lots of factors to take into consideration when buying and storing spices for sweet-making. There is no sense in buying a block of excellent chocolate (at a substantial price) and then infusing it with a stale, tainted liquorice or aniseed flavouring. Follow these tips to ensure the best taste in your confections:
• A poor-quality, inexpensive spice will always be inferior in taste to a top-quality one, even if it is stored carefully.
• Buy spices from a store with a high turnover of stock. If a spice has been sitting on a shelf for months, the flavour will certainly have deteriorated.
• Do not store spices for too long at home, for the same reason as above. It is advised to use spices within 6 months.
• Powdered spices can pick up the taints of other spices if stored in the same cupboard or drawer. Do not keep sweet spices near strong-smelling ingredients such as chilli powder or garlic granules.
• Light and heat affect the potency of spices and extracts as well. Glass jars may look pretty on show in the kitchen, but they are not ideal for the storage of spices and herbs – a canister or a dark cupboard is the best place to store them.

Aniseed, anise extract and star anise

The flavour of aniseed and anise extract is strong and a little goes a long way. It is not for everyone, but for those who enjoy its sharp, woody flavour, it is a very special treat. Star anise is from a different family, but it is related to aniseed in flavour. This pretty spice is native to China and is often used in savoury cooking there. The production of anise extract from the aniseed plant is costly, and in recent times it has been overtaken in markets around the world by anise extract made from star anise. The flavours are not the same, but they do complement each other well.

Both aniseed and star anise marry well with liquorice, and the three together can make a wonderful conbination in all kinds of delightful traditional forms, from hard candies to chewy sweets. Always use the crushed seeds or oils sparingly – their flavour can quickly become overpowering.

Using star anise

Star anise can be ground using a spice grinder or a mortar and pestle, and added to sugar syrups. This gives an intense flavour. It can also be added whole, which will impart a more subtle flavour and leave the texture of the finished confection smooth.

1 Add whole star anise to a sugar syrup to impart their taste. The strength of flavour will depend on the length of time they are in the syrup, so you can make it to your taste. When the mixture is ready to be poured into moulds or on to a baking sheet, strain it through a sieve (strainer) to remove the star anise. Discard the star anise.

Using aniseed

Aniseed (also known as anise seeds) can be ground in a mortar and pestle, and used to flavour sweets like Aniseed Twists (*see* page 74). Anise extract can be used instead to give a smoother finish, but fresh aniseed gives the deepest flavour.

1 Grind the aniseed using a mortar and pestle, or alternatively grind it in a spice grinder. Make sure the aniseed is very finely ground, as large, unpleasant lumps of the spice will spoil your confections.

2 Add the ground spice to a sugar syrup mixture according to the recipe. It should normally be added once the sugar syrup has been brought to the correct setting stage, and just before the cooking is halted in an ice-water bath.

Traditional Sweets

Aniseed and liquorice are ancient ingredients and some of the world's best-loved confections use these flavours. Aniseed Twists, Pontefract Cakes and Liquorice Sticks are just a few that can be found in this book.

Liquorice root

The root of the liquorice plant has a pungent flavour, married with a subtle sweetness. An excess of liquorice is said to raise the blood pressure and will react with some medications, so moderation is advised. All kinds of liquorice confections have become traditional favourites, from liquorice allsorts to the Dutch kind flavoured with salt. Liquorice is also used in drinks such as herbal tea mixtures, and in savoury recipes, particularly in China. The tough root can be chewed as it is, but it can also be used in different ways to extract its flavour for confectionery.

Grinding liquorice root

Liquorice root can be ground down to a fine powder. It is just about possible to pulverize the root in a mortar with a pestle, but a spice grinder will save a lot of time and effort.

1 Break the liquorice root into smaller pieces, then use a mortar and pestle or a spice grinder to pulverize it.

2 Use a sieve (strainer) to sift the ground liquorice root. Place any larger pieces left in the sieve back into the spice grinder or mortar, and grind again until they are fine enough to be sifted.

Flavouring a sugar syrup

You can infuse a sugar syrup with the delicious taste of liquorice root.

1 Break the liquorice root in half and add it to a mixture of sugar and water. Leave to infuse.

2 Strain the liquorice-infused syrup through a sieve (strainer) and discard the used liquorice root. This syrup can now be used in a recipe.

Making liquorice sweets

Liquorice sweets can be either hard or soft and chewy. The hard versions are essentially a boiled-down sugar syrup with liquorice flavouring, and are often mixed with a little anise oil (*see* Liquorice Shards, page 188). The soft versions (for example Liquorice Sticks, page 190) are more like caramel in structure. Liquorice-flavoured cream or sweetened condensed milk is boiled with sugar and butter until it reaches the firm-ball stage, or 118°C/244°F on a sugar thermometer. These sweets can be made even more intensely flavoured by the addition of black treacle (molasses), and black food colouring gives them a professional appearance. You can also omit the anise extract and use red colouring instead.

SHAPING SOFT LIQUORICE

Soft chewy liquorice can be poured into a shallow tin (pan) to set, and once it is ready, it can be cut into nearly any shape you like. Here are a few ideas:

Cut the set mixture into strips to make simple liquorice sticks. These sticks can then be left flat or twisted.

Cut the liquorice into bitesize rounds with a tiny cookie cutter to make a sweet that resembles the traditional British confection, Pontefract cakes.

Once you have cut them into rounds, you can use a stamp designed for sealing wax or the bottom of a pretty tartlet mould to leave elaborate marks on them.

PREPARING CHOCOLATE

Chocolate can be an intimidating ingredient. Words such as split, separate, break, bloom and seize are often associated with the preparation of this delicious substance. What is more, there is the percentage of cocoa bean solids to consider, many brands to choose from and myriad ingredients to pair with it. But before you start to get creative, take a little time to learn the basics that will help in achieving chocolate success.

It is possible to buy professional chocolate in pellets (also called beans or pastilles, depending on the manufacturer). The pellets are easier to measure and use, but the large blocks are ideal for making chocolate curls, and they are less expensive.

Chopping chocolate

It is best to use a heavy chef's knife to chop blocks of chocolate. If it is a very large block, break it into smaller pieces first.

1 Starting at one corner, chop the chocolate with a large, heavy knife, using your non-dominant hand to hold the tip of the knife down.

2 Once you have chopped all the way along, turn the board 90° and repeat until all the chocolate is chopped finely.

Melting chocolate

Many recipes in this book will require melted chocolate. Although, for speed, you can melt chocolate in a microwave, the best method is described here.

1 If you are using a block of chocolate, break it into small pieces. Place the chocolate in a heatproof bowl and set it above a pan of barely simmering water. Do not let the water touch the bottom of the bowl.

2 Allow the chocolate to melt, stirring occasionally, until it is smooth.

Grating chocolate

It is a good idea to chill chocolate before grating, to stop it melting in your hands.

1 Use a box grater to grate the chocolate, using different sides for different effects.

Tempering chocolate

The tempering process is used when chocolate is being melted to use as a decoration or finishing touch, for example coating little cakes or dipping fruit or nuts into chocolate. It gives a shiny, professional finish. Without tempering, melted chocolate may well end up with a grainy or chalky finish. Tempering means melting the chocolate very carefully to a specific temperature, cooling it and reheating, so that the right kind of crystals predominate in the mixture, which gives it the glossy, smooth finish.

Once it has been tempered properly, chocolate is much more resistant to higher temperatures later in the cooking process. Chocolate that has not been tempered correctly will not set properly and hardens very slowly at room temperature. Untempered chocolate has a gritty texture, will not release properly from moulds, and can have a blotchy appearance which will spoil the look of carefully prepared cake coverings or truffles.

Tempered chocolate is wonderful for making very simple chocolate treats, such as pretty lollipops or chocolate coins. If, however, appearance is not important for the confections or the occasion in question, you can just melt the chocolate and not bother with the tempering process.

COOK'S TIP

Some recipes call for just a small amount of tempered chocolate, but it is easier to temper at least 300g/10½oz of chocolate and it is not recommended to try tempering less than this. If the particular recipe does not need all the tempered chocolate, simply pour it out on to a piece of baking parchment and let it set. This chocolate can be recycled into brownies, cakes or any recipe where the chocolate will be cooked and does not need to have a shiny finish. Whatever you do, do not waste it!

Tempering technique

Different types of chocolates temper at different temperatures, so find out which chocolate is right for the recipe and then work out the temperatures for tempering (*see* chart). Domestic tempering machines are available that will take the guesswork out of this process, but they are expensive to buy.

It is vital to use a special chocolate thermometer, which records very low temperatures. All melting should be done in a heatproof bowl over a pan of barely simmering water, and the bottom of the bowl should not touch the water. The heat may not need to be turned on again for the second melting as the water beneath may still be hot enough to melt the mixture.

Use at least 300g/10½oz chocolate, either in pellets (or beans or pastilles) or as a chopped block.

TEMPERING TEMPERATURE CHART			
Type of chocolate	First melt to:	Cool to:	Melt again to:
Dark (bittersweet)	40–45°C/104–113°F	27–28°C/80–82°F	31–32°C/88–89°F
Milk	32.5°C/90°F	27–28°C/80–82°F	30°C/86°F
White	30.5°C/87°F	27°C/80°F	28°C/82°F

2 Use a chocolate thermometer to melt the chocolate to the 'first melt to' temperature on the chart above. When the chocolate has almost melted to this temperature, it should be removed from above the pan of simmering water and placed on a folded dish towel.

5 Allow the chocolate to continue to cool down on its own. Use a chocolate thermometer to cool it to the 'cool to' temperature on the chart above. This should take about 10–15 minutes. Do not leave the chocolate unattended or stop watching the thermometer.

1 Take two-thirds of the chopped chocolate or chocolate pellets and place it in a heatproof bowl. Place the bowl over a pan of barely simmering water, making sure no water comes into contact with the bottom of the bowl and no steam or water ever comes into contact with the chocolate.

3 Use a wooden spoon or heatproof rubber spatula to stir the chocolate gently once or twice. Add a spoonful of the remaining third of the chopped chocolate and stir – this will lower the temperature of the melted chocolate. This additional chocolate is known as the 'seed' chocolate.

4 Once the first spoonful of seed chocolate has melted in, add another spoonful and stir until it has melted completely. Continue in this way until the seed chocolate no longer melts when added. Stop adding the seed chocolate at this stage.

6 The chocolate must then be reheated to the third temperature on the chart. Bring it back up to this higher temperature by placing the bowl back over the pan. Be very careful at this stage not to overheat it. You may not need to have the heat on underneath the pan – the water may still be hot enough to increase the temperature of the chocolate.

7 Now the chocolate is ready to be used in the recipe. If the chocolate becomes too firm, warm it again, but do not exceed the final reheating temperature for the particular type of chocolate you are using.

COOK'S TIP

Never walk away from chocolate while it is being tempered. Variations in the air temperature inside or outside can cause the chocolate to melt more slowly or quickly on one day than it did the previous day. If it melts too rapidly, it may lose that wonderful, glossy shine.

Working with Chocolate

Once the tempering process is mastered, as described on the previous pages, working with chocolate is infinitely easier. Understanding this complex treatment will also help to solve any other problems that may arise as you begin to make delicious chocolate confections.

Chocolate ganache

Ganache is a mixture of chocolate, cream and butter, and is a wonderfully versatile paste. It can be infused with many flavours, including citrus fruit and spices. The ganache can become the creamy centre of a chocolate-coated truffle, or form the entire truffle itself. While warm, ganache is often poured over cakes, enrobing them in dense and delicious chocolate, but once it has begun to set, it is excellent for decorative piping and a whole host of confectionery.

Making a basic ganache

The two most important things to consider when making ganache are mixing and temperature. The temperature must be controlled – a chocolate thermometer that shows very low temperatures is essential for making ganache.

MAKES 60–100 TRUFFLES

350g/12oz dark (bittersweet) chocolate (66–70% cocoa solids), chopped

120ml/4fl oz/½ cup double (heavy) cream

50g/2oz/4 tbsp unsalted butter, softened (it needs to be very soft)

1 Melt the dark chocolate in a heatproof bowl over a pan of barely simmering water (*see* page 56) to 46°C/115°F on a chocolate thermometer.

2 Meanwhile, gently warm the double cream to the same temperature in a separate pan. When both the melted chocolate and the cream have reached the required temperature, they are ready to be emulsified. Take them both off the heat.

3 Gently pour the warmed cream over the melted chocolate.

4 Mix them together into a silky mass. The easiest way to blend them is with a hand blender, but a wire whisk will work just as well. If the ganache separates, it can sometimes be salvaged with the addition of a small amount of warmed cream.

5 Add the very soft butter, bit by bit, blending well between each addition.

6 Transfer the mixture to a square cake tin (pan) lined with clear film (plastic wrap). If the ganache is left to cool in a round bowl, the sides can harden before the centre, causing lumps to form, but in a square tin (pan) it cools evenly. Allow the ganache to set at room temperature until it begins to firm up.

Piping ganache

If you are piping your ganache, the trick is to allow it to set enough to hold its shape, but not so hard that it is stiff and difficult to work with. When the ganache is at the desired consistency for piping, spoon a small amount into a piping (pastry) bag fitted with a suitable nozzle. The heat from your hands may cause the ganache to melt, so it is best to work quickly in small batches. It can be piped on to mini cupcakes using a star-shaped nozzle for a pretty effect, or it can be piped into truffles.

Piping truffles

The standard method of making truffles is provided on the next page, but spherical truffles can also be made by piping, as shown here. You will need to fit a piping bag with a large round nozzle for this, rather than star-shaped.

1 Using a piping bag fitted with a large round nozzle, pipe even-sized blobs on to a baking sheet lined with baking parchment. Place in the refrigerator for about 20 minutes, or until firm, then roll each blob into a ball in your hands. Chill again for 10 minutes, until firm.

Cook's Tip

If the recipe calls for an infused cream to flavour the ganache, leave the cream to infuse in the refrigerator with the flavouring before straining and warming it. Taste it before heating the cream, but remember that it should taste slightly too strong. When the cream is whisked into the chocolate, the flavour will be diluted.

Making basic round truffles

A truffle is a confection, usually round, made of a soft ganache, and sometimes covered with chocolate or other coatings. It can be simple or luxurious, often containing alcohol or other flavourings. Here is a step-by-step guide to making simple truffles, using the ganache recipe from the previous page.

1 First make the ganache following the method on page 58, then leave it to set for a couple of hours at room temperature, then in the refrigerator until firm. Once set, turn the ganache out on to a board.

2 Cut the ganache into truffle-sized squares – this quantity should make 60–100 truffles depending on how big you make the squares. Prepare a bowl of unsweetened cocoa powder and dust your hands with it.

> COOK'S TIP
>
> Warm hands can spoil truffles. Cool them down by clasping some ice in a plastic bag. Rubber or latex gloves will also help keep the truffles from melting on the fingers.

3 Take the squares one by one and roll them into balls between your cocoa powder-dusted palms. Place on a baking parchment-lined baking tray. You can shape them into more rustic shapes, if you like.

4 Roll the truffles in another layer of cocoa powder and serve immediately. If you wish to store them, store them in an airtight container dusted with extra cocoa powder, in the refrigerator. Remove them 30 minutes before serving as they are best served at room temperature. They will keep for about three weeks in the refrigerator or two months in the freezer.

Dipping truffles

The next step in the hierarchy of truffles is the dipped version. Dipping chocolate truffles into tempered chocolate will result in a lovely, smooth finish. It also gives a surprising texture, as the crisp outer shell of tempered chocolate gives way to a creamy ganache centre. For round truffles, follow the shaping steps above, but instead of rolling them in unsweetened cocoa powder in step 4, use a dipping fork to dip them into tempered chocolate and then place them on a baking parchment-lined baking tray or a wire rack to set.

Making square dipped truffles

For square truffles, first make the ganache following the method on page 58, then leave it to set for a couple of hours at room temperature, then in the refrigerator until firm. Once set, turn the ganache out on to a board and cut it into truffle-sized squares – it should make 60–100 depending on the size of your squares. You will need to prepare some tempered chocolate of your choice (*see* pages 56–57).

1 Use a dipping fork to dip each square of ganache into the tempered chocolate. Lift them back up and drag the bottom of the fork along the side of the bowl to remove any excess tempered chocolate.

2 Leave them to set on a baking parchment-lined baking tray. If you wish to add any decoration to a dipped truffle, you must do so immediately before the chocolate sets. Silver balls, flakes of pink peppercorns or chopped candied peel make great embellishments – for example, a truffle flavoured with Cointreau would taste even better when rolled in finely chopped candied clementine peel. These coated truffles will keep for 3 weeks at cool room temperature. Do not refrigerate.

Making filled chocolates

Chocolate moulds come in many shapes and sizes, and produce some of the most beautiful and professional-looking truffles. The moulds should be clean, dry and free from scratches. Professional chocolate-makers use stiff polycarbonate moulds that are extremely durable and give the shiniest finish. Most of the clear plastic moulds available from cake stores are perfect for the home chocolate-maker, though they will not last long and are generally considered disposable.

1 Fill moulds with tempered chocolate, swirl the chocolate around the mould and then, using a metal spatula or palette knife, scrape any excess tempered chocolate from the edges into another bowl. Invert the mould on a cooling rack and let all the excess chocolate drip out. Leave to set for 12 minutes, until the chocolate is thickened but not set.

2 Scrape the drips clean with the metal spatula again and leave to set for a further 12 minutes. Now the moulds are ready to be filled. First, make sure the remaining chocolate for the outer shell is still in temper.

3 Fill the moulds with your filling (a squeeze bottle is useful for this), but leave enough space to add one more layer of tempered chocolate. The filling must be at room temperature or it could cause the chocolate to go out of temper.

4 Spoon over enough tempered chocolate to cover the filling and scrape any excess chocolate from the moulds. Leave to set for about 2 hours before inverting them on to a board.

Making chocolate curls

The simplest way to make curls is to drag a heavy chef's knife across a large chunk or slab of chocolate placed on the work surface, with a cloth between it and your body. Hold the knife at a 45° angle and very carefully drag it towards you. However, good quality chocolate with a high percentage of cocoa solids is quite brittle, so for attractive curls, follow the Chocolate Curls recipe.

CHOCOLATE CURLS

MAKES 210G/7½OZ

25g/1oz/2 tbsp butter

185g/6½oz dark (bittersweet) chocolate (55–70% cocoa solids), finely chopped

1 Line a small loaf tin (pan) with clear film (plastic wrap) and set aside.

2 Place the butter in a small pan over the lowest possible heat. As soon as the butter begins to melt, remove from the heat. As the butter melts, the white milk solids will sink to the bottom of the pan. The transparent golden liquid is clarified butter.

3 Slowly pour the clarified butter into a bowl, leaving the milk solids in the pan. Discard the milk solids.

4 Place the chocolate in a heatproof bowl with 7.5ml/1½ tsp of the clarified butter and set over a pan of barely simmering water. Leave to melt slowly.

5 Transfer the chocolate to the tin to form a layer in the bottom. Tap the tin on a surface to remove any air bubbles. Chill it for 2 hours.

6 Lift the chocolate out of the tin by the sides of the clear film to avoid marking it with your fingers, then place it on a clean board, on its side. Create curls with a sharp knife, vegetable peeler or cheese slicer by running the blade down the block.

7 Use the curls immediately or store in an airtight container in a cool place for up to 1 week. Position the curls with a cocktail stick (toothpick) to avoid getting fingerprints on the chocolate.

VARIATION

You can substitute the clarified butter with coconut oil. Coconut oil is solid at temperatures below 24°C/76°F, but is easily melted in a bowl over a pan of barely simmering water.

CHOCOLATE MINT LEAVES

MAKES 20

20 fresh mint leaves

100g/3¾oz dark (bittersweet) chocolate, tempered (*see* pages 56–57)

1 drop peppermint oil

1 Use a soft pastry brush to remove any dirt from the leaves. Place a couple of wooden spoons on a clean work surface.

2 Add the peppermint oil to the tempered chocolate and stir well to combine.

3 Using a small, clean pastry brush or new paintbrush, coat the underside of each leaf with the melted chocolate.

4 Carefully wipe away any melted chocolate that gets on the top side of the leaf.

5 Drape the leaves over the handles of the wooden spoons and leave the chocolate to set. This will take about 30 minutes.

6 When the chocolate is set, use kitchen tweezers to gently take hold of the chocolate and pull them away from the leaves. Try not to touch the chocolate with your fingers.

7 Serve immediately or store in an airtight container in the refrigerator for up to 1 week.

VARIATIONS

• Any edible leaves can be used for this technique – rose or camellia leaves are ideal. The more robust the leaves, the easier they will be to handle, and they will form a sturdier base on which the chocolate can set.
• Try painting the chocolate on to the tops of some leaves and on to the bottom of others for added variation and interest.

Making Easter eggs

A home-made chocolate Easter egg is a wonderful project to tackle at home with older children. Chocolate eggs can be left plain and simple or painted with edible gold or silver, which gives an elegant finish and is a clever way to conceal any imperfections. You will need an Easter egg mould, which you can buy from specialist cooking stores or from on-line retailers, and some tempered chocolate of your choice.

1 Pour tempered chocolate into two half-egg moulds, swirling it around so that all of the surface inside the mould is coated. Allow it to set for 30 minutes.

2 Once it is set, repeat the process to create a second layer of chocolate, then leave to set. Repeat a third time, if necessary.

3 Remove the chocolate from the moulds once set.

4 The halves can be filled with sweets or kept hollow before gluing them together with a little more melted chocolate. To conceal the seam, pipe a decorative edge round the egg with chocolate ganache, if you like.

Boiled Sweets, Lollipops, Pulled Taffies and Fondants

Everyone has their favourite boiled sweet (hard candy) or pulled taffy, and whether you suck them slowly or crunch them up, they provide a satisfying taste experience. Made with sugar syrup and a variety of other ingredients, they require a little effort to make, but the results are well worth it. Fondants are made using a slightly different process, giving them a softer, more chewy texture. All types can be made in many flavours and colours, so get creative!

LEMON DROPS

Adorable miniature lemon-shaped drops are a classic sweet around the world. Opaque yellow with a sugary coating, they have a certain sparkle and should be put in beautiful little dishes to entice your family and friends to eat them. Lemon drops are also known as Lemon Sherbets. Be sure to use a high quality lemon extract or oil. Lemon extract is usually lemon oil diluted with water, so you will need to use double the quantity to get the strong lemony flavour. Artificial flavourings are never recommended.

MAKES ABOUT 600G/1LB 6OZ

grapeseed or groundnut (peanut) oil, for greasing

400g/14oz/2 cups caster (superfine) sugar

15ml/1 tbsp liquid glucose or golden (light corn) syrup

150ml/¼ pint/⅔ cup water

2.5ml/½ tsp lemon oil or 5ml/1 tsp lemon extract

2 drops yellow food colouring

200g/7oz/1 cup caster sugar, for dusting

1 Grease a marble slab, a metal scraper and a pair of kitchen scissors. Prepare an ice-water bath.

2 Combine the sugar, liquid glucose or golden syrup, and water in a medium heavy pan and bring to the boil.

3 Reduce the heat to medium and cook, without stirring, until the mixture reaches the soft-crack stage (143°C/290°F).

4 Remove the pan from the heat and stir in the lemon oil or extract and yellow food colouring. Stir until the mixture stops bubbling, then arrest the cooking by placing the pan in the ice-water bath.

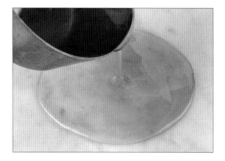

5 Pour the syrup on to the oiled marble slab and allow it to cool until a skin forms. Using the oiled scraper, begin to fold the edges into the centre of the pool until it is cool enough to handle.

6 Oil your hands and, with the aid of the scraper, lift the syrup up off the marble and work it into a cylindrical shape. Pull it out from either end to make a long strand.

7 Take hold of the ends of the syrup strand and pull them up toward you to form a 'U' shape.

8 Twist the two sides together into a rope, then pull again from both ends to make the 'U' shape.

9 Repeat these steps for about 15–20 minutes, until the syrup rope becomes opaque and a lot lighter in colour. You need to keep working it constantly so that it remains supple. If it becomes too hard, you can put it in a cool oven for a few minutes until it softens enough to work with again.

10 Gently pull the syrup into a long, thin strand again, then fold it in half and then in half again so that you have four even lengths. Twist them up into an even rope and pull until the diameter is about 2cm/1in.

11 Use oiled scissors to cut the pulled syrup into small, even pieces. Roll the pieces into little ovals using oiled hands. Pinch each end into a point.

12 Place the caster sugar in a bowl and toss the lemon drops in it to coat. Serve immediately, or wrap in baking parchment or waxed paper and store in an airtight container.

Energy 2412kcal/10289kJ; Protein 3g; Carbohydrate 639.7g, of which sugars 633g; Fat 0g, of which saturates 0g; Cholesterol 0mg; Calcium 319mg; Fibre 0g; Sodium 59mg

PEAR DROPS

These simple drops look especially pretty when poured into little moulds. If you can get your hands on an antique mould, use that. Otherwise, pour them out free-form on to an oiled marble slab or baking sheet. Pear drops are a traditional favourite in many countries, and jars of them are still common in many old-fashioned sweet shops.

MAKES ABOUT 600G/1LB 6OZ

grapeseed or groundnut (peanut) oil, for greasing

450g/1lb/2¼ cups caster (superfine) sugar

50ml/2fl oz/1¼ cup water

175ml/6fl oz/¾ cup pear juice

1.25ml/¼ tsp cream of tartar

30ml/2 tbsp lime juice

1 drop green food colouring

VARIATION
Pour the mixture into an oiled Swiss roll tin (jelly roll pan). Once set, drop the tin on the counter to shatter it.

1 Grease a sweet (candy) mould or a baking sheet with the oil. Prepare an ice-water bath or fill the sink with a little cold water.

2 Put the sugar, water, 150ml/¼ pint/ ⅔ cup of the pear juice, and the cream of tartar in a heavy pan. Heat over a moderate heat until the sugar has dissolved.

3 Turn the heat up to high and boil until it reaches the soft-ball stage (114°C/238°F). Add the lime juice, the rest of the pear juice and the food colouring. Do not stir as this could cause it to crystallize.

4 Bring back to the boil. Cook until it reaches the hard-crack stage (154°C/310°F). Remove from the heat and place over the cold water to arrest the cooking.

5 Spoon immediately into the mould or drop spoonfuls on to the baking sheet.

6 Cool completely. Remove the sweets with the tip of a knife. Serve immediately, or wrap in baking parchment or waxed paper and store in an airtight container.

Energy 1841kcal/7860kJ; Protein 2.4g; Carbohydrate 488.1g, of which sugars 488.1g; Fat 0.2g, of which saturates 0g; Cholesterol 0mg; Calcium 251mg; Fibre 0g; Sodium 31mg

SOUR DROPS

People either love or hate sour sweets. For me, there is nothing more satisfying than a hard, sugary sweet with a mouth-puckering tang. Sour drops were originally called 'acidulated drops' in 19-century Britain. They are also known as acid drops and sourballs. The sour taste comes from the addition of tartaric acid.

MAKES ABOUT 600G/1LB 6OZ

grapeseed or groundnut (peanut) oil, for greasing

450g/1lb/2¼ cups caster (superfine) sugar

150ml/¼ pint/⅔ cup water

2.5ml/½ tsp cream of tartar

2.5ml/½ tsp lemon juice

5ml/1 tsp tartaric acid

icing (confectioners') sugar, for dusting

1 Grease a marble slab. Prepare an ice-water bath or fill the sink with a little cold water.

2 Put the sugar, water and cream of tartar in a heavy pan over a moderate heat, and leave for about 5 minutes until the sugar has dissolved.

3 Once the sugar has dissolved completely, turn the heat up to high and boil the mixture until it begins to turn yellow in colour and reaches the soft-ball stage (116°C/240°F).

4 Add the lemon juice to the syrup, but resist the temptation to stir it, as this could cause the syrup to crystallize. Continue boiling until it reaches the hard-crack stage (154°C/310°F), then remove from the heat. Place the pan briefly over the ice-water bath or cold water to arrest the cooking.

5 Sprinkle over the tartaric acid and quickly stir it into the syrup.

6 Holding the pan of syrup low over the marble, carefully pour it out to form small drops, about the size of a large coin, or spoon it on to the marble with a spoon.

7 Allow the discs to harden and cool. Using an offset spatula, loosen the discs from the marble. Dust with icing sugar, then shake off any excess. Serve immediately, or wrap in baking parchment or waxed paper and store in an airtight container.

COOK'S TIP
Although it sounds like a chemical, tartaric acid is actually an organic by-product of winemaking. If you cannot find tartaric acid, you may have an easier time finding citric acid. The two are interchangeable. Websites that sell home brewing kits usually sell tartaric acid.

Energy 1862kcal/7984kJ; Protein 1g; Carbohydrate 476g, of which sugars 475g; Fat 0g, of which saturates 0g; Cholesterol 0mg; Calcium 59mg; Fibre 0g; Sodium 25mg

Rhubarb and Custards

Inspired by a delicious dessert made from stewed rhubarb and vanilla-flavoured custard that was once common in schools, these iconic two-tone treats are one of the most popular and enduring British boiled sweets. Using two colours requires a pre-heated oven so that you can keep the unworked portion of syrup warm.

MAKES ABOUT 600G/1LB 6OZ

grapeseed or groundnut (peanut) oil, for greasing

450g/1lb/2¼ cups granulated (white) sugar, plus extra for tossing

150ml/¼ pint/⅔ cup water

1.5ml/¼ tsp cream of tartar

15ml/1 tbsp golden (light corn) syrup

10ml/2 tsp tartaric acid

½ vanilla pod (bean), scraped

2–3 drops pink food colouring

1 Grease a marble slab, a metal scraper and a pair of kitchen scissors. Prepare an ice-water bath. Preheat the oven to 150°C/300°F/Gas 2.

2 Combine the sugar, water, cream of tartar and golden syrup in a medium, heavy pan and stir over a medium heat to dissolve the sugar. Bring to the boil.

Variation
Traditionally these are made without vanilla, comprising a plain, yellowish-white sweet on one side and a slightly tart pink one on the other, but the addition of fresh vanilla in this recipe perfectly balances the flavours and makes them more special. You could omit the vanilla, if you prefer, or use 2 drops of vanilla extract instead.

3 Reduce the heat to medium and cook, without stirring, until it reaches the soft-crack stage (143°C/290°F). Add the tartaric acid and swirl the pan around.

4 Place the pan in an ice-water bath for a few moments to arrest the cooking, then pour the syrup on to the oiled marble and leave to cool until a skin forms. Using the oiled scraper, cut off half the syrup and place it back in the pan. Place the pan in the warm oven to keep the syrup soft.

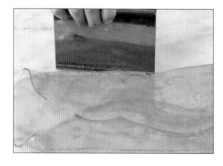

5 Using the scraper, begin to fold the edges into the centre of the larger portion of syrup until it is cool enough to handle. Add the scraped vanilla seeds to the syrup.

6 Oil your hands and, with the aid of the scraper, lift the syrup up off the marble and work it into a cylindrical shape, mixing the scraped vanilla seeds into the centre as you go. Pull it out from both ends to make a long strand.

7 Take hold of the ends of the syrup strand and pull them up towards you to form a 'U' shape. Twist the two sides together into a rope, then pull again from both ends to make the 'U' shape.

8 Repeat these steps for 15–20 minutes, until the syrup rope becomes opaque and a lot lighter in colour. Keep working it constantly so that it remains supple. If it becomes too hard, you can put it in the oven for a few minutes to soften.

9 Remove the un-pulled piece of syrup from the pan and replace it with the vanilla-flavoured piece. Set the pan aside. Working quickly, add the pink food colouring to the unworked syrup with the scraper and form it into a thick log.

10 Press the vanilla piece alongside the pink one. Pull the whole thing gently at both ends, until the combined strand is the required thickness. Cool slightly.

11 Using oiled scissors, cut small, even pieces from the strand. Toss in sugar. Serve immediately or wrap in baking parchment or waxed paper and store in an airtight container.

Energy 2015kcal/8595kJ; Protein 2.5g; Carbohydrate 534.4g, of which sugars 534.4g; Fat 0g, of which saturates 0g; Cholesterol 0mg; Calcium 269mg; Fibre 0g; Sodium 71mg

BULL'S EYES

Another Victorian-era confection, bull's eyes are slightly sour because of the addition of tartaric acid, which contrasts well with the deep caramel taste of the brown sugar. The pulling of the syrup lightens it, as air is incorporated; pulling half of the mixture and leaving the rest brown creates the two colours.

MAKES ABOUT 600G/1LB 6OZ

grapeseed or groundnut (peanut) oil, for greasing

425g/15oz/scant 2 cups soft dark brown sugar

75ml/5 tbsp water

0.75ml/⅛ tsp cream of tartar

2.5ml/½ tsp lemon extract

0.75ml/⅛ tsp tartaric acid or citric acid

1 Grease a marble slab, a metal scraper and a pair of kitchen scissors. Prepare an ice-water bath. Preheat the oven to 150°C/300°F/Gas 2.

2 Combine the soft dark brown sugar, water, and cream of tartar in a medium, heavy pan and heat gently until the sugar dissolves, then bring to the boil.

3 Reduce the heat to medium and cook, without stirring, until it reaches the soft-crack stage (143°C/290°F).

4 Add the lemon extract and tartaric acid or citric acid, then arrest the cooking by setting the pan into the ice-water bath.

5 Pour the syrup on to the oiled marble slab and allow it to cool until a skin forms.

6 Using the oiled scraper, cut off one-third of the syrup and put it back into the pan. Place the pan in the warm oven to prevent the syrup from hardening.

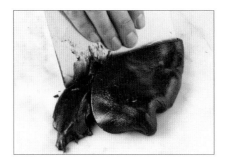

7 Using the scraper, begin to fold the edges of the remaining, larger portion of syrup into the centre, until it is cool enough to handle.

8 Oil your hands and, with the aid of the scraper, lift the syrup up off the marble and work it into a cylindrical shape. Pull it out from either end to make a long strand.

9 Take hold of the ends of the syrup strand and pull them up toward you to form a 'U' shape.

10 Twist the two sides together into a rope, then pull again from both ends to make the 'U' shape.

11 Repeat these steps for about 15–20 minutes, until the syrup rope becomes opaque and a lot lighter in colour. You need to keep working it constantly so that it remains supple. If it becomes too hard, you can put it in the oven for a few minutes until it softens enough to work with again.

12 Gently pull the syrup into a flat rectangle and place it on the marble slab.

13 Remove the smaller portion of syrup from the pan and roll it into a sausage shape that is as long as the longest side of the rectangle. Place it on one side of the rectangle. Roll the rectangle around it, so the darker syrup is enclosed.

14 Take hold of the ends and begin to pull as before, to form an upside-down 'U', then twist and pull into a long 2cm/¾in wide rope.

15 Using oiled scissors, cut it into small, even pieces. With oiled hands, roll the pieces into little balls. Serve immediately, or wrap in baking parchment or waxed paper and store in an airtight container.

Energy 1644kcal/7018kJ; Protein 0g; Carbohydrate 456g, of which sugars 456g; Fat 0g, of which saturates 0g; Cholesterol 0mg; Calcium 252mg; Fibre 0g; Sodium 140mg

PEPPERMINT HUMBUGS

'Humbug', meaning a hoax or hypocrite, was a term used frequently in the 18th and 19th centuries, most famously by Charles Dickens in *A Christmas Carol*. The sweet was developed in England around the same time, and was perhaps given the name because of the unexpected intensity of the peppermint flavour, which belies the appearance of the sweet. Traditionally a hard brown or black and white confection with a chewy centre, humbugs can now range in texture from minty toffees to hard sweets, as here.

MAKES ABOUT 600G/1LB 6OZ

grapeseed or groundnut (peanut) oil, for greasing

450g/1lb/2¼ cups granulated (white) sugar

150ml/¼ pint/⅔ cup water

1.5ml/¼ tsp cream of tartar

15ml/1 tbsp golden (light corn) syrup

10ml/2 tsp peppermint extract

2–3 drops black food colouring

1 Grease a marble slab, a metal scraper and a pair of kitchen scissors. Prepare an ice-water bath. Preheat the oven to 150°C/300°F/Gas 2.

2 Combine the sugar, water, cream of tartar and golden syrup in a medium, heavy pan and heat gently until the sugar dissolves, then bring to the boil.

3 Reduce the heat to medium and cook, without stirring, until it reaches the soft-crack stage (143°C/290°F). Add the peppermint extract.

4 Remove the pan from heat and arrest the cooking by momentarily placing the base of the pan in the ice-water bath.

5 Pour the syrup on to the oiled marble slab and leave it to cool until a skin forms.

6 Using the oiled scraper, cut off one-third of the syrup and place it back in the pan. Place the pan in the warm oven to prevent the syrup from hardening.

7 Using the scraper, begin to fold the edges of the larger portion of syrup into its centre until cool enough to handle.

8 Oil your hands and, with the aid of the scraper, lift the syrup up off the marble and work it into a cylindrical shape. Pull it out from both ends to form a long strand.

9 Take hold of the ends of the syrup strand and pull them up toward you to form a 'U' shape. Twist the two sides together into a rope, then pull again from both ends to make the 'U' shape.

10 Repeat these steps for 15–20 minutes, until the syrup rope becomes opaque and a lot lighter in colour. You need to work it constantly so that it remains supple. If it becomes too hard, you can put it in the oven for a few minutes to soften.

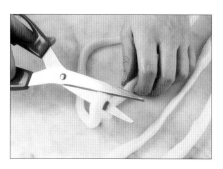

11 Divide the pulled syrup into four sections and pull these out to form strands of equal length and thickness.

12 Remove the un-pulled piece of syrup from the pan. Working quickly, add the black food colouring to it with the scraper, and shape it into a log that is the same length as the white pieces but quite a lot thicker.

13 Press the four white ropes of pulled syrup alongside and around the black log, spacing them evenly around the central black piece. Pull the whole thing gently at both ends until the combined piece is the required thickness of the sweets. Twist it once or twice so that the white strands spiral around the black. If the humbug taffy is still too soft, let it cool slightly and firm up a bit more, then cut it into small, even pieces.

14 Serve immediately, or wrap in baking parchment or waxed paper and store in an airtight container.

Energy 1621kcal/6914kJ; Protein 2g; Carbohydrate 429.9g, of which sugars 429.9g; Fat 0g, of which saturates 0g; Cholesterol 0mg; Calcium 216mg; Fibre 0g; Sodium 65mg

Aniseed Twists

Also known as anise candy, these little, hard twists have a wonderful depth of flavour. They can be made with anise extract for a smooth consistency, or you can use fresh aniseed, which is a great alternative – the tiny, flavourful seeds give a nice contrast to the sweetness. If you can get your hands on the lovely twisted moulds traditionally used to shape these confections, use them. If not, follow the directions below.

MAKES ABOUT 600G/1LB 6OZ

grapeseed or groundnut (peanut) oil, for greasing

400g/14oz/2 cups caster (superfine) sugar

100ml/3½fl oz/scant ½ cup water

100ml/3½fl oz/scant ½ cup liquid glucose or golden (light corn) syrup

15ml/1 tbsp red food colouring or 3 drops concentrated colour paste or gel

15ml/1 tbsp pulverized aniseed or 10ml/2 tsp anise extract

1 Grease a marble slab, a metal scraper and a pair of kitchen scissors. Prepare an ice-water bath.

2 Combine the sugar, water and liquid glucose or golden syrup in a medium, heavy pan and heat gently until the sugar dissolves, then bring to the boil.

3 Reduce the heat to medium and cook, without stirring, until the mixture reaches the soft-crack stage (143°C/290°F). Add the food colouring and aniseed or anise extract. Arrest the cooking by placing the pan briefly in the ice-water bath.

4 Pour the sugar syrup on to your prepared marble and let it cool until a skin forms on the surface.

5 Using the oiled scraper, begin to fold the edges into the centre of the pool until it is cool enough to handle.

6 Oil your hands and, with the aid of the scraper, lift the syrup up off the marble and work it into a cylindrical shape. Pull it out from both ends to make a long, thick strand.

7 Take hold of the ends of the syrup strand and pull them up towards you to form a 'U' shape. Twist the two sides together into a rope shape.

8 Continue to stretch the rope, twisting all the time, until it is 1cm/½in thick. Working quickly, use oiled scissors to cut the strand into even, bitesize pieces.

9 Wrap the individual pieces in cellophane and either serve immediately or store in an airtight container.

Energy 1894kcal/8079kJ; Protein 2g; Carbohydrate 502.7g, of which sugars 458.2g; Fat 0g, of which saturates 0g; Cholesterol 0mg; Calcium 220mg; Fibre 0g; Sodium 17mg

BARLEY SUGAR STICKS

Barley sugar was originally made with the water left over from cooking pearl barley, but it is essentially a hard-boiled sweet flavoured with lemon. You could try making them using the strained cooking water from boiled pearl barley, if you like. The flavour will be rich and earthy, slightly different from the taste of the commercially produced types. It will also make the sweets considerably more nutritious.

MAKES ABOUT 600G/1LB 6OZ

grapeseed or groundnut (peanut) oil, for greasing

450g/1lb/2¼ cups granulated (white) sugar

150ml/¼ pint/⅔ cup water

thinly peeled rind of 1 lemon

1.5ml/¼ tsp cream of tartar

juice of ½ lemon

1 Grease a marble slab, a palette knife or metal spatula, and a pair of kitchen scissors. Prepare an ice-water bath.

2 Place the sugar and water in a heavy pan and bring to the boil. Add the lemon rind and cream of tartar.

3 Boil the syrup until it reaches the soft-ball stage (114°C/238°F). Add the lemon juice, then continue to boil until it reaches the hard-crack stage (154°C/310°F).

4 Remove the pan from the heat. Arrest the cooking by placing it momentarily over the ice-water bath. Remove the lemon rind with a fork and discard.

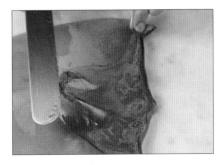

5 Pour the syrup on to the marble and allow it to cool for 1 minute. Using the oiled palette knife or metal spatula, fold each side into the centre of the pool.

6 Gently pull the two ends to make a longer, thinner, flat piece of syrup. Using oiled scissors, cut 1cm/½in strips.

7 Working quickly, twist the strips into corkscrew shapes. Serve immediately, or wrap the sweets in baking parchment or waxed paper and store in an airtight container.

Energy 1777kcal/7579kJ; Protein 0g; Carbohydrate 473g, of which sugars 473g; Fat 0g, of which saturates 0g; Cholesterol 0mg; Calcium 47mg; Fibre 0g; Sodium 23mg

CANDY CANES

These colourful confections are fun to create and make great holiday gifts. They can be used to decorate a Christmas tree, adding the finishing festive touch, which children in particular will love. This recipe uses peppermint extract and red food colouring, but you could experiment with other colours and flavours.

MAKES ABOUT 600G/1LB 6OZ

grapeseed or groundnut (peanut) oil, for greasing

450g/1lb/2¼ cups granulated (white) sugar

150ml/¼ pint/⅔ cup water

1.5ml/¼ tsp cream of tartar

15ml/1 tbsp golden (light corn) syrup

10ml/2 tsp peppermint extract

2–3 drops red food colouring

1 Grease a marble slab, a metal scraper and a pair of kitchen scissors. Prepare an ice-water bath. Preheat the oven to 150°C/300°F/Gas 2.

2 Combine the sugar, water, cream of tartar and golden syrup in a medium, heavy pan, and stir over a medium heat to dissolve the sugar.

3 Once the sugar has dissolved, bring it to the boil.

4 Reduce the heat to medium and cook the syrup, without stirring, until it reaches the soft-crack stage (143°C/290°F).

5 Add the peppermint extract. Place the base of the pan over the ice-water bath momentarily to arrest the cooking.

6 Pour the syrup on to the oiled marble slab and allow it to cool until a skin forms on the surface.

7 Using the oiled scraper, cut off half the syrup and place it back in the pan. Place the pan in the warm oven to prevent the syrup from hardening while you work the other half.

8 Using the oiled scraper, begin to fold the edges of the syrup into the centre until it is cool enough to handle.

9 Oil your hands and, with the aid of the scraper, lift the syrup up off the marble and work it into a cylindrical shape. Pull it out from both ends to make a long strand.

10 Take hold of the ends of the syrup strand and pull them up toward you to form a 'U' shape.

11 Twist the two sides together into a rope, then pull again from both ends to make the 'U' shape.

12 Repeat these steps for about 15–20 minutes, until the syrup rope becomes opaque and a lot lighter in colour. You need to keep working it constantly so that it remains supple. If it becomes too hard, you can put it in the oven for a few minutes until it softens enough to work with again.

13 Remove the un-pulled piece of syrup from the pan. Place the pulled piece in the warm pan and set it aside.

14 Working quickly, add the red food colouring to the unworked syrup with the scraper.

15 Work the red syrup into a thick log that is about the same length as the white piece of syrup.

16 Retrieve the white piece from the warm pan and press it alongside the red piece. Pull the whole thing gently at both ends until the strands are about 1cm/½in thick. Twist the rope to create a swirl pattern. Leave it to cool slightly.

17 Using oiled scissors, cut the pulled syrup into long, even lengths, and bend a curve in the top of each, to form canes. Leave to harden completely. Serve immediately, or wrap in baking parchment or waxed paper and store in an airtight container.

Energy 1775kcal/7570kJ; Protein 0g; Carbohydrate 473g, of which sugars 473g; Fat 0g, of which saturates 0g; Cholesterol 0mg; Calcium 45mg; Fibre 0g; Sodium 23mg

ROSE WATER EDINBURGH ROCK

Edinburgh rock was one of those cooking mishaps that turned into a triumph. It is nothing like conventional British rock. The story goes that some boiled sweets were exposed to air overnight, and as a result went soft and powdery, causing a revelation. These can be made in any flavour, but delicate, aromatic rose water works particularly well with these pretty confections.

5 Using the scraper, fold the edges into the centre until cool enough to handle.

6 Dust your hands with icing sugar. Lift the syrup and form it into a cylindrical shape. Take hold of the ends and pull them toward you to form a 'U' shape. Press the two sides together and form it into the 'U' shape again. Do not twist it. Continue for 10 minutes until opaque.

7 Pull it into a long strip, then cut it into small pieces with scissors. Leave it out at room temperature for 24 hours, until soft and powdery. Serve immediately, or store in an airtight container after that.

MAKES ABOUT 675G/1½LB

grapeseed or groundnut (peanut) oil, for greasing

450g/1lb/2¼ cups granulated (white) sugar

15ml/1 tbsp liquid glucose or golden (light corn) syrup

2.5ml/½ tsp cream of tartar

200ml/7fl oz/scant 1 cup water

10ml/2 tsp pink food colouring, or 2 drops concentrated colour paste or gel

10ml/2 tsp rose water

icing (confectioners') sugar, for dusting

1 Grease a marble slab, a metal scraper and a pair of kitchen scissors. Prepare an ice-water bath.

2 Combine the sugar, liquid glucose or golden syrup, cream of tartar and water in a medium heavy pan. Heat gently over medium heat until the sugar dissolves.

3 Bring it to the boil. Boil until it reaches the soft-crack stage (143°C/290°F).

4 Stir in the colouring and rose water and immediately place the pan over the ice-water bath to arrest the cooking. Pour the syrup on to the oiled marble slab and allow it to cool until a skin forms.

Energy 1821kcal/7768kJ; Protein 2.3g; Carbohydrate 483g, of which sugars 476.3g; Fat 0g, of which saturates 0g; Cholesterol 0mg; Calcium 240mg; Fibre 0g; Sodium 50mg

SALT-WATER TAFFY

Supposedly made with sea water, salt-water taffy is originally from Atlantic City, though you used to be able to find it along the boardwalks at most American seaside towns. Although it is not as common today, it is still available from traditional candy stores. Soft and chewy and with the addition of a pinch of salt, it is the perfect treat. Chewing on these, you can almost hear the seagulls.

MAKES ABOUT 400G/14OZ

grapeseed or groundnut (peanut) oil, for greasing

200g/7oz/1 cup caster (superfine) or granulated (white) sugar

15ml/1 tbsp cornflour (cornstarch)

150ml/¼ pint/⅔ cup liquid glucose or golden (light corn) syrup

25g/1oz/2 tbsp unsalted butter

120ml/4fl oz/½ cup water

1.5ml/¼ tsp sea salt

1 Grease a marble slab, a metal scraper and a pair of kitchen scissors. You will need waxed paper for wrapping.

2 Combine the sugar and cornflour in a large, heavy pan. Add the liquid glucose or golden syrup, butter, water and salt, and heat gently until the sugar dissolves, then boil over medium heat until it reaches the hard-ball stage (130°C/266°F).

3 Pour the taffy on to the prepared marble slab. Allow the taffy to cool for a few minutes until it can be handled.

VARIATION
Add food colouring or flavours to the syrup just as it reaches the hard-ball stage. Traditionally, it comes in pastel shades.

4 Oil your hands and, with the aid of the scraper, lift the syrup up off the marble slab and work it into a cylindrical shape.

5 Pull the syrup out from both ends to make a long, thick strand. Take hold of the ends of the syrup strand and pull them up toward you to form a 'U' shape.

6 Twist the two sides into a rope, then continue in this way, twisting the whole time, for 10 minutes, until it is lighter and firm enough to hold a shape. Stretch the strand until it is 2.5cm/1in in diameter.

7 Using oiled scissors, cut the strand into bitesize pieces. Wrap in waxed paper and twist the ends to seal. Serve immediately, or store in an airtight container.

Energy 1502kcal/6378kJ; Protein 1.2g; Carbohydrate 350g, of which sugars 269.3g; Fat 21g, of which saturates 14g; Cholesterol 58mg; Calcium 124mg; Fibre 0g; Sodium 1022mg

HONEY AND STAR ANISE CHEWS

Star anise is usually found whole, but it is easily ground in a coffee bean grinder or blender. It adds a wonderful depth of flavour to these simple chews, and combines perfectly with the honey and sesame seeds. Choose any variety of honey you like – each type will give a slightly different taste.

MAKES ABOUT 25

50g/2oz/4 tbsp sesame seeds

225ml/7½fl oz/scant 1 cup honey

6ml/1¼ tsp ground star anise
(*see* Cook's Tip)

COOK'S TIP
Grinding your own spices gives more flavour, but the aroma can linger. To clean a spice grinder, wash it with warm soapy water and dry it well. Place a little stale bread in the grinder and whizz it around. It will gather most of the residual scent.

1 Place a dry frying pan over medium heat. When it gets hot, add the sesame seeds. Watch them carefully, as they burn easily. Toss the sesame seeds around until they are a light golden brown, but not too dark. Transfer them to a small bowl.

2 Place about 25 mini cake or sweet cases on a baking sheet and set aside.

3 In a small pan, cook the honey and star anise together over a low heat until the mixture reaches the firm-ball stage (120°C/248°F).

4 When the honey reaches the firm-ball stage, remove it from the heat and spoon it into the prepared cases.

5 Leave to cool, then sprinkle with the sesame seeds. Serve immediately or store in an airtight container.

Energy 38kcal/160kJ; Protein 0g; Carbohydrate 7g, of which sugars 7g; Fat 1g, of which saturates 0g; Cholesterol 0mg; Calcium 15mg; Fibre 0g; Sodium 1mg

MAPLE CREAM CANDY

Walnuts and maple syrup are wonderful together, though if you prefer a creamy maple candy with no nuts, you can omit them. These candies have a soft, chewy consistency, and are particularly popular in the US, where maple syrup is a much-loved ingredient in muffins and drizzled over pancakes.

MAKES ABOUT 675G/1½LB

400g/14oz/2 cups granulated (white) sugar

225g/8oz/⅔ cup maple syrup

120ml/4fl oz/½ cup double (heavy) cream

120ml/4fl oz/½ cup water

1 vanilla pod (bean)

25g/1oz/2 tbsp unsalted butter, plus extra for greasing

40g/1½oz/⅓ cup walnuts, finely chopped

2.5ml/½ tsp salt

about 25 walnut halves

1 Place about 25 mini cake or sweet cases on a baking sheet. Alternatively, grease a 20cm/8in square cake tin (pan) and line it with baking parchment.

2 Combine the sugar, maple syrup, cream and water in a heavy pan. Split the vanilla pod and scrape the seeds into the pan. Add the pod, too. Place over a medium heat and stir until the sugar has dissolved.

3 Bring to the boil, then boil, without stirring, until the mixture reaches the soft-ball stage (114°C/238°F).

4 Add the butter and stir to combine. Pour the mixture into a shallow bowl and leave to cool to 43°C/110°F.

5 Beat the syrup with a wooden spoon until it is light and fluffy (alternatively, use an electric mixer). Stir in the nuts and salt.

6 Press the mixture into the cake cases or the prepared tin. If using a tin, score the surface to create about 25 portions. Top each with a walnut half. Leave to go cold, then cut along the markings.

7 Serve immediately, or store in an airtight container for a few days.

Energy 3773kcal/15818kJ; Protein 20g; Carbohydrate 577g, of which sugars 562g; Fat 168g, of which saturates 60g; Cholesterol 222mg; Calcium 366mg; Fibre 7g; Sodium 1060mg

FONDANT-STUFFED PECANS

These traditional sweets may seem dated, but they are delicious and beautiful. The hard caramel shell glistens in the sunlight and sparkles in candlelight, so whether you take them to a picnic or present them after supper, they will impress. Display them in lovely paper cases and pack them tightly in little gift boxes for presents.

MAKES ABOUT 900G/2LB

750g/1lb 11oz/3¾ cups caster (superfine) sugar

200ml/7fl oz/scant 1 cup water

200g/7oz/2 cups pecan halves

15ml/1 tbsp Grand Marnier or Cointreau

finely grated rind of 1 orange

1.5ml/¼ tsp cream of tartar

icing (confectioners') sugar, for dusting

1 Dampen a marble slab, a metal scraper and a wooden spatula with cold water. Prepare an ice-water bath.

2 Combine 400g/14oz/2 cups of the caster sugar and 150ml/¼ pint/⅔ cup water in a large, heavy pan and heat until the sugar has dissolved. Bring to the boil, then lower the heat and cook until it reaches the soft-ball stage (114°C/238°F).

3 Arrest the cooking by placing the pan in the ice-water bath. Pour the syrup on to the prepared marble slab and leave it to cool for 3 minutes.

4 Using the damp metal scraper, begin to fold the edges into the centre of the pool until the mixture becomes glossy.

5 With the wooden spatula, work the syrup in a figure-of-eight movement for 10 minutes, or until thick and opaque.

6 First using the metal scraper and then with moist hands, work and knead the fondant for 10 minutes to remove all lumps and create a smooth paste.

VARIATION
You can experiment with the flavouring in the fondant. Preserved cherry and Kirsch would make a tasty alternative to orange.

7 Moisten a bowl and place the fondant inside. Cover with a damp dish towel and rest for 12 hours in the refrigerator.

8 Check through the pecan halves, setting aside any that are broken or unattractive for another recipe. Line a baking tray with baking parchment.

9 Add the liqueur and rind to the fondant. Knead the fondant until it is incorporated.

10 Dust your hands with icing sugar, then break off small pieces of fondant and roll them into small balls.

11 Press a pecan on either side of the fondant, and place on the baking tray.

12 Prepare an ice-water bath. Combine the remaining caster sugar and water in a heavy pan with the cream of tartar, then heat gently. Stir until the sugar has dissolved, then cook, without stirring, until the mixture becomes a caramel colour. As soon as it reaches the right colour, arrest the cooking by placing the pan briefly in the ice-water bath.

13 Drop a few fondant balls at a time into the syrup, lifting out with a fork and placing on a cooling rack positioned over a piece of baking parchment to catch the drips. (You could place them directly on to the baking parchment, but this will leave the candies with a little 'foot' of caramel.)

14 After about an hour, the caramel will have hardened and the balls can be placed into individual mini cupcake or truffle cases and served. They will keep in an airtight container for a few days.

Energy 4377kcal/18445kJ; Protein 29g; Carbohydrate 799g, of which sugars 798g; Fat 137g, of which saturates 11g; Cholesterol 0mg; Calcium 263mg; Fibre 12g; Sodium 52mg

LEMON CREAM DREAMS

Soft, lemony, chewy morsels, these are wonderful sweets for sunny afternoons. They can be served alongside scones at a tea party, or dressed down by wrapping the cooled, set sweets in little squares of baking parchment to pack for picnics. They will make a great little energy booster on a long walk or cycle ride as well. The fondant needs to chill overnight, so start preparations the day before you need them.

MAKES 25–30

400g/14oz/2 cups caster (superfine) sugar

150ml/½ pint/⅔ cup water

60ml/4 tbsp lemon juice

finely grated rind of 1 lemon

50g/2oz candied lemon peel

25g/1oz/¼ cup chopped pistachios

1 Dampen a marble slab, metal scraper and wooden spatula with cold water. Prepare an ice-water bath.

2 Combine the sugar and water in a large, heavy pan and heat until the sugar dissolves.

3 Bring to the boil, then lower the heat and cook until it reaches the soft-ball stage (114°C/238°F).

4 Arrest the cooking by placing the pan in the ice-water bath. Pour the syrup on to the prepared marble and leave it to cool for 3 minutes.

5 Using the damp metal scraper, begin to fold the edges into the centre of the pool until the mixture becomes glossy.

6 With the wooden spatula, work the syrup in a figure-of-eight movement for about 10 minutes, until it is thick and opaque.

7 First using the metal scraper and then with moist hands, work and knead the fondant for 10 minutes to remove all lumps and create a smooth paste.

8 Moisten a bowl and place the fondant inside. Cover with a damp dish towel and rest for 12 hours in the refrigerator.

9 Set out 25–30 mini cake cases on a baking sheet. Chop the candied peel.

10 Place the fondant in a heatproof bowl over a pan of barely simmering water. The water should reach the same level as the fondant in the bowl.

11 Stir until just melted, then add the lemon juice and rind. If you melt it too much, it will go clear and then never set.

12 Pour the melted fondant into the mini cake cases, and sprinkle with the chopped peel and pistachios.

13 Leave to cool at room temperature, then serve. These can be stored in an airtight container for a few days.

Energy 62kcal/262kJ; Protein 0.2g; Carbohydrate 15g, of which sugars 15g; Fat 0.5g, of which saturates 0.1g; Cholesterol 0mg; Calcium 10mg; Fibre 0.1g; Sodium 10mg

FRUIT SHERBET

Kids love fizzy, sweet-yet-acidic sherbet, and it is very easy to make at home. You could even recreate a childhood classic combination by making the Raspberry Lollipops on the opposite page to dip in the powder. This combination evokes nostalgia on both sides of the Atlantic.

2 Transfer the sugar to a large mixing bowl, and add the tartaric acid or citric acid and the lemon or orange extract.

3 Add the yellow or orange food colouring to the sugar.

4 Mix well with a wooden spoon or spatula until the colour is evenly distributed throughout the sugar. This may take a few minutes.

MAKES 500G/1¼LB

500g/1¼lb/2½ cups caster (superfine) sugar

15ml/1 tbsp tartaric acid or citric acid

10–12 drops lemon or orange extract

1–2 drops yellow or orange food colouring

COOK'S TIP
To make a tasty drink, simply combine 1–2 tsp of the powder with a glass of water.

1 Put the caster sugar into the bowl of a food processor or blender, and blend until the sugar is in extremely fine crystals. This should take a few minutes.

5 Leave the sherbet to dry before storing in an airtight container. Serve in bags for dipping lollipops into, or use the powder to make a refreshing drink (see Cook's Tip).

Energy 1970kcal/8405kJ; Protein 2.5g; Carbohydrate 522.5g, of which sugars 522.5g; Fat 0g, of which saturates 0g; Cholesterol 0mg; Calcium 265mg; Fibre 0g; Sodium 30mg

RASPBERRY LOLLIPOPS

Fruit juice lollipops are one of the best ways to preserve the natural flavour of perfectly ripe berries. These raspberry lollipops have a wonderful colour, and taste even better than they look. Experiment with different berries or fresh fruit juices to make a range of fun and delicious lollipops.

MAKES ABOUT 675G/1½LB

grapeseed or groundnut (peanut) oil, for greasing

300g/11oz/2 cups raspberries

400g/14oz/2 cups caster (superfine) sugar

1 Grease a baking sheet and prepare an ice-water bath.

2 Put the raspberries in a heavy pan, and heat gently until the fruits have softened and the juices have run. Do not stir.

3 Strain through a sieve (strainer) placed over a large bowl to catch the juices. Resist the temptation to push the berries through the sieve with a spoon or other implement, as this will cause the juice to go cloudy.

4 Put the sugar in a heavy pan and add the strained raspberry juice. Stir the mixture over medium heat until the sugar has dissolved, then bring the mixture to the boil.

5 Boil, without stirring, over medium heat until the syrup reaches the hard-crack stage (154°C/310°F). You must not stir the syrup at this stage. If sugar crystals form around the edge of the pan, use a dampened pastry or silicone brush to coax them back into the syrup. Arrest the cooking by placing the pan in the ice-bath.

6 Pour spoonfuls of the syrup on to the prepared baking sheet, about 5cm/2in apart. Press lollipop sticks into the syrup. Pour another drop of syrup over the top of the stick to seal it in.

7 Allow the lollipops to cool completely before removing and wrapping them individually in cellophane.

Energy 1651kcal/7051kJ; Protein 6.2g; Carbohydrate 432g, of which sugars 432g; Fat 1g, of which saturates 0.3g; Cholesterol 0mg; Calcium 287mg; Fibre 7.5g; Sodium 33mg

JEWELLED LOLLIPOPS

Lollipops are always popular with children. They are usually round or oval-shaped and come in many colours. These beautiful jewelled ones are wonderfully simple to make, using pretty dried fruits and nuts for texture and decoration. You can use whatever fruits and nuts you like.

MAKES 12

grapeseed or groundnut (peanut) oil, for greasing

100ml/3½fl oz/scant ½ cup water

400g/14oz/2 cups caster (superfine) sugar

15ml/1 tbsp liquid glucose or 5ml/ 1 tsp cream of tartar

40g/1½oz/¼ cup assorted dried fruits, such as cranberries, sultanas (golden raisins) and chopped apricots

25g/1oz/3 tbsp shelled pistachio nuts

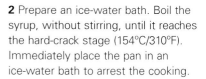

1 Grease a marble slab or baking sheet, or line it with a silicone mat. Put the water, sugar and liquid glucose or cream of tartar in a large, heavy pan. Stir over medium heat until the sugar has dissolved.

2 Prepare an ice-water bath. Boil the syrup, without stirring, until it reaches the hard-crack stage (154°C/310°F). Immediately place the pan in an ice-water bath to arrest the cooking.

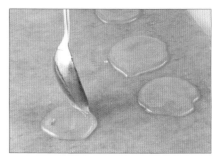

3 Spoon 12 circles of syrup on to the prepared surface, reserving about one-fifth of the syrup.

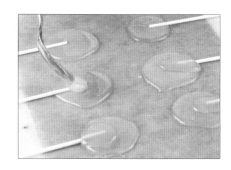

4 Working quickly, press a lollipop stick into each lollipop, then pour a drop of the remaining syrup over the top of each stick so that it is sealed in.

5 Press in the dried fruits and nuts to make a random pattern.

6 Leave the lollipops to harden for about 10 minutes, then remove them carefully from the surface by holding on to the stick; go slowly, they will release eventually. You may have some breakage, but the recipe makes plenty to account for this.

7 Serve immediately, or wrap in baking parchment or waxed paper and store for a few days in an airtight container.

Energy 157kcal/668kJ; Protein 0.6g; Carbohydrate 38.4g, of which sugars 37.8g; Fat 1.2g, of which saturates 0.2g; Cholesterol 0mg; Calcium 22mg; Fibre 0.2g; Sodium 16mg

CHOCOLATE LOLLIPOPS

These simple lollipops use chocolate rather than sugar syrup, and are extremely versatile. Here I have made lacy swirls and heart shapes, but you could make them into any shape or size. These treats are whimsical and jolly; children will enjoy helping to make them, or you can serve them to friends.

MAKES 6

200g/7oz dark (bittersweet) chocolate, chopped

edible silver dust and chopped candied fruits, rose petals and violets, to decorate (optional)

1 Line a baking sheet with baking parchment or a silicone mat, and line six lollipop sticks in a row, leaving about 7.5cm/3in between each one.

2 Place 150g/5oz of the chocolate in a heatproof bowl. Bring a pan of water to the boil, then remove from the heat.

3 Place the bowl of chocolate over the steaming water, making sure the water does not touch the bottom of the bowl. Stir the chocolate once or twice as it melts, then leave the chocolate to stand for 10 minutes and stir again.

4 Meanwhile, chop the remaining chocolate into fine shards.

5 Add the shards of chocolate, a spoonful at a time, to the melted chocolate, stirring each time until completely smooth and the chocolate reaches 30°C/86°F exactly. You may not need all of the chocolate shards.

6 Remove the bowl from the pan of water and set it aside. Put the pan of water back on the heat and bring it to the boil, then remove it from the heat.

7 Place the bowl of chocolate back over the hot water for a few seconds to bring the temperature up to 32°C/89°F.

8 Using a pastry (piping) bag fitted with a medium round nozzle, pipe the chocolate in swirly shapes over the lollipop sticks. Alternatively, spoon solid circles of chocolate on to the sticks. You can write letters or numbers, or shape them however you wish.

9 Decorate with edible dust or candied fruits and flowers, if you like.

10 Place the baking sheet in the refrigerator for 5 minutes, then remove and leave to stand at room temperature for 15 minutes before removing the lollipops from the parchment. Serve immediately, or store in an airtight container for up to a week.

Energy 170kcal/712kJ; Protein 2g; Carbohydrate 21g, of which sugars 21g; Fat 9g, of which saturates 6g; Cholesterol 2mg; Calcium 11mg; Fibre 0g; Sodium 2mg

Toffees, Caramels and Nut Brittles

An amazing range of textures can be achieved when sugar is combined with other ingredients, such as butter, cream and golden syrup, and heated to a specific temperature. From chewy toffees to firmer butterscotch and light-as-air honeycomb, there is sure to be something for everyone in this chapter. Delicious on their own, these treats can be further enhanced by the addition of chocolate, nuts or seeds, or embellished with gold leaf for an extra-special touch.

CARAMEL APPLES

These delicious treats are popular at fairs and fêtes around the world. The buttery, chewy caramel contrasts well with the crisp apple, though eating these is a messy experience. Wooden dowels are sturdy enough to hold apples, and are available at hardware stores. Make sure there are no sharp points, especially when serving to children.

3 Place all of the remaining ingredients in a pan and warm over a medium heat. Stir to dissolve everything together into an emulsified mass.

4 Once the sugar has dissolved, bring the mixture to the boil and cook until it reaches the soft-ball stage (114°C/238°F).

5 Remove the caramel from the heat and arrest the cooking by placing the pan over the ice-water bath.

6 Leave the mixture to cool to 82°C/180°F before dipping the apples into the caramel, holding them by their sticks.

7 Place the caramel-covered apples on the parchment-lined baking sheet, stick- or dowel-end up, and allow them to cool and set.

8 If the caramel slips off of the apple skin at all, leave it to cool slightly, then dip the apple again. Serve immediately, or store in the refrigerator for up to 3 days.

MAKES 8

8 small or medium eating apples, washed and dried

115g/4oz/½ cup unsalted butter

200g/7oz/1 cup granulated (white) sugar

150ml/¼ pint/⅔ cup double (heavy) cream

15ml/1 tbsp soft light brown sugar

125g/4¼oz/⅓ cup golden (light corn) syrup

2.5ml/½ tsp vanilla extract

1.5ml/¼ tsp salt

1 Push wooden dowels or ice lolly (popsicle) sticks into the stem-end of the apples.

2 Prepare an ice-water bath and line a baking tray with baking parchment.

Energy 366kcal/1534kJ; Protein 0.8g; Carbohydrate 47g, of which sugars 47g; Fat 22g, of which saturates 13.4g; Cholesterol 57mg; Calcium 33mg; Fibre 1.1g; Sodium 160mg

PECAN TOFFEES

This rich, deep and dark toffee recipe comes originally from New Orleans. Its French-Creole name is La Colle, which means 'glue'; when made correctly, it should have a luxuriously thick and very smooth texture, interspersed with crunchy pecans.

MAKES ABOUT 550G/1LB 5OZ

125g/4¼oz/¾ cup pecans

50ml/2fl oz/¼ cup water

425g/15oz/scant 2 cups soft dark brown sugar

1 Preheat the oven to 160°C/325°F/ Gas 3. Spread the pecans out on a baking sheet and place in the oven.

2 Set a timer for 7 minutes and then check the nuts, giving them a toss. They will probably need another few minutes. Test whether they are done by breaking one in half. It should be slightly golden but not brown. You will just start to smell them when they are ready.

3 Remove the pecans from the oven. Allow them to cool for a few minutes, then transfer them to a chopping board.

4 Chop the pecans roughly, then sift them to separate the fine powder from the nut pieces. Save the nut powder and set them both aside.

5 Put the water into a heavy pan and add the soft dark brown sugar. Heat over low heat until the sugar has dissolved completely.

VARIATION
Substitute the soft dark brown sugar with black treacle (molasses), but use only 225g/8oz/⅔ cup.

6 Once the sugar has dissolved, turn the heat up to medium-high and bring the mixture to the boil. Boil until it reaches the soft-crack stage (143°C/290°F).

7 Stir in the toasted, chopped pecans.

8 Spoon the mixture into mini paper cake or sweet cases, then sprinkle with the fine nut powder and leave to cool completely. Once cool, serve immediately or store them in an airtight container.

Energy 2536kcal/10698kJ; Protein 13.6g; Carbohydrate 451.4g, of which sugars 449.5g; Fat 87.6g, of which saturates 7.1g; Cholesterol 0mg; Calcium 302mg; Fibre 5.9g; Sodium 27mg

Nutty Chocolate Toffee

This toffee is crunchy and buttery and could be made with any one of your favourite nuts. The combination of dark chocolate and macadamia works wonderfully, making this treat rich and luxurious, but different nuts, such as pecans or hazelnuts, would be equally delicious.

MAKES ABOUT 850G/1LB 12OZ

200g/7oz/generous 1 cup macadamia nut halves

60ml/4 tbsp water

350g/12oz/1¾ cups caster (superfine) sugar

125g/4¼oz/8½ tbsp unsalted butter

15ml/1 tbsp black treacle (molasses)

1.5ml/¼ tsp sea salt

5ml/1 tsp vanilla extract

1.5ml/¼ tsp bicarbonate of soda (baking soda)

150g/5oz dark (bittersweet) chocolate (60–70% cocoa solids), finely chopped

1 Preheat the oven to 160°C/325°F/ Gas 3. Spread the macadamias out on a baking sheet and place in the oven.

2 Set a timer for 5 minutes and then check the nuts, giving them a toss. They will probably need another few minutes. They should be slightly golden but not brown. Macadamia nuts contain a lot of oil so they can burn easily. Remove them from the oven and set aside.

3 Line a shallow baking tray with baking parchment. Spread three-quarters of the macadamias out on the tray, tightly packed so that you cannot see the bottom. Set the rest aside for the topping.

4 Combine the water, sugar, butter, black treacle and salt in a heavy pan. Place over a low heat and heat until the sugar has dissolved.

5 Bring to the boil and boil, without stirring, until the syrup reaches the hard-crack stage (154°C/310°F).

6 Immediately remove from the heat and stir in the vanilla and bicarbonate of soda. Be sure to stir thoroughly to incorporate these ingredients.

7 Quickly pour the mixture over the nuts. Shake the baking tray and tap it on the counter to get an even covering of toffee all over the nuts.

8 Sprinkle the chocolate evenly on top (the chocolate will melt into the toffee).

9 Roughtly chop the reserved macadamia nuts, and sprinkle them on top of the chocolate.

10 Leave to cool completely, then break into pieces and serve. Store in an airtight container at room temperature.

Energy 4254kcal/17814kJ; Protein 61g; Carbohydrate 498g, of which sugars 478g; Fat 238g, of which saturates 109g; Cholesterol 301mg; Calcium 456mg; Fibre 12g; Sodium 993mg

BONFIRE TOFFEE

Dark, intensely flavoured and satisfyingly hard and brittle to crunch on, this traditional British toffee is the perfect accompaniment to fireworks and fun on Bonfire Night. The dark shards taste strongly of black treacle, but the flavour is rounded by the demerara sugar and the richness of the butter.

MAKES ABOUT 600G/1LB 6OZ

125g/4¼oz/8½ tbsp unsalted butter, plus extra for greasing

225ml/7½fl oz/scant 1 cup black treacle (molasses)

200g/7oz/scant 1 cup demerara (raw) sugar

tiny pinch of salt

1 Grease a shallow baking tray. Place the butter in a large, heavy pan and melt it over low heat.

2 Add the black treacle and demerara sugar and, still over a low heat, let them gently dissolve into the butter.

3 Once the sugar has dissolved, turn the heat up to medium and bring the mixture to the boil. Boil until the mixture is just below the hard-crack stage (140°C/280°F).

4 Immediately pour the syrup into the prepared baking tray and leave to cool for about 10 minutes.

5 When the toffee is completely cold, break it into bitesize shards using a palette knife or metal spatula.

6 Wrap each shard in greaseproof or waxed paper and store them in an airtight container.

Energy 2386kcal/10037kJ; Protein 4.5g; Carbohydrate 386g, of which sugars 386g; Fat 102g, of which saturates 68g; Cholesterol 288mg; Calcium 1263mg; Fibre 0g; Sodium 1167mg

CINDER TOFFEE

Like golden cinders from the fire, this toffee is an old favourite in many parts of the world. It is known by many names, including yellow man, puff candy, hokey pokey, sponge candy, sea foam and angel food candy. To make it into an extra-special treat, dip the toffee pieces into melted chocolate and allow them to set.

MAKES ABOUT 300G/11OZ

butter, for greasing

60ml/4 tbsp water

225g/8oz/generous 1 cup caster (superfine) sugar

15ml/1 tbsp golden (light corn) syrup

1.5ml/¼ tsp bicarbonate of soda (baking soda), sifted

5ml/1 tsp warm water

4 Remove the thermometer and place it in the jug of warm water. Remove the syrup from the heat and place it over the ice-water bath to arrest the cooking.

5 Dissolve the bicarbonate of soda in the warm water, then pour it into the sugar syrup. At this point, it should bubble and froth up, so take great care.

6 Quickly stir the mixture to disperse the bubbles, then pour the mixture into the prepared baking tray.

1 Prepare an ice-water bath and a jug (pitcher) of warm water large enough to hold your sugar thermometer. Grease a shallow baking tray and set it aside.

2 Put the water in a heavy pan and add the sugar and golden syrup. Heat gently until the sugar dissolves.

3 Increase the heat and bring to the boil, then boil, without stirring, until it reaches just above the hard-crack stage (154°C/310°F) and takes on a little colour.

7 When cooled, break into pieces. Serve immediately or wrap the shards in cellophane, baking parchment or waxed paper and store in an airtight container.

Energy 931kcal/3973kJ; Protein 1.2g; Carbohydrate 247g, of which sugars 247g; Fat 0g, of which saturates 0g; Cholesterol 0mg; Calcium 123mg; Fibre 0g; Sodium 54mg

HONEYCOMB TOFFEE

Equally traditional, this is a richer version of honeycomb than Cinder Toffee. To make it lighter in colour and taste, you can replace the black treacle with honey. The bicarbonate of soda gives this its light, airy texture. Be sure to sift it before adding it in, or lumps of bicarbonate can get caught in the toffee.

MAKES ABOUT 750G/1LB 13OZ

125g/4¼oz/generous ½ cup unsalted butter, plus extra for greasing

30ml/2 tbsp cider vinegar or white wine vinegar

100ml/3½fl oz/scant ½ cup black treacle (molasses)

200ml/7fl oz/scant 1 cup golden (light corn) syrup

400g/14oz/1¾ cups demerara (raw) sugar

2.5ml/½ tsp bicarbonate of soda (baking soda), sifted

5 Pour the mixture into the prepared tin and leave it to cool. When it begins to set (after about 30 minutes), score the toffee with a knife into bitesize squares.

6 Leave it to cool completely for a few hours before taking hold of the sides of the paper and lifting the block out of the tin. Break into squares along the scored lines. Store in an airtight container.

1 Grease a 20cm/8in square cake tin (pan). Line it with a sheet of baking parchment so that each end of the paper comes up the sides of the tin. This will make it easier to remove the honeycomb.

2 Melt the butter gently in a large, heavy pan over a low heat. Add the vinegar, black treacle, golden syrup and demerara sugar. Stir gently until the sugar has dissolved into the butter.

3 Turn the heat up to medium then, without stirring, heat the syrup until it reaches the hard-crack stage (154°C/310°F).

4 Remove the pan from the heat and immediately stir in the sifted bicarbonate of soda. As the mixture begins to froth, stir it once again. Take great care as the hot syrup bubbles up.

Energy 3350kcal/14147kJ; Protein 4.4g; Carbohydrate 643g, of which sugars 643g; Fat 102g, of which saturates 68g; Cholesterol 288mg; Calcium 783mg; Fibre 0g; Sodium 1598mg

BURNT CARAMEL SHARDS

A very different method for making toffee, this recipe does not require a sugar thermometer. Gold leaf is expensive, but it makes the caramel shards look beautiful. You could crush the caramel to make a crunchy ice cream topping, in which case, do not bother with the gold leaf.

MAKES ABOUT 400G/14OZ

100g/3¾oz/scant ½ cup unsalted butter, plus extra for greasing

300g/11oz/1½ cups caster (superfine) sugar

2 sheets of edible loose gold leaf (optional)

1 Grease a baking tray with butter and set it aside.

2 Melt the butter gently in a heavy pan. Add the sugar.

3 Over medium heat, stir the butter and sugar mixture constantly using a wooden spoon until it is a dark caramel colour; this will take about 10 minutes. The sugar and butter may separate during the cooking, but should come back together again in an emulsified mass by the time the mixture is the right colour.

4 Carefully pour the caramel mixture on to the prepared baking tray and leave to cool.

5 Apply the gold leaf (if using) to the surface of the caramel. (*See* Cook's Tip.)

6 Break into shards. Serve immediately or store in an airtight container.

COOK'S TIP

Gold leaf can come in two different forms: loose leaf or pressed to paper. Loose gold leaf, used here, should be applied with a clean, dry paint or pastry brush. Gently lift pieces from between the sheets of paper and lower it on to the surface you want to cover with the gold. You could use the pressed type instead, if you like. Pressed gold leaf should be rubbed on to the caramel by inverting the paper on to it and rubbing it with your finger.

Energy 1919kcal/8074kJ; Protein 2g; Carbohydrate 314g, of which sugars 314g; Fat 82g, of which saturates 54g; Cholesterol 230mg; Calcium 174mg; Fibre 0g; Sodium 768mg

SALTED CARAMELS

These extra-dark caramels have the wonderful crunch of sea salt. Although it may be a surprising addition to the confection, the salt cuts the sweetness of the caramel and creates a lovely balance. Play around with the types of salt you use. Fleur de sel is suggested in the recipe, but Maldon Sea Salt is also an interesting choice.

MAKES ABOUT 1KG/2¼LB

450ml/¾ pint/scant 2 cups double (heavy) cream

1 vanilla pod (bean), split down the side

225g/8oz/⅔ cup golden (light corn) syrup

400g/14oz/2 cups caster (superfine) or granulated (white) sugar

65g/2½oz/⅓ cup unsalted butter

7.5ml/1½ tsp fleur de sel or other fine sea salt

1 Line a 23cm/9in square cake tin (pan) with baking parchment so that the paper comes up the sides of the tin on all sides.

2 Gently heat the cream in a heavy pan. Scrape the seeds from the vanilla pod and add them, along with the pod, to the cream.

3 Bring the cream and vanilla to just under the boil, being careful not to scorch it. When it is ready, it will start to exude wisps of steam and have a thin layer of frothy foam beginning to form at the edges of the pan.

4 In another heavy pan, heat the golden syrup and sugar gently until the sugar dissolves, then boil until it reaches the hard-crack stage (154°C/310°F). Once the cream has heated to the required stage, strain it through a sieve (strainer), discarding the vanilla pod.

5 Add the butter, 5ml/1 tsp salt and the strained cream to the sugar mixture. Stir enough to combine, then bring the whole mixture back up to the firm-ball stage (120°C/248°F).

6 Pour the caramel into the prepared tin and tamp it down to release any air bubbles. Sprinkle the remaining salt over the surface.

7 Leave it to cool completely for a few hours before taking hold of the sides of the paper and lifting the caramel block out of the tin. Cut it into bitesize rectangles using a sharp knife.

8 Wrap the caramels individually in foil squares, and store in an airtight container at room temperature. They will keep for about 10 days.

Energy 4746kcal/19870kJ; Protein 11g; Carbohydrate 608g, of which sugars 608g; Fat 295g, of which saturates 170g; Cholesterol 735mg; Calcium 505mg; Fibre 0g; Sodium 1286mg

CARAMEL-PECAN CHEWS

These extra-dark caramels are silky and chewy, with the added crunch of toasted pecans. They are almost like a bitesize pecan pie without the pastry. Pecans are native to the southern United States and they make a natural pairing with caramelized sugar. Use unlined foil cases, if possible, to prevent the caramels from sticking.

5 When the cream has reached the required temperature, strain it through a sieve (strainer), discarding the vanilla pod.

6 Add the butter, salt and the strained cream to the sugar mixture. Stir to combine only, then bring it back up to the firm-ball stage (120°C/248°F).

7 Stir in the toasted, chopped pecans. Retrieve and discard the vanilla pod.

8 Spoon the caramel into the foil cases, then gently tap the baking sheet on the work surface to release any air bubbles. Leave to cool completely before serving. Store in an airtight container for about 10 days.

MAKES 48

450ml/¾ pint/scant 2 cups double (heavy) cream

1 vanilla pod (bean), split down the side

225g/8oz/⅔ cup golden (light corn) syrup

400g/14oz/2 cups granulated (white) sugar

65g/2½oz/⅓ cup unsalted butter

5ml/1 tsp fleur de sel or other fine sea salt

100g/3¾oz/scant 1 cup toasted, chopped pecans

edible gold leaf (optional)

1 Arrange 48 mini foil sweet cases on one or two baking sheets and set aside.

2 Gently heat the cream in a heavy pan. Scrape the seeds from the vanilla pod and add to the cream, along with the pod.

3 Bring the cream to just under the boil, being careful not to scorch it. When it is ready, it will exude wisps of steam and have a thin layer of frothy foam forming at the edges of the pan.

4 In another heavy pan, heat the golden syrup and sugar gently until the sugar dissolves, then boil until it reaches the hard-crack stage (154°C/310°F).

Energy 113kcal/473kJ; Protein 0.4g; Carbohydrate 12.8g, of which sugars 12.8g; Fat 7.6g, of which saturates 3.7g; Cholesterol 15mg; Calcium 12mg; Fibre 0.1g; Sodium 27mg

Fresh Coconut and Cardamom Caramels

This might seem like an unusual flavour combination for caramel, but it works very well. The texture of fresh coconut suspended in chewy caramel is a lovely surprise, while the distinctive flavour of the cardamom cuts through the sweetness. The rum adds the finishing touch to make these a tropical taste sensation!

MAKES ABOUT 1KG/2¼LB

freshly grated flesh of 1 coconut

500g/1¼lb/2½ cups caster (superfine) sugar

200ml/7fl oz/scant 1 cup golden (light corn) syrup

225ml/7½fl oz/scant 1 cup double (heavy) cream

50g/2oz/¼ cup unsalted butter, cut into small cubes, plus extra for greasing

1.5ml/¼ tsp ground cardamom

10ml/2 tsp white rum

1 Grease and line a 20 x 30cm/8 x 12in baking tin (pan) with baking parchment.

2 Heat a large, heavy pan and drop the grated coconut into it, in batches, stirring constantly until it is dry and flaky. Put the coconut into a bowl and set aside.

3 Put the sugar, golden syrup and cream in a heavy pan over medium heat, and stir to dissolve the sugar. Add the butter, cardamom and coconut, and stir to melt.

4 When the butter is melted, bring the pan to the boil and, without stirring, let the mixture go at a slow rolling boil for about 10 minutes, or until it reaches the soft-ball stage (114°C/238°F).

5 Remove the pan from the heat and stir in the rum.

6 Pour the mixture into the prepared tin and leave to cool completely. This can take up to 8 hours.

7 Cut into squares and wrap in waxed paper or foil candy wrappers. Store in an airtight container at room temperature. They will keep for about 10 days.

Energy 4419kcal/18575kJ; Protein 12g; Carbohydrate 692g, of which sugars 692g; Fat 208g, of which saturates 135g; Cholesterol 408mg; Calcium 454mg; Fibre 10g; Sodium 1049mg

BUTTERSCOTCH

Depending on who you talk to you will get a very different answer to the question of which is the most traditional of all sweets, but butterscotch will certainly be a popular choice. The butterscotch in this recipe is similar to a caramel, but the syrup is cooked a little longer to get a more brittle result to suck on rather than chew.

MAKES ABOUT 800G/1¾LB

400g/14oz/2 cups caster (superfine) or granulated (white) sugar

150ml/¼ pint/⅔ cup double (heavy) cream

150ml/¼ pint/⅔ cup water

1 vanilla pod (bean), split down the side

1.5ml/¼ tsp cream of tartar

100g/3¾oz/scant ½ cup unsalted butter, cut into small cubes, plus extra for greasing

1 Grease a 20cm/8in square cake tin, and line it with baking parchment so that the paper comes all the way up the sides.

2 Place the sugar, cream and water in a heavy pan over a low heat and stir gently until the sugar is dissolved.

3 Scrape the vanilla seeds from the pod into the pan and add the pod as well. Add the cream of tartar. Place over medium heat and boil until it reaches the soft-ball stage (114°C/238°F).

4 Add the butter and boil until the mixture reaches the soft-crack stage (143°C/290°F).

5 Pour the mixture into the prepared tin, retrieving and discarding the vanilla pod.

6 Let it cool slightly and score the top to make it easy to break into squares when it has cooled.

7 When it is completely cold, break it into squares and wrap them in waxed paper, cellophane or foils. Store in an airtight container at room temperature. They will keep for about 10 days.

Energy 2987kcal/12529kJ; Protein 5g; Carbohydrate 422g, of which sugars 422g; Fat 162g, of which saturates 99g; Cholesterol 425mg; Calcium 302mg; Fibre 0g; Sodium 830mg

HONEY-SESAME CRUNCH CANDIES

These are wholesome and energizing little confections. You often see a similar product in health food stores, but this version tastes much better. Densely packed with sesame seeds and lightly sweetened with honey and brown sugar, they make a great afternoon pick-me-up.

MAKES ABOUT 400G/14OZ

butter and grapeseed or groundnut (peanut) oil, for greasing

100g/3¾oz/8 tbsp soft light brown sugar

100g/3¾oz/scant ½ cup honey

200g/7oz/scant ½ cup raw sesame seeds

1 Grease a baking sheet with butter and set aside. Grease a rolling pin and a palette knife or metal spatula with oil.

2 Heat the sugar and honey gently in a small, heavy pan, stirring constantly, until the sugar dissolves.

3 Add the sesame seeds and stir for about 10 minutes until golden brown.

VARIATIONS
• Try adding different seeds to the mixture, such as flax seeds.
• For a sweet and tangy mixture, add 25g/1oz finely chopped dried apricots with the sesame seeds.

4 Spread the mixture out on the baking sheet to a thickness of about 5mm/¼in using the palette knife or metal spatula. Run the oiled rolling pin over it to smooth the surface.

5 Leave to cool slightly, but cut it into diamonds while still warm or it will be too brittle and may shatter. Once cooled, keep in an airtight container or wrap individually.

Energy 1878kcal/7850kJ; Protein 37.3g; Carbohydrate 183g, of which sugars 182g; Fat 116g, of which saturates 17g; Cholesterol 0mg; Calcium 1398mg; Fibre 15.8g; Sodium 57mg

PEANUT POPCORN

A mixture of peanuts and popcorn coated in caramel is a popular snack in the US, traditionally sold in cardboard boxes. Today they are more likely to be sold in a bag, but the delicious flavours, replicated in this recipe, remain the same. You can buy cardboard boxes for serving this from specialist stores or on-line.

4 Combine the golden syrup, brown sugar and vinegar in a separate heavy pan. Stir gently over a low heat to dissolve the sugar, then turn up the heat to medium. Boil the syrup until it reaches the thread stage (111°C/233°F).

5 Pour the syrup over the popcorn and mix well. Spread the mixture out on a baking sheet lined with baking parchment, and leave it to cool completely before breaking apart.

6 Serve immediately in cardboard boxes, or keep for a few days in an airtight container or sealed bags.

MAKES ABOUT 675G/1½LB

30ml/2 tbsp vegetable oil

100g/3¾oz dried popcorn kernels

25g/1oz/2 tbsp butter

2.5ml/½ tsp salt

250g/9oz/1½ cups raw peanuts

225g/8oz/1⅔ cups golden (light corn) syrup

90g/3½oz/scant ½ cup soft dark brown sugar

2.5ml/½ tsp white wine vinegar or cider vinegar

1 Warm the oil in a heavy pan with a lid over a medium-high heat.

2 Add the popcorn and cover with the lid. Cook, shaking occasionally, until the popping stops (it will take a few minutes). Transfer the popcorn to a large bowl.

3 Drop the butter into the hot pan to melt it, then drizzle the butter over the popcorn. Sprinkle with the salt and toss. Stir in the peanuts.

Energy 3570kcal/14934kJ; Protein 74g; Carbohydrate 381g, of which sugars 295g; Fat 205g, of which saturates 30g; Cholesterol 81mg; Calcium 177mg; Fibre 16g; Sodium 257mg

CARAMEL-BUTTERED POPCORN

Gooey, buttery, caramel-coated popcorn is a fabulous treat. This recipe is very simple and is a great one to make on a Saturday afternoon. Children love the popping of the popcorn and will be especially delighted that they can eat the delicious results immediately.

MAKES 300G/11OZ

30ml/2 tbsp vegetable oil

100g/3¾oz dried popcorn kernels

100g/3¾oz/scant ½ cup butter

100g/3¾oz golden (light corn) syrup

3 Melt the butter and golden syrup together in a separate heavy pan, stirring constantly until the mixture is combined.

4 Pour the syrup mixture over the popcorn and stir well to coat. Serve immediately, or keep for a few days in an airtight container or sealed bags.

1 Warm the oil in a heavy pan with a lid over medium-high heat. Add the popcorn and cover the pan with the lid.

2 Cook, shaking occasionally, until the popping stops (it will take a few minutes). Transfer the popcorn to a large bowl.

Energy 1440kcal/6054kJ; Protein 6.3g; Carbohydrate 232.8g, of which sugars 186.3g; Fat 60g, of which saturates 6g; Cholesterol 54mg; Calcium 18mg; Fibre 0g; Sodium 168mg.

PEANUT BRITTLE

It is the addition of bicarbonate of soda that gives brittle its unique texture. The raising action introduces thousands of tiny air bubbles into the sugar syrup, making it crunchy and airy. The stretching process also adds air and gives the brittle an almost opalescent quality.

MAKES 600G/1LB 6OZ

grapeseed or groundnut (peanut) oil, for greasing

175g/6oz/scant 1 cup caster (superfine) sugar

115g/4oz/⅓ cup golden (light corn) syrup

5ml/1 tsp salt

250g/9oz/1½ cups raw peanuts

25g/1oz/2 tbsp unsalted butter, cubed

2.5ml/½ tsp vanilla extract

2.5ml/½ tsp bicarbonate of soda (baking soda)

1 Line a baking sheet with parchment and grease it lightly.

2 Combine the sugar, golden syrup and salt with 60ml/4 tbsp water in a large, heavy pan. Heat the mixture gently over a low heat until the sugar dissolves.

3 Turn the heat up to medium and boil until the syrup reaches the hard-ball stage (130°C/266°F).

4 Add the peanuts and stir until the syrup reaches the hard-crack stage (154°C/310°F).

5 Transfer to a heatproof bowl and stir in the butter and vanilla.

6 Dissolve the bicarbonate of soda in 5ml/1 tsp warm water and fold into the peanut mixture. Pour out on to the prepared baking sheet.

7 Leave the mixture until it is cool enough to touch. With oiled hands, pull the brittle from the sides to stretch it and make holes.

8 Leave to cool completely before breaking it up with the back of a spoon.

9 Serve immediately, or store in an airtight container for a few days.

Energy 2626kcal/11011kJ; Protein 65g; Carbohydrate 305g, of which sugars 289g; Fat 135g, of which saturates 34g; Cholesterol 58mg; Calcium 276mg; Fibre 16g; Sodium 514mg

PISTACHIO CRACKNEL

Honey makes an excellent partner for pistachios. Native to the Middle East, pistachios have been a food source for thousands of years. This cracknel is wonderful sprinkled over ice cream in the summer or folded into whipped cream for a rich accompaniment to a winter pudding. Alternatively, eat it as it is for a lovely, crunchy sweet!

MAKES ABOUT 350G/12OZ

grapeseed or groundnut (peanut) oil, for greasing

175g/6oz/scant 1 cup caster (superfine) sugar

75g/3oz/⅓ cup clear honey

100g/3¾oz/⅓ cup pistachios, shelled

1 Grease a marble slab or baking sheet and a rolling pin.

2 Dissolve the sugar and honey in a heavy pan over a medium heat, stirring constantly.

3 Add the pistachios, increase the heat and boil until the mixture reaches the hard-crack stage (154°C/310°F), stirring occasionally.

4 Pour the mixture out on to the oiled marble slab and roll flat with the oiled rolling pin.

5 Leave to cool slightly, then break into pieces. Serve immediately, or store in an airtight container for a few days.

Energy 1507kcal/6347kJ; Protein 18g; Carbohydrate 249g, of which sugars 247g; Fat 55g, of which saturates 7g; Cholesterol 7mg; Calcium 131mg; Fibre 0g; Sodium 547mg

Hazelnut Praline

The key to this delectable recipe is toasting the hazelnuts to perfection. If under-toasted, they will not release their oils and therefore not reach their full flavour potential. If they are over-toasted, they will impart a bitter, unpleasant taste. The smell will alert you to check them, and always taste periodically throughout the toasting.

4 Grease a sheet of baking parchment with butter and use it to line the bottom of a baking tray. Transfer the toasted, skinned nuts on to it so they are in a single layer.

5 Now make the caramel. Combine the water, sugar and cream of tartar in a heavy pan. Place over a medium heat and bring to the boil, stirring to dissolve the sugar.

6 Once the sugar has dissolved, stop stirring. Boil the syrup until it reaches the hard-crack stage (154°C/310°F), then continue cooking for a further 1 minute.

7 Remove the pan from the heat and immediately pour the syrup over the toasted nuts.

8 Allow the caramel to cool completely before breaking it into bitesize pieces using your hands. Serve immediately, or store in an airtight container. This praline can also be processed to a fine powder and sprinkled over ice cream or other desserts.

MAKES 600G/1LB 6OZ

200g/7oz/1¼ cups whole hazelnuts, with skins

butter, for greasing

60ml/4 tbsp water

400g/14oz/2 cups caster (superfine) sugar

1.5ml/¼ tsp cream of tartar

COOK'S TIP
Always buy the freshest hazelnuts you can and use them quickly. It is best to buy them with the skins on as they have better flavour.

1 Preheat the oven to 180°C/350°F/ Gas 4. Spread the hazelnuts out on a baking sheet so that they are all in one layer, and place in the oven.

2 Set a timer for 7 minutes and then check them. They should have a golden colour and a good, firm texture. Cook them for a little longer, if necessary, checking them often, until they reach this stage.

3 When the nuts are properly toasted, remove them from the oven. Empty the tray into a clean dish towel and, while the nuts are still warm, rub them with the towel until the skins have all come off.

Energy 2876kcal/12094kJ; Protein 30.2g; Carbohydrate 430g, of which sugars 426g; Fat 127g, of which saturates 9.4g; Cholesterol 0mg; Calcium 492mg; Fibre 13g; Sodium 36mg

SALTY CASHEW CROCCANTE

This delicious, crunchy croccante could be made with any of your favourite nuts, but the classic salty-sweet combination of cashew nuts and toffee works especially well in this recipe. Ensure you use fresh, raw, unsalted cashews rather than the salted type, or the croccante will taste far too salty.

MAKES ABOUT 425G/15OZ

grapeseed or groundnut (peanut) oil, for greasing

200g/7oz/1¼ cups raw unsalted cashew nuts

60ml/4 tbsp water

200g/7oz/1 cup caster (superfine) sugar

25g/1oz/2 tbsp butter, cubed

2.5ml/½ tsp sea salt

6 Sprinkle the surface lightly with the sea salt and then allow the croccante to cool until it is cool enough to touch.

7 Stretch it out with oiled hands. Leave to cool completely, then break it into pieces. Serve immediately or store in an airtight container.

1 Preheat the oven to 180°C/350°F/Gas 4. Grease a marble slab and a rolling pin.

2 Spread the cashew nuts out on a baking sheet and cook them in the preheated oven for about 7 minutes, or until the cashews are very lightly toasted. Watch them closely so that they do not burn.

3 Meanwhile, combine the water and sugar in a heavy pan. Place over a low heat to dissolve the sugar.

4 Once the sugar has dissolved and the syrup starts to colour, stir in the hot cashews. Continue to cook, stirring constantly, until the syrup reaches the hottest soft-crack stage (143°C/290°F).

5 Remove the pan from the heat and stir in the butter. Immediately pour the mixture out on to the oiled marble. Roll the oiled rolling pin over it to flatten it out evenly.

Energy 2121kcal/889kJ; Protein 36g; Carbohydrate 246g, of which sugars 219g; Fat 117g, of which saturates 33g; Cholesterol 58mg; Calcium 94mg; Fibre 0g; Sodium 1010mg

FUDGES, AND FRUIT AND NUT CONFECTIONS

THERE IS AN ALMOST LIMITLESS ARRAY OF RECIPES FOR
FUDGES, BUT THE SUCCESS OF THEM ALL RELIES ON EXACT
PROPORTIONS OF INGREDIENTS, COOKED TO THE
CORRECT TEMPERATURE AND COMBINED WITH
COMPLEMENTARY FLAVOURS. SLIGHTLY LESS RICH,
BUT NO LESS DELICIOUS, CONFECTIONS MADE WITH FRUIT
AND NUTS RANGE FROM DENSE PANFORTE TO LIGHT,
SWEET COCONUT ICE. THEY MAKE A TASTY TREAT AT ANY
TIME OF DAY AND ARE PERFECT FOR GIFTS.

VANILLA FUDGE

This classic recipe makes a delicious and simple fudge, which can be used as the base for a variety of different flavours. The beating of the mixture gives it its typical grainy texture. If you want the grains to be larger, stir the fudge when it is hotter. Letting the fudge cool down before you work it will result in finer grains.

3 When the sugar is dissolved and the butter is melted, bring the mixture to the boil. Cover with a tight-fitting lid for 2 minutes, then remove the lid.

4 Without stirring, leave the mixture to cook at a slow rolling boil until it reaches the soft-ball stage (114°C/238°F). This will take about 10 minutes.

5 Immediately place the base of the pan in the ice-water bath for a few seconds. Remove the vanilla pod with a fork or slotted spoon and discard it. Stir in the vanilla extract and salt.

6 Place the pan in a cool part of the kitchen until it is lukewarm or about 43°C/110°F. Do not stir.

7 Once it reaches this temperature, beat the fudge with a wooden spoon until it is thick, smooth and creamy.

8 Pour into the prepared tin and allow to cool completely. Cut it into sqaures, then lift it out by the sides of the baking parchment. Serve immediately, or store in an airtight container.

MAKES ABOUT 1KG/2¼LB

300ml/½ pint/1¼ cups full-fat (whole) milk

½ vanilla pod (bean), seeds scraped

900g/2lb/4½ cups caster (superfine) sugar

125g/4¼oz/generous ½ cup unsalted butter, cut into 1cm/½in cubes, plus extra for greasing

10ml/2 tsp vanilla extract

tiny pinch of salt

COOK'S TIP
Work quickly, so the fudge does not have time to seize up.

1 Grease a 20cm/8in square baking tin (pan) and line with baking parchment or waxed paper. Prepare an ice-water bath.

2 Put the milk, scraped vanilla seeds and pod, sugar and butter in a large, heavy pan and cook over moderate heat, stirring constantly, until the sugar dissolves.

Energy 4665kcal/19743kJ; Protein 15g; Carbohydrate 955g, of which sugars 955g; Fat 114g, of which saturates 75g; Cholesterol 330mg; Calcium 841mg; Fibre 0g; Sodium 1157mg

OLD-FASHIONED CHOCOLATE FUDGE

This timeless classic is a smooth fudge that is not worked. Instead it is simply melted to the perfect temperature and poured into a tin to set. This version uses dark chocolate, which cuts through the sweetness of the sugar, but you could use milk chocolate, if you prefer.

MAKES ABOUT 1.2KG/2½LB

800g/1¾lb/4 cups caster (superfine) sugar

250ml/8fl oz/1 cup full-fat (whole) milk

75g/3oz/6 tbsp unsalted butter, cut into 1cm/½in cubes, plus extra for greasing

350g/12oz dark (bittersweet) chocolate (55–60% cocoa solids), cut into small pieces

5ml/1 tsp vanilla extract

1 Grease a 20 x 30cm/8 x 12in rectangular baking tin (pan) and line with baking parchment or waxed paper. Prepare an ice-water bath.

2 Put the sugar, milk and butter in a large, heavy pan and cook over a medium heat, stirring constantly, until the sugar has dissolved.

3 When the sugar has dissolved and the butter has melted, stop stirring. Bring the mixture to the boil.

COOK'S TIP
If you want the fudge to have a grainier texture, you can stir it with a spoon while it cools down. (*See* the recipe for Vanilla Fudge, opposite.) Take care when following this method, as this will cause the fudge to harden quickly and it can suddenly seize up, resulting in a crumbly texture.

4 Without stirring, let the mixture cook at a slow rolling boil until it reaches the soft-ball stage (114°C/238°F). This will take about 10 minutes. Stir in the chocolate.

5 Immediately place the base of the pan in the ice-water bath for a few seconds. Stir in the vanilla extract.

6 Pour into the prepared baking tin and leave to cool completely.

7 Lift the fudge out of the tin by the sides of the baking parchment and place it on a cutting surface. Cut into squares and serve immediately, or store in an airtight container.

Energy 5707kcal/24098kJ; Protein 29g; Carbohydrate 1075g, of which sugars 1056g; Fat 173g, of which saturates 105g; Cholesterol 239mg; Calcium 856mg; Fibre 0g; Sodium 787mg

ALMOND MILK FUDGE

This fudge is inspired by the Indian sweets that are popular in restaurants all over the world. The clarified butter adds a nutty flavour and the ground almonds give it a grainy texture. The edible silver leaf is an optional finishing touch that makes it look really special. This is a simple recipe and does not require a sugar thermometer.

MAKES ABOUT 800G/1¾LB

115g/4oz/½ cup unsalted butter, plus extra for greasing

500ml/17fl oz/generous 2 cups double (heavy) cream

175g/6oz/scant 1 cup caster (superfine) sugar

500g/1¼lb/5 cups ground almonds

edible silver leaf (optional)

1 Begin by clarifying the butter. Place the butter in a small pan on the lowest heat. Leave to melt without disturbing it.

2 When it has melted, skim any white foam off the top. The milk solids should have sunk to the bottom at this point, so pour the yellow, 'clarified' liquid into a jar, leaving any white milk solids behind. Do not worry about leaving a tiny amount of the fat in the pan if it means keeping the clarified butter completely free from the milk solids. You may not need all of the clarified butter, but whatever you do not use can be kept in an airtight container in the refrigerator for up to 2 weeks.

3 Grease a 20cm/8in square baking tin (pan) and line with baking parchment.

4 Place the cream into a heavy pan over medium heat, bring to the boil and boil for 10 minutes. Add the sugar and stir until dissolved.

5 Add the ground almonds and 50g/2oz of the clarified butter. Stir constantly for a further 5 minutes. Do not let it scorch.

6 Pour the mixture into the prepared tin and press down with a palette knife or offset metal spatula. Cover with a sheet of baking parchment and weight it down with a block of wood (such as a chopping board) and some weights. Leave to cool for 10 minutes.

7 Remove the board and the top layer of baking parchment. Lift the fudge from the tin using the edges of the baking parchment. Decorate the surface with edible silver leaf, if you like, using a clean paint brush or pastry brush to transfer the leaf from the paper to the fudge.

8 While the fudge is still slightly warm, cut it into diamond shapes. Leave to cool completely, then remove from the tin and serve. Store in an airtight container.

Energy 6842kcal/28342kJ; Protein 116g; Carbohydrate 231g, of which sugars 217g; Fat 642g, of which saturates 236g; Cholesterol 915mg; Calcium 1560mg; Fibre 37g; Sodium 1128mg

PEANUT BUTTER FUDGE

This fudge has a fabulous texture. The combination of smooth, creamy peanut butter and melted milk chocolate result in a silkiness that cannot be attained any other way. Use a high-quality natural peanut butter with no added sugars or fats. Using the best milk chocolate will also make a huge difference.

MAKES ABOUT 1.3KG/3LB

750g/1lb 11oz/3¾ cups caster (superfine) sugar

250ml/8fl oz/generous 1 cup golden (light corn) syrup

300ml/½ pint/1¼ cups double (heavy) cream

75g/3oz/6 tbsp unsalted butter, cut into 1cm/½in cubes, plus extra for greasing

200g/7oz/scant 1 cup smooth peanut butter

150g/5oz/scant 1 cup roasted and salted peanuts, chopped

100g/3¾oz milk chocolate, chopped

1 Grease a 20cm/8in square baking tin (pan) and line with baking parchment or waxed paper.

2 Put the sugar, golden syrup, cream and butter in a large, heavy pan and cook over a medium heat, stirring constantly, until the sugar has dissolved.

3 When the sugar has dissolved and the butter has melted, bring the mixture to the boil.

VARIATION
You could use crunchy peanut butter instead of smooth, if you prefer, but this will change the consistency of the fudge.

4 Without stirring, let the mixture cook at a slow rolling boil until it reaches the soft-ball stage (114°C/238°F). This will take about 10 minutes.

5 Remove the pan from the heat and stir in the peanut butter.

6 Fold in the nuts and chocolate, then pour into the prepared tin. Allow to cool completely. This can take up to 8 hours.

7 Lift the fudge out of the tin by the sides of the parchment paper and place on a cutting surface. Cut into squares and serve. Store in an airtight container.

Energy 8274kcal/34696kJ; Protein 97g; Carbohydrate 1091g, of which sugars 1068g; Fat 435g, of which saturates 185g; Cholesterol 572mg; Calcium 791mg; Fibre 19.8g; Sodium 2705mg

Espresso-Macadamia Fudge

Macadamia nuts make the perfect partner for fudge, as their oily yet slightly crunchy texture complements the creaminess of the fudge. The addition of coffee extract is merely to give it a little lift. If you own an espresso maker then, by all means, add a short shot of espresso. A really strong blend would be absolutely delicious here. Be sure to use the freshest nuts possible, as macadamia nuts have a short shelf life.

5 Remove from the heat and quickly stir in the chocolate, nuts, butter, and coffee extract or espresso. Keep stirring until the chocolate and butter have completely melted and are thoroughly combined.

6 Pour the fudge mixture into the prepared baking tin and leave it to cool completely. This can take up to 8 hours.

7 Lift the fudge out of the tin by the sides of the baking parchment, and place it on a cutting surface. Cut into squares and serve immediately, or store in an airtight container.

MAKES ABOUT 1.3KG/3LB

750g/1lb 11oz/3¾ cups caster (superfine) sugar

250ml/8fl oz/generous 1 cup golden (light corn) syrup

300ml/½ pint/1¼ cups double (heavy) cream

375g/13oz milk chocolate, chopped

250g/9oz macadamia nuts, chopped

75g/3oz/6 tbsp unsalted butter, cut into 1cm/½in cubes, plus extra for greasing

5ml/1 tsp coffee extract or instant espresso powder, dissolved in 10ml/2 tsp boiling water

1 Grease a 20 x 30cm/8 x 12in rectangular baking tin (pan) and line it with baking parchment or waxed paper, making sure the paper comes right up the sides of the tin.

2 Put the sugar, golden syrup and cream in a large, heavy pan and cook over moderate heat, stirring constantly, until the sugar dissolves.

3 When the sugar has dissolved, bring the mixture to the boil.

4 Without stirring, let the mixture cook at a slow rolling boil until it reaches the soft-ball stage (114°C/238°F). This will take about 10 minutes.

Energy 9614kcal/40330kJ; Protein 134g; Carbohydrate 1257g, of which sugars 1224g; Fat 502g, of which saturates 227g; Cholesterol 675mg; Calcium 1665mg; Fibre 22g; Sodium 1851mg

CANDIED CLEMENTINE FUDGE

Divine nuggets of beautiful candied clementine peel make this fudge truly special. You should definitely try making your own, as the flavour will be much brighter and truer than in store-bought varieties. In order to buy candied clementine, you will need to go to speciality delicatessens or department stores with food halls. If all else fails, you can make this fudge with candied orange or lemon peel instead.

MAKES ABOUT 1.3KG/3LB

750g/1lb 11oz/3¾ cups caster (superfine) sugar

50ml/2fl oz/¼ cup golden (light corn) syrup

300ml/½ pint/1¼ cups double (heavy) cream

100g/3¾oz/scant ½ cup unsalted butter, cut into 1cm/½in cubes, plus extra for greasing

15ml/1 tbsp grated clementine rind

350g/12oz white chocolate, chopped

150g/5oz/¾ cup candied clementine peel, chopped

30ml/2 tbsp clementine juice

30ml/2 tbsp lemon juice

1 Grease a 20 x 30cm/8 x 12in baking tin (pan) with butter and line with baking parchment or waxed paper.

2 Put the sugar, golden syrup, cream, butter and clementine rind in a large, heavy pan and cook over a moderate heat, stirring constantly, until the sugar has dissolved and the butter has melted.

3 Bring the mixture to the boil and, without stirring, let the mixture cook at a slow rolling boil until it reaches the soft-ball stage (114°C/238°F). This will take about 10 minutes.

4 Remove the fudge from the heat and stir in the white chocolate, two-thirds of the candied clementine peel, the clementine juice and the lemon juice. Pour the fudge mixture into the prepared baking tin.

5 Sprinkle over the remaining peel and allow to cool completely. (This can take up to 8 hours.) Lift the fudge out of the tin by the sides of the paper and cut it into squares. Serve immediately, or store in an airtight container.

Energy 7450kcal/31305kJ; Protein 38.9g; Carbohydrate 1132.5g, of which sugars 1132.5g; Fat 355.4g, of which saturates 209.5g; Cholesterol 620mg; Calcium 1746mg; Fibre 7.2g; Sodium 1860mg

PENUCHE FUDGE

This is an old-fashioned fudge in which the key ingredient is brown, or raw, sugar (in Spanish, *panocha* means raw sugar). You can experiment with different raw and brown sugars until you find the taste you like best. The sugar is what gives the fudge its signature caramel taste.

MAKES ABOUT 675G/1½LB

400g/14oz/1¾ cups soft dark brown sugar

100ml/3½fl oz/scant ½ cup golden (light corn) syrup

225ml/7½fl oz/scant 1 cup double (heavy) cream

50g/2oz/4 tbsp unsalted butter, cut into 1cm/½in cubes, plus extra for greasing

200g/7oz/1¼ cups walnuts, chopped

7.5ml/1½ tsp vanilla extract

VARIATION
Walnuts are used here but pecans are equally delicious and make the fudge reminiscent of pecan praline.

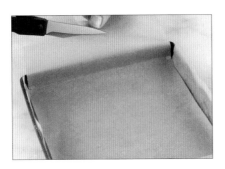

1 Grease a 20cm/8in square baking tin (pan) and line with baking parchment or waxed paper. Prepare an ice-water bath.

2 Put the sugar, golden syrup, cream and butter in a large, heavy pan and cook over a medium heat, stirring constantly, until the sugar has dissolved and the butter has melted. Then bring the mixture to the boil.

3 Without stirring, let the mixture cook at a slow rolling boil until it reaches the soft-ball stage (114°C/238°F). This will take about 10 minutes.

4 Remove from the heat and dip the base of the pan into the ice-water bath. Leave until it is lukewarm (about 50°C/122°F).

5 Stir in the nuts and vanilla extract, and beat until creamy.

6 Pour into the prepared tin, smooth the surface and leave to cool completely. Lift the fudge out with the sides of the paper. Cut it into squares. Serve immediately, or store in an airtight container.

Energy 4611kcal/19281kJ; Protein 34g; Carbohydrate 495g, of which sugars 493g; Fat 299g, of which saturates 113g; Cholesterol 423mg; Calcium 546mg; Fibre 12g; Sodium 1463mg

YOGURT PECAN FUDGE

This delectable treat is similar to penuche fudge, in which brown sugar is the main flavouring. In this modern twist, yogurt is used in place of double (heavy) cream for a lighter, tangier flavour. Do not use Greek (US strained plain) yogurt in this recipe. For instructions on toasting pecans at home, *see* Pecan Toffees, page 93.

MAKES ABOUT 550G/1LB 4OZ

225ml/7½fl oz/scant 1 cup natural (plain) yogurt

5ml/1 tsp bicarbonate of soda (baking soda)

400g/14oz/1¾ cups soft light brown sugar

30ml/2 tbsp golden (light corn) syrup

60g/2½oz/5 tbsp unsalted butter, plus extra for greasing

150g/5oz/1 cup chopped, toasted pecans

1 Combine the yogurt and bicarbonate of soda in a large, heavy pan, and set aside for 20 minutes.

2 Meanwhile, grease a 20cm/8in square baking tin (pan) and line with baking parchment or waxed paper. Prepare an ice-water bath.

3 Add the soft light brown sugar and golden syrup to the yogurt mixture, then place the pan over a medium heat and cook, stirring, until the sugar has dissolved.

4 Bring the mixture to the boil and then add the butter. Boil until the syrup reaches the soft-ball stage (114°C/238°F).

5 Remove from the heat and dip the base of the pan into the ice-water bath for a few seconds. Set aside and leave to cool until the mixture is lukewarm (about 50°C/122°F).

6 Beat the fudge until creamy, then stir in the chopped, toasted pecans. Pour the mixture into the tin and leave to cool completely.

7 Lift the fudge out of the tin by the sides of the baking parchment, and cut into thin wedges. Serve immediately, or store in an airtight container.

Energy 3267kcal/13719kJ; Protein 27.7g; Carbohydrate 467.3g, of which sugars 465g; Fat 156.4g, of which saturates 42.1g; Cholesterol 141mg; Calcium 748mg; Fibre 7g; Sodium 743mg

SOUR CHERRY PANFORTE

Panforte is a dense and spicy Italian fruit cake, made by stirring a range of ingredients into a fudgy sugar syrup. The cake is said to contain 17 ingredients to represent the 17 municipal wards, or *contrade*, of Siena – the town that is famous for this speciality. There are records of panforte-making going as far back as the 13th century. Many variations exist, but most are made up of a combination of candied citrus fruits, nuts, honey and spices. This version includes dried sour cherries, which add a pleasing tartness to the very sweet cake.

MAKES 2 CAKES

500g/1¼lb whole almonds, skins on

butter, for greasing

4 sheets of rice paper

100g/3¾oz/⅔ cup candied citron peel

100g/3¾oz/⅔ cup candied lemon peel

200g/7oz/1¼ cups candied orange or clementine peel

200g/7oz/1¼ cups dried sour cherries

250g/9oz/2¼ cups plain (all-purpose) flour, sifted, plus extra for dusting

2.5ml/½ tsp salt

5ml/1 tsp ground cinnamon

2.5ml/½ tsp freshly grated nutmeg

2.5ml/½ tsp ground black pepper

2.5ml/½ tsp ground cloves

0.75ml/⅛ tsp ground cayenne pepper

350g/12oz/scant 1 cup honey

300g/11oz/1½ cups granulated (white) sugar

175g/6oz/scant ½ cup golden (light corn) syrup

icing (confectioners') sugar, for dusting

1 Preheat the oven to 170°C/340°F/ Gas 3½. Spread the whole almonds out on a baking sheet lined with baking parchment, and place in the oven for 12 minutes. Test to see if they are done by tasting one. They should just be starting to look golden inside and taste lightly toasted.

2 Transfer the almonds to a large mixing bowl and set aside. Reduce the oven temperature to 150°C/300°F/Gas 2.

3 Grease and flour two 15–18cm/6–7in round cake tins (pans). Cut circles of rice paper to line the bottoms of the tins and then cut strips to line the sides.

4 Chop all of the candied peel and the dried cherries into small, even-sized pieces. Add the fruit to the toasted nuts in the bowl.

6 In a large, heavy pan, gently heat the honey, sugar and golden syrup until the sugar dissolves, then boil until the mixture reaches the soft-ball stage (114°C/238°F). Pour into the fruit and nut mixture and stir quickly to combine.

7 Divide the mixture between the tins, pressing down with a wooden spoon. Bake in the preheated oven for exactly 35 minutes.

8 Remove from the oven and leave to cool in the tins. When cool, carefully turn out on to a serving dish. Sift over plenty of icing sugar, cut into wedges, and serve immediately or store in an airtight container for up to 2 weeks.

COOK'S TIP
This recipe makes two panfortes, perfect for making as Christmas gifts. Halve the amounts should you only want to make one.

5 Add the flour, salt, cinnamon, nutmeg, black pepper, cloves and cayenne pepper to the fruit and nuts. Stir together.

Energy 4078kcal/17190kJ; Protein 71g; Carbohydrate 665.1g, of which sugars 559.6g; Fat 144.7g, of which saturates 12.2g; Cholesterol 0mg; Calcium 1228mg; Fibre 34g; Sodium 886mg

PINEAPPLE CHEWS

You can use home-made candied pineapple (*see* Candied Pineapple, page 158) or a good quality store-bought version to make these fruity morsels. The rum adds a lovely depth to the chews and cuts the sweetness. Be sure to use a white rum, as dark, spiced rum would overwhelm the pineapple flavour.

4 Add the chopped pineapple, white chocolate, lemon juice and rum.

5 Leave the mixture to cool slightly, then stir it twice. Leave it for 1–2 minutes to cool a bit further, then stir it twice more. Continue in this way, allowing it to cool between stirs. As it cools, it will thicken.

6 Transfer the fudge to the tin and press it down with an offset spatula. Press the 36 candied pineapple wedges on to the surface, evenly spacing them in rows of 6. Score the surface with a sharp knife and leave to set completely.

MAKES 36

25g/1oz/2 tbsp unsalted butter, plus extra for greasing

300g/11oz/1½ cups caster (superfine) sugar

120ml/4fl oz/½ cup full-fat (whole) milk

185g/6½oz Candied Pineapple (*see* p158), chopped, plus 50g/2oz Candied Pineapple, cut into 36 small wedges

25g/1oz white chocolate, chopped

2.5ml/½ tsp lemon juice

2.5ml/½ tsp white rum

1 Grease an 18cm/7in square baking tin (pan) and line with baking parchment or waxed paper.

2 Put the butter, caster sugar and milk in a large, heavy pan. Cook over a moderate heat, stirring constantly, until the sugar has dissolved and the butter has melted.

3 Bring the mixture to the boil and cook until it reaches the soft-ball stage (114°C/238°F). Remove from the heat.

7 Cut into 36 pieces. Serve immediately, or store in an airtight container.

Energy 61kcal/259kJ; Protein 0.2g; Carbohydrate 13.8g, of which sugars 13.8g; Fat 0.9g, of which saturates 0.6g; Cholesterol 2mg; Calcium 13mg; Fibre 0g; Sodium 9mg

COCONUT ICE

The pink food colouring used here is optional, but it looks lovely and gives it the iconic appearance of the store-bought variety. The use of coconut milk instead of milk in this version really brings out the coconut taste. You could also add a splash of rum, which is a classic partner to coconut and helps to balance the sweetness.

MAKES ABOUT 1.3KG/3LB

butter, for greasing

750g/1lb 13oz/3¾ cups caster (superfine) sugar

300ml/½ pint/1¼ cups coconut milk

2.5ml/½ tsp salt

275g/10oz/3 cups desiccated (dry unsweetened shredded) coconut

2–3 drops pink food colouring (optional)

1 Grease a 20cm/8in square tin (pan) and line with baking parchment or waxed paper.

2 Combine the caster sugar, coconut milk and salt in a heavy pan, and stir over a medium heat until the sugar has dissolved.

3 Bring the mixture to the boil, add the desiccated coconut and stir with a wooden spoon to combine.

4 Pour two-thirds of the mixture into the prepared tin.

5 Combine the remaining one-third with a few drops of pink food colouring and quickly pour over the first layer. Smooth the top with an offset spatula, pressing down slightly.

6 Allow it to cool completely. Lift out of the tin by the sides of the baking parchment or waxed paper and place on a cutting surface. Cut it into squares and serve immediately, or store in an airtight container.

VARIATIONS
- You could replace the coconut milk with an equal quantity of full-fat (whole) milk.
- You can use any food colouring you like; green or blue look good for a party.

Energy 4682kcal/19746kJ; Protein 20.1g; Carbohydrate 816.1g, of which sugars 816.1g; Fat 171.4g, of which saturates 147.4g; Cholesterol 0mg; Calcium 548mg; Fibre 37.7g; Sodium 452mg

COCONUT DATE ROLLS

Incredibly simple to make and attractive as after-dinner treats, these little morsels were once found primarily in health food stores. High in fibre, they are indeed better for you than many other confections, but they taste none the worse for it! Use unsweetened desiccated coconut rather than the sweetened variety.

MAKES 36

36 good quality dates, such as Medjool

150g/5oz/1½ cups desiccated (dry unsweetened shredded) coconut

1 Remove the skins from the dates.

2 Cut the dates in half and remove the stones (pits) using a small knife.

3 Place the dates in a small pan with 15ml/1 tbsp water. Simmer for 5 minutes, or until softened. Push the dates through a sieve (strainer) using the back of a spoon.

4 Roll the pulped dates into small balls, about the same size as the dates were originally.

5 Place the desiccated coconut in a shallow bowl or saucer and roll the date balls in it.

6 Place in paper cups and serve immediately, or store in an airtight container for a few days.

Energy 63kcal/264kJ; Protein 0.7g; Carbohydrate 9.7g, of which sugars 9.7g; Fat 2.6g, of which saturates 2.2g; Cholesterol 0mg; Calcium 7mg; Fibre 1.1g; Sodium 3mg

CHOCOLATE-STUFFED MACAROONS

These macaroons combine moist coconut with dark chocolate, and are a popular variety of cookie in the US. This recipe makes a chewy macaroon with a slightly toasted outer edge, filled with rich dark chocolate. Eat them immediately before the chocolate has set completely to experience them at their best.

MAKES ABOUT 18 COOKIES

2 egg whites

125g/4¼oz/⅔ cup caster (superfine) sugar

0.75ml/⅛ tsp salt

10ml/2 tsp clear honey

100g/3¾oz/generous 1 cup desiccated (dry unsweetened shredded) coconut

2.5ml/½ tsp vanilla extract

100g/3¾oz dark (bittersweet) chocolate, broken into pieces

1 Preheat the oven to 160°C/325°F/ Gas 3. Line a baking sheet with baking parchment.

2 Combine all of the ingredients, except the chocolate, in a heavy pan and cook over a medium heat for about 7 minutes, stirring constantly, until the mixture is opaque and sticky. The coconut should just begin to scorch on the bottom of the pan.

3 Transfer the coconut mixture to a mixing bowl. Allow it to cool completely.

COOK'S TIP
Instead of using a piping (pastry) bag, you could put the chocolate in a sealable food bag. Tilt the bag so the chocolate is in one corner, then snip off that corner to make a small hole through which the chocolate can be piped.

4 Drop tablespoonfuls of the mixture on to the baking sheet. Using the end of a wooden spoon, make small depressions in the centre of each macaroon.

5 Place in the oven and bake for about 12 minutes, until the macaroons are just golden around the edges.

6 Place the chocolate in a heatproof bowl and position over a pan of barely simmering water, making sure that the water does not touch the bottom of the bowl. Leave, stirring occasionally, until the chocolate has melted.

7 Transfer the melted chocolate to a piping (pastry) bag with a fine nozzle and fill the centre of each macaroon with chocolate.

8 Leave the macaroons to cool until the chocolate is almost set, then serve immediately. These macaroons are best eaten on the day they are made, while the chocolate is still slightly soft, but they can be stored in an airtight container for up to 2 days.

Energy 93kcal/390kJ; Protein 0.9g; Carbohydrate 11.6g, of which sugars 11.3g; Fat 5.1g, of which saturates 3.9g; Cholesterol 1mg; Calcium 7mg; Fibre 0.8g; Sodium 9mg

ROCKY ROAD FUDGE

Most often associated with ice cream, rocky road is a classic US treat. An impressive way to present this fudge is to put it into a loaf tin and then slice it like a terrine when it is set. The presentation is lovely and the fudge is appealing in different shapes. Be warned – this is very rich, so a thin slice will suffice!

4 Once the sugar has dissolved and the butter has melted, bring the mixture to the boil. Without stirring, allow it to cook at a slow rolling boil until it reaches the soft-ball stage (114°C/238°F). This will take about 10 minutes. Stir in the chocolate, vanilla extract and salt.

5 Pour about one-third of the chocolate fudge mixture into the prepared baking tin. Sprinkle with one-third of the marshmallows and half of the cherries and walnuts. Cover with half of the remaining fudge. Sprinkle with the rest of the cherries and walnuts, and half of the remaining marshmallows. Cover with the rest of the fudge mixture and sprinkle over the remaining marshmallows.

6 Place a piece of baking parchment over the top and press it down firmly with your hands. Set aside to cool.

MAKES ABOUT 3KG/6¾LB

75g/3oz/½ cup walnuts

1.4kg/3lb 2oz/7 cups caster (superfine) sugar

500ml/17fl oz/generous 2 cups full-fat (whole) milk

150g/5oz/10 tbsp unsalted butter, cut into 1cm/½in cubes

700g/1lb 11oz dark (bittersweet) chocolate (55–60% cocoa solids), cut into small pieces

10ml/2 tsp vanilla extract

1.5ml/¼ tsp salt

130g/4½oz mini marshmallows or large marshmallows, cut into pieces

90g/3½oz amarena cherries or sour cherries in syrup, sliced in half

1 Line a 10 x 23cm/4 x 9in loaf tin (pan) with clear film (plastic wrap) so that it comes out of the tin and over the sides.

2 Chop the walnuts roughly. Set aside.

3 Put the sugar, milk and butter in a medium, heavy pan. Cook over a moderate heat, stirring constantly, until the sugar has dissolved and the butter has melted.

7 When ready to serve, lift the fudge from the tin by holding the sides of the clear film, and transfer to a chopping board. Cut 1cm/½in slices. Serve immediately, or store in an airtight container for up to 1 week.

Energy 11632kcal/49052kJ; Protein 73.2g; Carbohydrate 2067.8g, of which sugars 2006g; Fat 397.8g, of which saturates 215.5g; Cholesterol 478mg; Calcium 1695mg; Fibre 3.2g; Sodium 1611mg

VANILLA TABLET

Scotch tablet is a hybrid of fudge and toffee that dates back to the early 18th century in Scotland. It has a grainy texture, similar to fudge, but is harder. Traditionally it was made using just sugar and cream, but since this has a tendency to burn, the recipe has been adapted over time to incorporate sweetened condensed milk.

MAKES ABOUT 1KG/2¼LB

900g/2lb/4½ cups caster (superfine) sugar

125g/4¼oz/generous ½ cup unsalted butter, plus extra for greasing

150ml/¼ pint/⅔ cup water

150ml/¼ pint/⅔ cup full-fat (whole) milk

1 vanilla pod (bean)

200ml/7fl oz/scant 1 cup sweetened condensed milk

1 Grease a 20cm/8in square baking tin (pan) or 23cm/9in square baking dish, and line with baking parchment.

2 Put the sugar, butter, water and milk in a heavy pan and stir over a low heat to combine.

3 Split the vanilla bean down the centre and scrape the seeds from inside using a small knife. Add the seeds and the pod to the pan. Stir gently until the sugar has dissolved and the butter has melted.

COOK'S TIP
Versions of tablet are made all over the world. In Quebec it is called *sucre à la crème* and is made with maple syrup; in South America it is called *tableta de leche*, and it is known as *borstplaat* in the Netherlands and is eaten during the festival of *Sinterklaas*.

4 Turn the heat up to medium and bring to the boil. Do not stir the syrup at this point as this could cause crystallization.

5 Boil the mixture until it reaches the soft-ball stage (114°C/238°F), then stir in the condensed milk. Bring the mixture back up to 114°C/238°F, then remove the pan from the heat.

6 Leave the tablet mixture to cool for 5 minutes, then remove the vanilla pod with a fork and discard.

7 Using a wooden spoon, stir the syrup vigorously for a few minutes until it becomes creamy and lighter in colour.

8 Pour the mixture into the tin through a sieve (strainer). Leave to cool completely.

9 Turn out on to a board and cut it into squares. Serve immediately, or store in an airtight container.

Energy 5232kcal/22142kJ; Protein 26.9g; Carbohydrate 1058.7g, of which sugars 1058.7g; Fat 128.2g, of which saturates 83.7g; Cholesterol 381mg; Calcium 1248mg; Fibre 0g; Sodium 1354mg

FIG TABLET

This recipe has a wonderful texture: fudgy tablet bursting with fig seeds and vanilla seeds. Tablet works well with any dried fruit, but this particular combination is lovely. Try dried apricots or prunes, if you like. Do not use fresh figs, as they hold too much juice and the tablet will not set properly.

MAKES ABOUT 1.3KG/3LB

100g/3¾oz/⅔ cups dried figs, chopped

150ml/¼ pint/⅔ cup full-fat (whole) milk

50g/2oz/¼ cup unsalted butter,
plus extra for greasing

2.5ml/½ tsp salt

900g/2lb/4½ cups caster (superfine)
or granulated (white) sugar

1 vanilla pod (bean)

1 Grease a 20cm/8in square baking tin (pan) or 23cm/9in square baking dish and line with baking parchment.

2 Place the chopped figs in a small bowl and cover with about 50ml/2fl oz/¼ cup boiling water. Set them aside to soak for about 30 minutes.

3 Put 150ml/¼ pint/⅔ cup water in a large, heavy pan with the milk, butter, salt and sugar, and place over a low heat. Stir to combine.

4 Split the vanilla pod down the centre.

5 Scrape the seeds from the pod using a small knife. Add the scraped seeds and the pod to the pan.

6 Stir gently until the sugar has dissolved and the butter has melted, then turn the heat up to medium and bring the mixture to the boil.

7 Boil the mixture until it reaches the soft-ball stage (114°C/238°F).

8 Meanwhile, strain the figs and pat them dry using kitchen paper.

9 As soon as the syrup has reached the soft-ball stage, stir in the figs. Remove from the heat and leave to cool for 5 minutes. Remove the vanilla pod with a fork and discard.

COOK'S TIP
Instead of discarding the vanilla pod, you can rinse it, dry it out near an open oven and place it in a jar of sugar. In a few days you will have vanilla-flavoured sugar.

10 Using a wooden spoon, stir the syrup vigorously for a few minutes until it becomes creamy and lighter in colour.

11 Pour the tablet mixture into the prepared tin and leave it to set and cool completely.

12 Turn the tablet out on to a board and cut it into squares to serve. Store in an airtight container.

VARIATIONS
• Replace the figs with desiccated (dry unsweetened shredded) coconut, and add 15ml/1 tbsp Bacardi rum or Malibu.
• It is perfectly fine to use 10ml/2 tsp vanilla extract in place of the seeds of the vanilla pod for a more economical version of this recipe.

Energy 4223kcal/17946kJ; Protein 12.9g; Carbohydrate 996.3g, of which sugars 996.3g; Fat 48.2g, of which saturates 30.6g; Cholesterol 136mg; Calcium 887mg; Fibre 6.9g; Sodium 569mg

MARSHMALLOWS, NOUGATS AND SUGAR SHAPES

EGG WHITES ARE THE MAIN INGREDIENT IN THIS
COLLECTION OF MELT-IN-THE-MOUTH RECIPES. FROM
LIGHT-AS-AIR MARSHMALLOWS TO DELECTABLE DENSE
NOUGATS, THESE CONFECTIONS TRANSFORM SIMPLE SUGAR
SYRUPS AND FRESH EGG WHITES INTO VARIOUS PRETTY
AND TASTY TREATS. FOR SPECIAL OCCASIONS, IT IS
WELL WORTH TRYING YOUR HAND AT MOULDING SUGAR
TO MAKE SUGAR MICE OR A SUGARY ALTERNATIVE TO A
TRADITIONAL CHOCOLATE EASTER EGG.

VANILLA MARSHMALLOWS

Wonderfully fluffy and delicious, home-made marshmallows are nothing like the store-bought version. The texture is completely different because these are meant to be eaten within days, rather than months, and are not full of preservatives. You can add many flavours and colours – the possibilities are limitless.

MAKES ABOUT 900G/2LB

vegetable oil, for greasing

50g/2oz/½ cup icing (confectioners') sugar

50g/2oz/½ cup cornflour (cornstarch)

2 egg whites

400g/14oz/2 cups caster (superfine) sugar

15ml/1 tbsp glucose syrup

½ vanilla pod (bean), split and seeds scraped

375ml/13fl oz/generous 1½ cups cold water

60ml/4 tbsp powdered gelatine

30ml/2 tbsp vanilla extract

1 Grease a baking tray. Combine the icing sugar and cornflour in a mixing bowl. Pass the mixture through a sieve (strainer) into another bowl positioned underneath to ensure it is well mixed. Liberally sift some of the mixture over the greased baking tray.

COOK'S TIP

These pretty marshmallows make a fabulous gift and look attractive when presented in cellophane bags. Make sure you have dusted them liberally with the cornflour and icing sugar mixture to stop them sticking together. Tie the bag with a ribbon.

2 Whisk the egg whites until they form firm peaks (preferably in a stand mixer or with a powerful hand-held electric whisk). Set aside. They will separate slightly, but you can whisk them up again just before you need them.

3 Combine the caster sugar, glucose syrup, the seeds from the vanilla pod and the scraped pod, and half of the water in a small pan over a low heat. Stir to dissolve the sugar.

4 Bring the syrup to the boil and boil until it reaches the hard-ball stage (130°C/266°F).

5 Meanwhile, combine the gelatine with the other half of the cold water in a small pan, off the heat. Just before the sugar syrup reaches the hard-ball stage, place the gelatine mixture over a low heat and stir to dissolve.

6 When the syrup reaches the correct temperature and the gelatine has dissolved, combine the two into one pan and stir. Add the vanilla extract.

7 Turn the electric whisk on again and whisk the egg whites constantly, while pouring in the syrup and gelatine mixture in a slow, steady stream. Continue until all of the mixture has been incorporated.

8 Whisk on medium-high for at least 7 minutes, until the mixture is almost stiff. Pour the marshmallow into the prepared baking tray.

9 Smooth the top with an oiled offset metal spatula. Allow to set for 5 hours.

10 Dust a work surface with most of the remaining cornflour and icing sugar mixture, and turn the marshmallow out on to it. Cut it into cubes and allow to dry out for a couple of hours.

11 Serve immediately, or store in an airtight container or in pretty cellophane bags. Dust with the remaining cornflour and icing sugar mixture to keep the marshmallows from sticking together.

Energy 2224kcal/9481kJ; Protein 59g; Carbohydrate 529g, of which sugars 476.3g; Fat 0.3g, of which saturates 0.1g; Cholesterol 0mg; Calcium 250mg; Fibre 0.1g; Sodium 197mg

RASPBERRY HEART MARSHMALLOWS

You can add almost any flavour to marshmallows. Berry-flavoured ones are especially wonderful, because the acidity in the fruit balances the sweetness of the fluffy, sugary mass. The colour of the berries also transfers to the finished confections, in this case creating a delicate, soft pink.

MAKES ABOUT 800G/1¾LB

vegetable oil, for greasing

50g/2oz/½ cup icing (confectioners') sugar

50g/2oz/½ cup cornflour (cornstarch)

2 egg whites

400g/14oz/2 cups caster (superfine) sugar

15ml/1 tbsp glucose syrup

175ml/6fl oz/¾ cup cold water

60ml/4 tbsp powdered gelatine

200ml/7fl oz/scant 1 cup puréed raspberries, strained (see Cook's Tips)

10ml/2 tsp vanilla extract

1 Grease a baking tray. Combine the icing sugar and cornflour in a mixing bowl. Pass the mixture through a sieve (strainer) into another bowl positioned underneath to ensure it is well mixed. Liberally sift some of the mixture over the greased baking tray.

2 Whisk the egg whites until they form firm peaks (preferably in a stand mixer or with a powerful hand-held electric whisk). Set aside. They will separate slightly, but you can whisk them up again just before you need them.

COOK'S TIPS
• To make the raspberry purée, place 350g/12oz/2 cups raspberries in a small pan and cook for 10 minutes, or until they release their juices. Strain through a sieve (strainer), pushing them with the back of a spoon to get all the juice.
• Cutting these pink marshmallows into heart shapes is perfect for a romantic occasion such as Valentine's Day. They look charming floating in a cup of hot chocolate.

3 Combine the sugar, glucose syrup and 75ml/5 tbsp of the cold water in a small pan over a low heat. Stir to dissolve the sugar.

4 Bring the syrup to the boil and boil until it reaches the hard-ball stage (130°C/266°F).

5 Meanwhile, combine the gelatine with the rest of the cold water in a small pan, off the heat. Just before the sugar syrup reaches the hard-ball stage, place the gelatine mixture over a low heat and stir until the gelatine has dissolved.

6 When the syrup has reached the correct temperature, pour the dissolved gelatine mixture into the syrup and stir.

7 Add the raspberry purée and the vanilla extract and stir to combine.

8 Using a hand whisk, electric whisk or stand mixer, whisk the egg whites constantly while pouring in the syrup, gelatine and raspberry mixture in a slow, steady stream. Continue until all of the mixture has been incorporated.

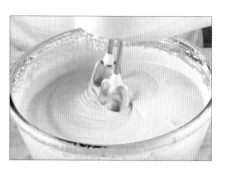

9 Using an electric whisk or stand mixer, whisk on medium-high for at least 7 minutes, until the mixture is almost stiff. Pour the marshmallow into the baking tray and smooth the top with an offset spatula. Allow to set for 5 hours.

10 Dust a work surface with most of the remaining cornflour and icing sugar mixture and turn the marshmallow out on to it. Cut into heart shapes with a cookie cutter (or just cut into squares, if you prefer) and allow to dry out for a couple of hours.

11 Serve immediately or store in an airtight container or in pretty cellophane bags. Dust with the remaining cornflour and icing sugar mixture to keep the marshmallows from sticking together.

Energy 2274kcal/9699kJ; Protein 61.8g; Carbohydrate 538.2g, of which sugars 485.5g; Fat 0.9g, of which saturates 0.3g; Cholesterol 0mg; Calcium 300mg; Fibre 5g; Sodium 203mg

PEPPERMINT MARSHMALLOWS

The delightful minty green colour of these fresh-tasting sweets comes from food colouring. Here, traditional liquid food colouring is used, but if you are using gel or paste food colouring, you will only need the tiniest amount. The green colour should be subtle and light, so do not use too much!

MAKES ABOUT 900G/2LB

vegetable oil, for greasing

50g/2oz/½ cup icing (confectioners') sugar

50g/2oz/½ cup cornflour (cornstarch)

2 egg whites

400g/14oz/2 cups caster (superfine) sugar

15ml/1 tbsp glucose syrup

375ml/13fl oz/generous 1½ cups cold water

60ml/4 tbsp powdered gelatine

10ml/2 tsp peppermint extract

2.5ml/½ tsp liquid green food colouring, a drop of gel colouring, or a tiny dab of colouring paste from the end of a cocktail stick (toothpick)

1 Grease a baking tray. Combine the icing sugar and cornflour in a mixing bowl. Pass the mixture through a sieve (strainer) into another bowl positioned underneath, to ensure it is well mixed. Liberally sift some of the mixture over the greased baking tray.

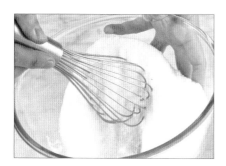

2 Whisk the egg whites in a clean, grease-free bowl until they form firm peaks (this will be easiest in a stand mixer or with a powerful hand-held electric whisk). Set the egg whites aside. They will separate slightly, but you can whisk them again just before you need them.

3 Combine the caster sugar, glucose syrup and half of the water in a small, heavy pan over a low heat. Stir to dissolve the sugar.

4 Bring the syrup to the boil and boil until it reaches the hard-ball stage (130°C/266°F).

5 Meanwhile, combine the gelatine with the rest of the cold water in a small pan, off the heat. Just before the sugar syrup reaches the hard-ball stage, place the gelatine mixture over a low heat and stir to dissolve the gelatine.

6 When the syrup reaches the correct temperature and the gelatine has dissolved, pour the gelatine mixture into the syrup and stir to combine.

7 Add the peppermint extract and green food colouring, and stir.

8 Turn the electric whisk on again and whisk the egg whites constantly while pouring in the syrup and gelatine mixture in a slow, steady stream. Continue until all of the mixture has been incorporated.

9 Whisk on medium-high for at least 7 minutes, until the mixture is almost stiff. Scrape the sides of the bowl down from time to time, using a spatula, to be sure of incorporating all of the green colouring. The marshmallow mixture should have a pale minty green hue.

10 Pour the marshmallow into the prepared baking tray and smooth the top with an offset spatula. Leave to set for 5 hours.

11 Dust a work surface with most of the remaining cornflour and icing sugar mixture, and turn the marshmallow out on to it. Cut into cubes and allow to dry out for a couple of hours.

12 Dust with the remaining cornflour and icing sugar mixture to keep the marshmallows from sticking together. Serve immediately, or store in an airtight container or in pretty cellophane bags.

Energy 2382kcal/10165kJ; Protein 9g; Carbohydrate 625g, of which sugars 566g; Fat 0g, of which saturates 0g; Cholesterol 0mg; Calcium 56mg; Fibre 0g; Sodium 144mg

MARSHMALLOW STICKS

This classic recipe for pretty two-tone marshmallows is a joy to make. The end result is wonderful in both texture and colour. The combination of pink and yellow is delightful, but you could always choose other colours, if you prefer. Try twisting them or tying them into pretzel-like knots.

MAKES ABOUT 900G/2LB

vegetable oil, for greasing

50g/2oz/½ cup icing (confectioners') sugar

50g/2oz/½ cup cornflour (cornstarch)

2 egg whites

400g/14oz/2 cups caster (superfine) sugar

15ml/1 tbsp glucose syrup

5ml/1 tsp vanilla extract

375ml/13fl oz/generous 1½ cups cold water

60ml/4 tbsp powdered gelatine

3 drops pink food colouring

3 drops yellow food colouring

1 Grease a baking tray. Combine the icing sugar and cornflour in a mixing bowl. Pass the mixture through a sieve (strainer) into another bowl positioned underneath to ensure it is well mixed. Liberally sift some of the mixture over the greased baking tray.

2 Whisk the egg whites in a grease-free bowl until they form firm peaks (this is easiest in a stand mixer or with a hand-held electric whisk). Set them aside. They will separate slightly, but you can whisk them again before you need them.

3 Combine the sugar, glucose syrup, vanilla extract and half of the water in a small pan over low heat. Stir to dissolve the sugar.

4 Bring to the boil and boil until it reaches the hard-ball stage (130°C/266°F).

5 Meanwhile, soften the gelatine with the rest of the cold water in a small pan, off the heat. Just before the sugar syrup reaches the hard-ball stage, place the gelatine mixture over a low heat and stir to dissolve.

6 When the syrup reaches the correct temperature and the gelatine has dissolved, pour the gelatine mixture into the syrup and stir to combine. Add the vanilla extract.

7 Turn the electric whisk on again, and whisk the egg whites constantly while pouring in the syrup and gelatine mixture in a slow, steady stream. Continue until all of the mixture has been incorporated.

8 Whisk on medium-high for at least 7 minutes, until the mixture holds soft peaks.

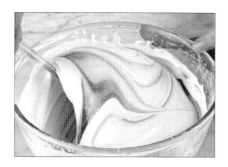

9 Divide the mixture between two bowls and add a different food colouring to each. Using an electric whisk or a stand mixer, continue to whisk both mixtures until almost stiff. (You will need to do this one at a time, working quickly, if you only have one mixer or whisk. If you have two, ask someone else to whisk one.)

10 Pour the yellow marshmallow mixture into the prepared baking tray and spread it out evenly using an offset spatula. Pour the pink mixture on top.

11 Spread the pink mixture out evenly on top of the yellow mixture, using an offset spatula. Allow to set for 5 hours.

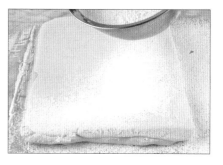

12 Dust a work surface with half of the remaining cornflour and icing sugar mixture, and turn the marshmallow out on to it. Dust the top with some more cornflour and icing sugar, then cut it into strips using an oiled knife. Dust the strips with the remaining cornflour and icing sugar to prevent them from sticking. Serve immediately, or store in an airtight container.

Energy 2224kcal/9481kJ; Protein 59g; Carbohydrate 529g, of which sugars 476.3g; Fat 0.3g, of which saturates 0.1g; Cholesterol 0mg; Calcium 250mg; Fibre 0.1g; Sodium 197mg

ALMOND MERINGUE KISSES

These nutty kisses should be slightly gooey in the middle and simply melt in your mouth. The salt in this recipe really brings out the toasty almond flavour. They are attractive and delicate little confections, and require only a few ingredients. To add an extra dimension, you could dip these treats in melted chocolate.

MAKES ABOUT 250G/9OZ

100g/3¾oz flaked (sliced) almonds

2 egg whites

115g/4oz/1 cup icing (confectioners') sugar

0.75ml/⅛ tsp salt

2.5ml/½ tsp vanilla extract

COOK'S TIP
Always make sure your bowls and equipment are scrupulously clean with no trace of grease when whisking egg whites. Stainless-steel bowls are best for this purpose. Adding a pinch of cream of tartar to the egg whites can help stabilize them.

1 Preheat the oven to 180°C/350°F/ Gas 4 and line two baking sheets with baking parchment or silicone mats.

2 Spread the flaked almonds out on another baking sheet and toast for 7 minutes, or until golden. Allow to cool.

3 Using a rolling pin, smash up the almonds into pieces that will fit through a large nozzle of a piping (pastry) bag.

4 In a stainless-steel bowl, combine the egg whites, icing sugar and salt, and place over a pan of just-simmering water. Whisk the ingredients to combine, then continue whisking until the whites reach 49°C/120°F.

5 Take the whites off the heat and transfer to a stand mixer or use an electric whisk. Add the vanilla extract and whisk the whites until stiff, glossy peaks form. Fold in the almonds.

6 Working quickly, use a piping (pastry) bag fitted with a large, round nozzle to pipe tablespoon-size blobs of mixture on to the prepared baking sheets, about 2.5cm/1in apart. Pull away from the tops quickly to create little points.

7 Place the sheets in the oven and keep the door ajar with a wooden spoon. Cook for about 20 minutes, until you can move the meringues along the paper easily. If they stick to the paper, they need a further 1–2 minutes. Bake for less time if you want the inside more gooey. Serve immediately, or store the kisses in an airtight container.

Energy 1088kcal/4565kJ; Protein 27.4g; Carbohydrate 127.1g, of which sugars 124.4g; Fat 55.8g, of which saturates 4.7g; Cholesterol 0mg; Calcium 304mg; Fibre 7.4g; Sodium 143mg

STRAWBERRY MERINGUE CLOUDS

These little sandwiches of meringue and strawberry-flavoured cream are even more delicious if they are assembled an hour or so before serving. Place them in an airtight container in the refrigerator to chill them through and allow the flavours to develop – excellent to make ahead when you have guests coming.

MAKES ABOUT 600G/1LB 6OZ

2 egg whites

115g/4oz/1 cup icing (confectioners') sugar

0.75ml/⅛ tsp salt

2.5ml/½ tsp vanilla extract

300ml½ pint/1¼ cups double (heavy) cream

100ml/3¾fl oz/scant ½ cup strawberry purée (*see* Cook's Tip, p134 – use 200g/7oz/1¾ cups strawberries for the purée)

50ml/2fl oz/¼ cup raspberry purée (*see* Cook's Tip, p134 – use 100g/3¾oz/⅔ cup raspberries for the purée)

30ml/2 tbsp caster (superfine) sugar

1 Preheat the oven to 180°C/350°F/Gas 4 and line two baking sheets with baking parchment or silicone mats.

2 Combine the egg whites, icing sugar and salt in a stainless-steel bowl, and place over a pan of just-simmering water. Whisk constantly until the whites reach 49°C/120°F.

3 Take the whites off the heat and transfer to a stand mixer or use an electric whisk. Add the vanilla extract and whisk the whites until stiff, glossy peaks form.

4 Working quickly, use a piping (pastry) bag fitted with a large, round nozzle to pipe tablespoon-size blobs on to the prepared baking sheets, about 2.5cm/1in apart. Pull away from the tops quickly to create little points.

5 Place in the oven and keep the door ajar with a wooden spoon. Cook for about 20 minutes, until you can move the meringues along the paper easily. If they stick to the paper, they need a further 1–2 minutes. Bake for less time if you want the inside more gooey.

6 Leave the meringues to cool completely, then pull them up from the paper, resting them back down on their sides.

7 Whisk the double cream into soft peaks and fold in the strawberry and raspberry purées, and the sugar.

8 Using a piping bag fitted with a large, round nozzle, pipe a blob of cream on to the flat side of half of the cooled meringues. Top with the remaining meringues to make little sandwiches. Place them in paper cake cases or pile high on a serving plate. Chill for an hour or, if you prefer, serve immediately.

Energy 1981kcal/8250kJ; Protein 13.1g; Carbohydrate 167.9g, of which sugars 167.9g; Fat 161.3g, of which saturates 90g; Cholesterol 390mg; Calcium 259mg; Fibre 2.4g; Sodium 249mg

MERINGUE MUSHROOMS

These lovely little meringues are baked in two parts and then glued together with melted chocolate. They end up looking just like field mushrooms, and kids in particular will love them. Use them to decorate a Yule log at Christmas, or make them in the autumn as a treat to share with friends after (or during) a good mushroom hunt.

5 Pipe out little stems. For these, you need to pipe upward, perpendicular to the baking sheet, so that the stems are upright.

6 Place in the oven and bake for 1 hour, or until you can move the meringues easily along the baking parchment.

7 Melt the chocolate over a pan of barely simmering water, stirring occasionally. Remove from the heat and allow to cool slightly.

MAKES ABOUT 200G/7OZ

2 egg whites

150g/5oz/¾ cup caster (superfine) sugar

50g/2oz dark (bittersweet) chocolate, chopped

unsweetened cocoa powder, for dusting

1 Preheat the oven to 110°C/225°F/ Gas ¼ and line a baking sheet with baking parchment or silicone mats.

2 Combine the egg whites and sugar in a stainless-steel bowl, and place over a pan of just-simmering water. Whisk until the whites reach 49°C/120°F.

3 Take the whites off the heat and transfer to a stand mixer or use a hand-held mixer with a whisk attachment. Whip the whites until stiff, glossy peaks form.

4 Working quickly, use a piping (pastry) bag fitted with a large, round nozzle to pipe little blobs to look like the tops of mushrooms.

8 Dip the tips of the stems into the chocolate and affix the mushroom tops. When completely cooled, dust the tops with cocoa powder.

Energy 875kcal/3712kJ; Protein 9g; Carbohydrate 189g, of which sugars 189g; Fat 14g, of which saturates 9g; Cholesterol 3mg; Calcium 37mg; Fibre 0g; Sodium 151mg

MELTING CHOCOLATE MERINGUES

These little meringues are both chewy and crunchy, and filled with delectable flecks of rich dark chocolate. When they are baked correctly, the meringue will be slightly gooey and, if served fresh from the oven, the chocolate will still be slightly melted. Confection perfection!

MAKES ABOUT 250G/9OZ

2 egg whites

115g/4oz/1cup icing (confectioners') sugar

0.75ml/⅛ tsp salt

2.5ml/½ tsp vanilla extract

100g/3¾oz dark (bittersweet) chocolate, chopped into pea-sized chunks

1 Preheat the oven to 180°C/350°F/ Gas 4 and line two baking sheets with baking parchment or silicone mats.

2 Combine the egg whites, icing sugar and salt in a stainless-steel bowl. Place over a pan of just-simmering water. Whisk the ingredients until the whites reach 49°C/120°F.

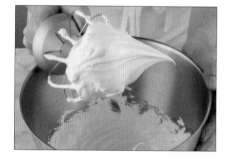

3 Take the whites off the heat and transfer to a stand mixer, or use a hand-held mixer with a whisk attachment. Add the vanilla extract and whip the whites until stiff and glossy peaks form.

4 Fold in the chopped chocolate.

5 Working quickly, transfer the mixture to a piping (pastry) bag fitted with a large, round nozzle.

6 Pipe tablespoon-size blobs on to the baking sheets, about 2.5cm/1in apart.

7 Put the sheets in the oven and keep the door ajar with a wooden spoon. Cook for about 20 minutes, until you can move the meringues easily along the paper. If they stick to the paper, they need a further 1–2 minutes. Bake for less time if you want the inside a little more gooey. Leave to cool completely.

8 Serve immediately, or store in an airtight container.

Energy 1001kcal/4228kJ; Protein 11g; Carbohydrate 185g, of which sugars 179.7g; Fat 29.2g, of which saturates 16.9g; Cholesterol 9mg; Calcium 102mg; Fibre 0g; Sodium 438mg

SEA FOAM

This delicious sweet is so named because of its resemblance to the sea foam that forms along the coast of the Irish Sea, where the sweet was originally made. Made using soft light brown sugar, it is a pale caramel colour studded with nuggets of crystallized ginger, which cuts the sweetness and gives it a spicy bite. Let the mixture fall from the end of your spoon to create irregular blobs of foam.

MAKES ABOUT 500G/1¼LB

160g/5¼oz/⅔ cup soft light brown sugar

160g/5¼oz/generous ¾ cup granulated (white) or caster (superfine) sugar

15ml/1 tbsp glucose syrup

0.75ml/⅛ tsp salt

50ml/2fl oz/¼ cup water

1 egg white

125g/4¼oz crystallized ginger, chopped into 5mm/¼in dice

1 Line a baking sheet with baking parchment or waxed paper.

2 Put the brown and white sugars, glucose syrup, salt and water in a heavy pan and place over a medium heat.

3 Stir to dissolve the sugar and then raise the heat. Boil the syrup until it reaches the firm-ball stage (120°C/248°F).

4 Meanwhile, place the egg white in a clean, grease-free bowl and whisk until it forms firm peaks.

5 When the syrup is ready, pour it into the whites in a steady stream, whisking the whole time.

6 Whip up into almost firm peaks, then add the chopped crystallized ginger.

7 Drop spoonfuls of the mixture on to the baking parchment or waxed paper. Allow the sea foam to set for about 20 minutes before serving on a plate, or transferring to mini paper cases. Store in an airtight container for 1 week.

Energy 1628kcal/6942kJ; Protein 3.5g; Carbohydrate 430.1g, of which sugars 423.4g; Fat 0g, of which saturates 0g; Cholesterol 0mg; Calcium 242mg; Fibre 1.1g; Sodium 104mg

WALNUT AND APRICOT DIVINITY DROPS

In the southern states of the US, divinity is a very common treat. It is often made with pecans, but the soft texture of fresh walnuts is delicious with this meringue-like confection. Since the recipe includes fresh walnuts, they are best eaten immediately. The optional addition of chopped dried apricots adds a contrast in flavour and a little colour, making these a decadent autumnal treat.

MAKES ABOUT 575G/1LB 7OZ

325g/11½oz/1⅔ cups granulated (white) or caster (superfine) sugar

50ml/2fl oz/¼ cup glucose syrup or golden (light corn) syrup

0.75ml/⅛ tsp salt

50ml/2fl oz/¼ cup water

1 egg white

5ml/1 tsp vanilla extract

75g/3oz/¾ cup chopped walnuts

75g/3oz/½ cup chopped dried apricots

1 Line a baking sheet with baking parchment or waxed paper.

2 Put the sugar, glucose or golden syrup, salt and water in a heavy pan, and place over a medium heat.

3 Stir to dissolve the sugar and then increase the heat. Boil the syrup until it reaches the firm-ball stage (120°C/248°F).

4 Meanwhile, place the egg white in a large, clean bowl and whisk until it forms firm peaks.

5 When the syrup is ready, pour it into the egg white in a steady stream, whisking constantly. Whisk the mixture to almost-firm peaks, then add the vanilla extract.

6 Whip up into almost-firm peaks again, then add the chopped walnuts and apricots, and stir to combine.

7 Drop spoonfuls of the mixture on to the baking parchment or waxed paper. Leave to set for about 20 minutes before serving either on a plate, or transferring to mini paper cases. Store in an airtight container for up to 1 week.

VARIATION
If you want to omit the apricots, use an extra 75g/3oz/¾ cup of chopped walnuts instead.

Energy 2273kcal/9620kJ; Protein 18.9g; Carbohydrate 461.2g, of which sugars 460.7g; Fat 51.8g, of which saturates 4.2g; Cholesterol 0mg; Calcium 339mg; Fibre 7.3g; Sodium 234mg

CHERRY DIVINITY DROPS

The white swirls of meringue in these sweets are offset by the bright red of glacé cherries. Use the best quality glacé cherries you can find, as they vary greatly in flavour. The vanilla and almond extracts add a delicate, subtle taste to the sweets, so that the cherries are not too cloying.

5 Meanwhile, place the egg whites in the clean bowl and whisk until they form firm peaks.

6 When the syrup is ready, pour it into the whites in a steady stream, whisking constantly. Whisk to almost-firm peaks, then add the vanilla and almond extracts. Whisk to almost-firm peaks again, then add the chopped cherries.

7 Drop spoonfuls of the mixture on to the baking parchment or waxed paper, then place a halved cherry on top of each. Leave to set for about 20 minutes.

8 Serve either as they are or transfer to mini paper cases. Store in an airtight container for up to 2 weeks.

COOK'S TIP
Play around with the shapes of the meringue swirls by using two spoons to help slide the mixture from the spoon on to the baking parchment or waxed paper.

MAKES ABOUT 850G/1LB 14OZ

200g/7oz glacé (candied) cherries

400g/14oz/2 cups caster (superfine) sugar

120ml/4fl oz/½ cup glucose syrup

2.5ml/½ tsp salt

120ml/4fl oz/½ cup water

2 egg whites

2.5ml/½ tsp vanilla extract

2.5ml/½ tsp almond extract

1 Line a baking sheet with baking parchment or waxed paper.

2 Chop 150g/5oz of the cherries into pieces, then slice the remaining 50g/2oz in half.

3 Put the sugar, glucose syrup, salt and water in a heavy pan and place over a medium heat.

4 Stir to dissolve the sugar and then increase the heat. Boil the syrup until it reaches the firm-ball stage (120°C/248°F).

Energy 2483kcal/10586kJ; Protein 8.6g; Carbohydrate 652.4g, of which sugars 599g; Fat 0g, of which saturates 0g; Cholesterol 0mg; Calcium 337mg; Fibre 1.8g; Sodium 380mg

PISTACHIO NOUGAT

Nougat is made slightly differently in every country. This is an Italian version, which is weighted down to make it slightly dense, but it is still gooey and light. The pure flavours of pistachio, honey and orange blossom water marry beautifully, and the bright green pistachios look attractive when the nougat is cut.

MAKES ABOUT 1KG/2¼LB

grapeseed or groundnut (peanut) oil, for greasing

rice paper

375g/13oz/scant 2 cups caster (superfine) sugar

15ml/1 tbsp glucose syrup

100ml/3½fl oz/scant ½ cup water

120ml/4fl oz/½ cup honey

2 egg whites

250g/9oz/1½ cups whole almonds, lightly toasted

200g/7oz/1¼ cups pistachios, warmed

5ml/1 tsp orange blossom water

1 Grease a Swiss roll tin (jelly roll pan), then line with the rice paper. Put 350g/12oz/1¾ cups of the caster sugar, the glucose syrup and water in a large, heavy pan and heat until it reaches the soft-crack stage (143°C/290°F).

2 Warm the honey in a separate pan until it just boils, then add to the syrup and bring everything up to 143°C/290°F again.

3 Meanwhile, whisk the egg whites with the remaining 25g/1oz/2 tbsp of the sugar until stiff peaks form.

4 Slowly pour the sugar and honey syrup into the whites in a stream, whisking constantly. Tiny lumps may form, but do not worry. Continue mixing until the mixture is stiff and glossy.

5 Add the warmed and toasted nuts and orange blossom water, and gently fold together. Pour the nougat into the tin.

6 Cover the mixture with more sheets of rice paper and weight down with a heavy board, such as a chopping board, and weights or dishes. If the chopping board smells strongly (of onions, for example), place something between it and the nougat or the nougat will take on the flavour. Leave to set for 4 hours.

7 Remove the weights and board, turn out on to a chopping board and trim the sides to neaten them. Slice into bars or squares and serve immediately, or store in an airtight container for 1 week.

Energy 4838kcal/20294kJ; Protein 103.3g; Carbohydrate 577.8g, of which sugars 554.5g; Fat 251.1g, of which saturates 21.1g; Cholesterol 0mg; Calcium 1293mg; Fibre 33.3g; Sodium 264mg

French Nougat with Candied Fruit

There are two main types of nougat: white and brown. The white type is made with beaten egg whites and has a softer texture than the brown version, given here, which is made with caramelized sugar. This recipe is for French nougat, which is thought to date back to the 18th century. It is a wonderful contrast in tastes and textures, with soft, chewy nougat studded with crisp nuts and sweet, flavoursome candied fruit.

MAKES ABOUT 1.2KG/2½LB

grapeseed or groundnut (peanut) oil, for greasing

rice paper

375g/13oz/scant 2 cups caster (superfine) sugar

15ml/1 tbsp glucose syrup or golden (light corn) syrup

100ml/3½fl oz/scant ½ cup water

350g/12oz/1½ cups honey

2 egg whites

300g/11oz good quality candied fruit

100g/3¾oz/⅔ cup whole almonds, lightly toasted

75g/3oz/½ cup hazelnuts, lightly toasted

75g/3oz/¾ cup flaked (sliced) almonds, lightly toasted

75g/3oz/½ cup pistachios, warmed

2.5ml/½ tsp fresh or dried culinary lavender buds

a pinch of salt

40g/1½oz/3 tbsp unsalted butter, cut into small pieces and softened

1 Grease a baking tray and line with rice paper, or grease a 15cm/6in square cake tin (pan) and line with the rice paper for a thicker nougat.

2 Put 350g/12oz/1¾ cups of the caster sugar, the glucose or golden syrup and water in a large, heavy pan, and heat to the soft-crack stage (143°C/290°F).

3 Warm the honey in a separate pan until it just boils, then add to the syrup and bring everything up to 143°C/290°F again.

4 Meanwhile, whisk the egg whites with the remaining 25g/1oz/2 tbsp of sugar until stiff peaks form.

5 Slowly pour the sugar and honey syrup into the whites in a stream, whisking constantly. Tiny lumps may form, but do not worry. Continue mixing until the mixture is stiff and glossy.

6 Chop one-third of the candied fruits and add to the mixture with the warm nuts, lavender buds and salt. Gently stir in. Add the butter and stir to combine.

7 Pour the nougat into the baking tray or tin and smooth the top with a spatula.

8 Decorate the surface with large pieces of the remaining candied fruits.

9 Leave to set at room temperature for 4–6 hours.

10 To remove the nougat from the tin, run an oiled paring knife around the edge and invert the cake tin, if using, or slip a metal offset spatula underneath the block if it is on a baking sheet.

11 Transfer to a chopping board and cut into small pieces and serve. Store in an airtight container for about 1 week. Do not refrigerate.

Cook's Tips

• Seek out top quality candied fruits if you are not able to make them yourself. Food halls of department stores and delicatessens stock them at Christmas. They are expensive because of the amount of time and effort that goes into their production, but you only need a small amount.
• It is important to toast all of the nuts in this recipe separately. Hazelnuts and almonds need a little time in the oven for their oils to be released, whereas pistachios simply require a few minutes.

Energy 5644kcal/23755kJ; Protein 62.8g; Carbohydrate 878.1g, of which sugars 859.8g; Fat 233.4g, of which saturates 36.8g; Cholesterol 92mg; Calcium 1171mg; Fibre 36.4g; Sodium 1388mg

Cocoa Nougat

Nougat can be a wonderful carrier for your favourite flavours. I love the texture of the chewy egg white with the melty bits of chocolate, and think the rice paper is the perfect finish. If you want a more chocolatey version, these would also be delicious if cut into squares and dipped in tempered chocolate. Another variation would be to use toasted hazelnuts, as they make such a natural companion to chocolate.

MAKES ABOUT 1KG/2¼LB

grapeseed or groundnut (peanut) oil, for greasing

rice paper

450g/1lb/2½ cups caster (superfine) sugar, plus 15g/½oz/1 tbsp

45ml/3 tbsp glucose syrup or golden (light corn) syrup

100ml/3½fl oz/scant ½ cup water

50g/2oz/½ cup unsweetened cocoa powder, plus extra for dusting

2 egg whites

200g/7oz/1¼ cups whole almonds, lightly toasted

100g/3¾oz dark (bittersweet) chocolate, finely chopped

5ml/1 tsp vanilla extract

1 Grease a Swiss roll tin (jelly roll pan), then line with the rice paper.

2 Put 400g/1lb/2½ cups of the caster sugar, the glucose or golden syrup and water in a large, heavy pan and heat to the soft-crack stage (143°C/290°F).

3 Add the cocoa powder to the syrup and bring back to 143°C/290°F again.

4 Meanwhile, whisk the egg whites with the remaining 15g/½oz/1 tbsp of the sugar until stiff peaks form.

5 Slowly pour the syrup into the whites in a stream, whisking constantly. Tiny lumps may form, but do not worry. Continue mixing until the mixture is stiff and glossy.

6 Add the warm nuts, chocolate pieces and vanilla and gently fold together. Pour the nougat into the prepared tin.

7 Cover the mixture with more sheets of rice paper and weigh down with a heavy board, such as a chopping board, and weights or dishes. If the chopping board smells of onions, for example, make sure you put it on a tray or place something in between it and the nougat, or the nougat will take on the flavour of the onions. Leave the nougat to set for 4 hours.

8 Remove the weights and board, and turn out on to a chopping board.

9 Dust the top with cocoa powder and trim the sides to neaten them.

10 Slice into diamonds. Serve immediately, or store in an airtight container for about 1 week.

Energy 3893kcal/16394kJ; Protein 62g; Carbohydrate 611g, of which sugars 570g; Fat 150g, of which saturates 32g; Cholesterol 6mg; Calcium 631mg; Fibre 26g; Sodium 751mg

SUGAR MICE

Sugar mice are traditionally found in the Christmas stockings of British children. They can be made from sugar set with egg whites or egg white powder, or they can be formed from soft sugar fondant. The former is made much like a sugar egg, using a mould. The latter can be made by hand and make a great project to do at home with children. Be creative with the decoration – small sweets could be used instead to decorate and embellish the mice.

MAKES 6

300g/12oz fondant (*see* page 38)

a few drops of pink food colouring

12 coffee beans

silver balls or other decorations, for the eyes

string, for the tail

1 Wearing latex gloves, colour half the fondant pink. If you like, you could leave all the fondant white. (You could also make it brown or grey, instead of pink.)

2 Shape the fondant into 6 pear shapes with flat bottoms; 3 white and 3 pink. Carefully mould the ears, using a sugar shaping tool or a wooden skewer, to form indentations the coffee beans can sit in snugly.

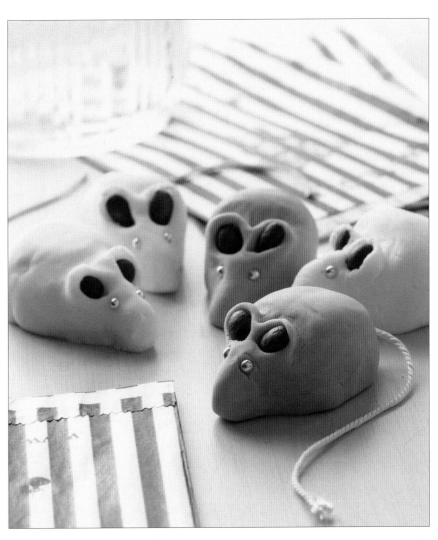

3 Push the coffee beans into the shaped ears, then add silver balls or other decorations for eyes. (You could add a ball for a nose, if you like.)

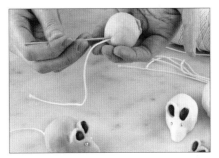

4 Cut lengths of string for the tails. Using sugar working tools or a wooden skewer, push them into place.

5 Allow the mice to dry completely overnight at room temperature.

COOK'S TIP

If you would like to add whiskers to your mice, cut the bristles from a new (but inexpensive) pastry brush and push them into place with a wooden skewer or sugar working tool. If you want edible whiskers and tail, try using thin liquorice laces.

Energy 194kcal/826kJ; Protein 0.9g; Carbohydrate 45.3g, of which sugars 43.2g; Fat 2.3g, of which saturates 1.4g; Cholesterol 0mg; Calcium 31mg; Fibre 0.1g; Sodium 18mg

SUGAR EASTER EGG

Looking inside a sugar Easter egg is like looking into a fairytale if you are a child. The panorama that you create inside the egg can set the imagination off on a little pastel-coloured adventure – if you let it. This recipe does require some patience, but the results are well worth the effort.

MAKES 1

FOR THE EGG:

400g/14oz/2 cups caster (superfine) sugar

2.5ml/½ tsp meringue powder

food colouring (optional)

30ml/2 tbsp water

cornflour (cornstarch), for dusting

sugar decorations

FOR THE ROYAL ICING:

45ml/3 tbsp meringue powder or egg whites

600g/1lb 6oz/5½ cups icing (confectioners') sugar

75–105ml/5–7 tbsp water

1 To make the egg, combine the sugar and meringue powder in a large bowl.

2 If you are colouring the egg, combine the desired amount of colour in with the water and blend well. Make a well in the sugar and add the water, and colouring, if using. With a wooden spoon, stir the mixture to an even colour. It will have the consistency of wet sand.

3 Dust a two-piece plastic egg mould and a cake board or cardboard disc with cornflour. Using a spoon, press the mixture into each half of the mould and pack it tightly. Using an offset spatula, scrape away any excess sugar so that the surface is flush with the mould.

4 Unmould the mixture immediately by placing the cornflour-dusted cake board over one egg half and inverting it. Remove the mould. Repeat with the other egg half.

5 Decide how you want the egg oriented and then trim a small portion off either the bottom (for an upright egg) or the side (for a landscape egg). To do this, you can use a metal spatula or a length of thread. Working quickly, saw about 5mm/¼in off. You need to trim both halves of the egg, so place the halves next to each other with the side you are trimming facing you so they will match up neatly when they are stuck together.

6 On the curved face of one half of the egg you need to cut out your 'window'. Using a thread, remove a piece of the egg that will leave a window of the size you desire. Leave the cut-off portion resting on top of the egg so that the area inside does not dry out. Leave to dry for 1–1½ hours.

7 Carefully remove the cut-off portion of egg and discard. Use a spoon to mark a 1cm/½in rim around the opening. Gently scoop out the centre within these marks.

8 When you have dug out as much as you can, carefully lift it up and remove the remaining mixture through the window. Put it back down very carefully. You will now have a hollow egg half with a window on the curved edge.

9 Carefully pick up the other half of the egg and, holding it in your hand, gently scoop out the centre, 5mm/¼in from the edge, following the contour of the egg. You should now have a hollow egg half.

10 Using your finger, smooth the opening on the inside of the egg halves. Place the egg halves right side-up on the cake boards and leave them to dry out for 24 hours.

11 The next day, prepare the royal icing. Combine the meringue powder or egg whites and sugar with 75ml/5 tbsp water in a large bowl. Using an electric mixer, beat for 8–10 minutes. The icing should form peaks. Add more water if needed. Divide the icing into small bowls. Leave one portion white and colour the others however you like. Green is needed if you want to have grass in your egg.

12 Holding the egg halves, one at a time, in the palm of your hand, file away any rough edges using a clean emery board.

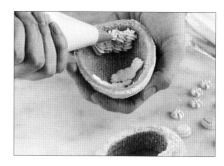

13 To decorate the egg, use a piping (pastry) bag to pipe royal-icing grass and clouds into the window-less egg half. Add sugar decorations and leave to set.

14 To join the halves, pipe icing around the flat rim of one egg half. Match the egg up with the other half and press together. Leave to dry for a few hours. Pipe a trim around the edge of the window and along the seam of the egg. Allow to set completely. Store in an airtight container at room temperature.

Energy 3956kcal/16879kJ; Protein 9.1g; Carbohydrate 1045g, of which sugars 1045g; Fat 0g, of which saturates 0g; Cholesterol 0mg; Calcium 532mg; Fibre 0g; Sodium 146mg

CANDIED FRUITS AND FLOWERS, AND JELLIED FRUITS

AN EXCELLENT PRESERVATIVE, SUGAR IS USED IN THIS
CHAPTER TO TRANSFORM FRUIT RINDS, JUICES AND
PURÉES INTO A RANGE OF STUNNING AND SOPHISTICATED
CONFECTIONS THAT ARE AS PLEASING TO THE EYE AS THEY
ARE TO THE PALATE. FROM INTENSE CANDIED PEEL,
PINEAPPLE AND PETALS TO FLAVOURFUL JELLIES AND
PASTES, AND CRISP SLIVERS OF PEAR, THESE JEWEL-LIKE
TREATS EVOKE MEMORIES OF SUMMER ABUNDANCE AND
PROVIDE THE PERFECT END FOR A SPECIAL DINNER.

Candied Citrus Peel

Fresh candied citrus peel is far superior to any that you can buy, with a brighter colour and fresher flavour. There will be slight variations in the thickness and bitterness of different citrus peels, so you will need to adjust the recipe accordingly: if the peel is thicker, blanch it for longer to soften the peel and remove more of the bitter oils.

MAKES ABOUT 1.2KG/2½LB

3 grapefruits, 4 oranges, or 12 clementines, preferably organic

800g/1¾lb/4 cups granulated (white) sugar

400ml/14fl oz/1⅔ cups water, plus extra for blanching

100g/3¾oz/½ cup caster (superfine) sugar

1 Wash the fruits. Cut them in half and juice them. Reserve the juice for drinking or using in another recipe. Place the juiced shells in a pan and cover with cold water. Bring to the boil and cook for 10 minutes.

2 Drain the peel, then return it to the pan and cover with fresh cold water. Bring to the boil again and drain. Repeat the blanching process a total of 5 times for grapefruit, 3 times for oranges and 2 times for clementines.

3 After the final blanching, test the tenderness of the peel by piercing it with the tip of a sharp knife. The knife should meet no resistance when pushed into the peel. If it still seems a little tough, blanch it once more.

4 Drain the peel and leave it until it is cool to the touch. Scrape away the soft pith using a spoon, then slice the peel into 1cm/½in strips with a sharp paring knife.

5 Place the sugar and water into a clean pan (do not reuse the pan you blanched the peel in without washing it, or the syrup could crystallize). Stir over medium heat to dissolve the sugar.

6 Once it has dissolved, stop stirring. Add the peel and bring to the boil. Boil for about 45 minutes, until the syrup reduces and small bubbles form on top (about 110°C/225°F). The peel will be slightly translucent. Leave the peel to cool in the syrup overnight.

7 Remove the peel from the syrup with a slotted spoon and lay it out on a wire rack placed over a piece of baking parchment to catch the drips. Leave it to dry for 24 hours.

8 The next day, touch the peel to see if it is almost dry. It should feel just sticky (if it is too moist, the sugar you toss it in will dissolve, but if it is too dry, the sugar will not adhere to the peel). Toss the strips in the caster sugar, spread them out on the wire rack and leave to dry for a few hours. Store in an airtight container for up to 6 months.

Energy 2772kcal/11808kJ; Protein 3.6g; Carbohydrate 709.2g, of which sugars 709.2g; Fat 10.8g, of which saturates 0g; Cholesterol 0mg; Calcium 1560mg; Fibre 57.6g; Sodium 3360mg

PRESERVED STEM GINGER

Peppery, sweet and aromatic, these golden chunks of ginger in syrup are a real treat. It is important to select heavy, plump-looking root ginger. If the root is at all shrivelled, it will not have the lovely spiciness that it needs to balance out the sweetness that comes from the preserving process.

MAKES ABOUT 1KG/2¼LB

300g/11oz fresh root ginger

500g/1¼lb/2½ cups granulated (white) sugar

550ml/18fl oz/2½ cups water, plus extra for blanching

15ml/1 tbsp glucose syrup

1 Peel the ginger with the edge of a spoon or a vegetable peeler, then cut it into 2cm/¾in chunks. Try to cut the chunks into appealing bulbous shapes.

2 Place the prepared ginger in a pan and cover with cold water. Bring to the boil and cook for 20 minutes.

3 Drain, then return the ginger to the pan and cover with fresh cold water. Bring to the boil again and drain. Repeat the blanching process 4 times in total.

4 Place the sugar, water and glucose syrup into a clean pan (do not use the pan you blanched the ginger in without washing it, or the syrup could crystallize).

5 Stir over medium heat to dissolve the sugar. Once it has dissolved, stop stirring and bring the syrup to the boil. Boil for about 45 minutes until the ginger becomes translucent. Leave the ginger to cool in the syrup overnight.

6 Using a slotted spoon, transfer the ginger from the syrup to a sterilized jar.

7 Pour syrup over the ginger to cover and store in the refrigerator.

8 Alternatively, you could strain the ginger and lay it on a wire rack to dry overnight. The next day, toss the ginger in granulated sugar and lay it out on a wire rack again to dry for a few hours.

Energy 2723kcal/11612kJ; Protein 3.7g; Carbohydrate 721.7g, of which sugars 721.7g; Fat 0g, of which saturates 0g; Cholesterol 0mg; Calcium 433mg; Fibre 2.7g; Sodium 111mg

CANDIED PINEAPPLE

Although this recipe takes an astonishingly long time (about two weeks) to prepare, the end result is golden-glazed, candied pineapple that is unlike any other candied fruit. The sweet taste of pineapple deepens and becomes concentrated by replacing the water content in the fruit with a reduced pineapple sugar syrup.

MAKES ABOUT 1.2KG/2½LB

1 pineapple

about 1kg/2¼lb/5 cups granulated (white) or caster (superfine) sugar

liquid glucose

1 Using a sharp knife, cut off the top and base of the pineapple. Stand the pineapple upright and, working in a circular motion to retain the shape of the pineapple, cut off the skin, starting at the top and finishing at the bottom of the fruit. You need to remove all of the sharp and spiny skin, without removing too much of the flesh. You may need to go back over the fruit to shave off any extra bits of skin.

2 Slice the pineapple into round discs about 1cm/½in thick. Using a small paring knife, cut out the hard inner core from each disc.

3 Weigh the pineapple and measure out 250ml/8fl oz/1 cup water per 500g/1¼lb of fruit. Put the water into a large pan.

4 Place the fruit gently in the water and cook over a medium heat for about 15 minutes, until the pineapple pieces are tender but not falling apart. Place a wire rack over a baking tray and, using a slotted spoon, remove the pineapple pieces from the pan and place them on the rack to drain. Reserve the liquid.

5 For every 250ml/8fl oz/1 cup of the reserved cooking liquid, add 150g/5oz/¾ cup sugar and 15ml/1 tbsp liquid glucose. Place the pan over a medium heat and stir until the sugar dissolves. Bring to the boil.

6 Line a large roasting pan with baking parchment or waxed paper, then arrange the pineapple pieces in the roasting pan in a single layer. Pour the boiling syrup over the pineapple to submerge it completely. Cover with another sheet of baking parchment or waxed paper and press down slightly. Set aside for 24 hours.

7 The following day, remove the paper, lift out the fruit on to a cooling rack and measure the remaining syrup. Pour the syrup into a heavy pan with an extra 50g/2oz/¼ cup sugar for every 300ml/½ pint/1¼ cups syrup. Bring to the boil.

8 Place the fruit back into the roasting pan and cover with the hot syrup. Cover once more with baking parchment or waxed paper, pressing down. Leave for another 24 hours.

9 Repeat steps 7 and 8 for a further 5 days.

10 On the eighth day, add 75g/3oz/scant ½ cup sugar for every 300ml/½ pint/1¼ cups of syrup, then let the fruit steep for 48 hours.

11 On the tenth day again add 75g/3oz/scant ½ cup sugar for every 300ml/½ pint/1¼ cups of syrup, then let the fruit steep for a further 4 days.

12 At the end of the 4 days, use a slotted spoon to lift the fruit from the syrup and place it on a cooling rack set over a baking tray to catch the juices. Preheat the oven to 110°C/225°F/Gas ¼. Place the tray in the oven, turn off the heat and leave the tray in the oven at least 4 hours to dry out the fruit.

13 Serve immediately, or store in an airtight container in the refrigerator for up to 6 months.

Energy 4186kcal/17866kJ; Protein 7.4g; Carbohydrate 1105.6g, of which sugars 1105.6g; Fat 1.2g, of which saturates 0g; Cholesterol 0mg; Calcium 638mg; Fibre 7.2g; Sodium 72mg

CANDY-COATED SOFT FRUITS

Coating soft fruits, such as berries, grapes, physalis or tangerine sections, in a thin layer of barely caramelized sugar lends them a completely different quality. The fruits retain their wonderful freshness but they are turned into something surprising. These look extremely pretty served in mini paper sweet cases. You must eat them within a few hours, or the juices of the fruit will start to dissolve the coating.

3 Pour the water into a heavy pan, then add the sugar. Place over a medium heat and swirl occasionally while the sugar dissolves. Do not stir it. If little crystals begin to form on the sides of the pan, brush them down with a wet, clean pastry brush (this must not have any oil residue on it). Alternatively, use a small spoon to drizzle water over the crystallized areas.

4 When the syrup reaches the hard-crack stage (154°C/310°F), remove the pan from the heat and place it on a folded dish towel or a hotplate, if you have one. The sugar syrup will continue to cook as it sits. This will give you a wonderful range of flavours – the fruits that are dipped first will be covered in a clear sugar shell, while ones dipped last will have a slightly caramelized covering.

5 Hold on to the stem, calyx, or end of a piece of fruit and dip it into the hot syrup to coat. Drag the bottom on the edge of the pot to remove any excess syrup and place the coated fruit into a sweet case to set. Working quickly, repeat until you have dipped all the fruit.

6 If the syrup becomes too hard before you have finished, simply place the pan back on the heat for a few minutes to re-melt it, then carry on dipping.

7 Serve the fruits as soon as their candy coating has set.

MAKES ABOUT 500G/1¼LB

250g/9oz soft fruit, such as cherries, strawberries, physalis or grapes

50ml/2fl oz/¼ cup water

250g/9oz/1¼ cups granulated (white) or caster (superfine) sugar

COOK'S TIP
Keep a bowl of cold water nearby in case your skin comes into contact with the hot sugar. If this happens, immediately plunge the affected area into the cold-water bath.

1 Select the prettiest pieces of fruit and wipe them clean with kitchen paper. Do not wash them in water, or the candy coating will not adhere to them.

2 Set out decorative paper or foil mini cake or sweet cases on a baking sheet.

Energy 1135kcal/4835kJ; Protein 1g; Carbohydrate 301g, of which sugars 301g; Fat 0g, of which saturates 0g; Cholesterol 0mg; Calcium 58mg; Fibre 2g; Sodium 18mg

SLICED CANDIED CLEMENTINES AND LEMONS

Candied citrus is one of the luxuries of life that is somewhat overlooked outside Italy and France, though it is now possible to buy good-quality candied fruit in delicatessens and some supermarkets. Although the process of making it takes a long time, it is worth making it yourself as it is easy and the result keeps well in a tightly sealed container in the refrigerator. Candied fruit is useful in many recipes and tastes divine dipped in chocolate, as here.

MAKES ABOUT 100–150

10 clementines and 5 lemons, sliced into 3mm/⅛in slices

2kg/4½lb/10 cups granulated (white) sugar

2 litres/3½ pints/8 cups water, plus extra for blanching

200g/7oz dark (bittersweet) chocolate (64–70% cocoa solids), broken into pieces

1 Put all of the clementine and lemon slices in a large pan and cover with water. Bring the water to the boil, then drain the slices in a colander. Return the fruit to the pan and cover again with cold water. Bring to the boil, then drain the fruit slices. Repeat this process a third time.

2 After the third blanching, leave the fruit in the colander while you wash out the pan. (A clean pan is important to avoid the sugar syrup crystallizing.)

3 Put the sugar and the 2 litres/3½ pints/8 cups water in the clean pan. Bring to the boil over a medium heat, stirring occasionally, to dissolve the sugar. Once the sugar has dissolved, stop stirring.

4 Add the sliced, blanched fruit and lower the heat so that the sugar syrup is at a very low simmer (with only tiny bubbles appearing on the surface). Simmer for 45 minutes, then turn off the heat. Leave the fruit to cool in the liquid.

5 Remove the fruit from the syrup and lay it out on a cooling rack positioned over some baking parchment to catch the drips. Discard the syrup.

6 The fruit will take at least 24 hours to dry out, sometimes longer if the weather is humid.

7 Once the fruit is dry, place the chocolate in a heatproof bowl set over a pan of barely simmering water. Leave the chocolate to melt, stirring occasionally. Remove the bowl from the heat and leave the chocolate to cool for 10 minutes.

8 Meanwhile, place a sheet of baking parchment on the work surface.

9 Dip pieces of candied fruit into the chocolate so they are half-coated. Scrape the bottom along the edge of the bowl to remove any excess chocolate.

10 Lay the dipped slices on to the baking parchment. Leave to set for 1 hour. Serve immediately or store in an airtight container for 2–3 weeks.

Energy 61kcal/260kJ; Protein 0.1g; Carbohydrate 15g, of which sugars 15g; Fat 0.4g, of which saturates 0.2g; Cholesterol 0.1mg; Calcium 3.6mg; Fibre 0g; Sodium 1mg

CRYSTALLIZED ROSE PETALS

If you have beautiful, fragrant roses growing in your garden you are very fortunate indeed! This is a wonderful use for the petals when you have a glut of flowers in the late spring and early summer, and the candied petals make a stunning decoration for desserts or cakes, or a glass of champagne.

MAKES HOWEVER MANY PETALS YOU
CHOOSE TO CRYSTALLIZE

unsprayed, fragrant garden roses

egg white

caster (superfine) sugar

1 Position sheets of baking parchment underneath cooling racks on a work surface to catch the sugar.

2 Gently separate the rose petals from the flowers, one rose at a time. Keep the other roses in water.

3 Very lightly brush the petals with egg white, using a new paintbrush. Do not dip the brush into the egg whites each time, as only a thin coating is required.

4 Sprinkle the painted petals with caster sugar.

5 Place the sugar-coated petals on the wire rack and leave them to dry for 24–36 hours.

6 Serve immediately, or store in an airtight container. The colour and flavour will fade, so enjoy them within 1 month.

(Approx. per petal) Energy 17kcal/75kJ; Protein 0.1g; Carbohydrate 4.5g, of which sugars 4.5g; Fat 0g, of which saturates 0g; Cholesterol 0mg; Calcium 2mg; Fibre 0g; Sodium 3mg

CRYSTALLIZED VIOLETS

Violets, like most roses, have a distinctive, intoxicating fragrance. Their perfume creates a wonderful flavour that works well as a sweet decoration. Their pretty purple hue is even more attractive when coated in a delicate layer of sugar. Make sure any flowers you use are edible and have not been sprayed with any chemicals.

MAKES HOWEVER MANY FLOWERS YOU
CHOOSE TO CRYSTALLIZE

unsprayed, fragrant sweet violets

egg white

caster (superfine) sugar

1 Position sheets of baking parchment under cooling racks on a surface to catch the sugar. You will also need a new, soft, small paintbrush.

2 Keep the violets in water while you are working with one flower at a time. Very lightly brush the petals on both sides, one at a time, with egg white. You do not need to dip the brush into the egg wash each time, as you want only a very thin coating of the egg white to make the sugar adhere.

3 Sprinkle the petals with sugar, and gently place on the cooling racks to dry. Leave for at least 24–36 hours.

4 Use to decorate all manner of cakes and desserts. Store in an airtight container. The colour and flavour will fade eventually, so enjoy them within 1 month.

COOK'S TIP
These sugared violets also make a delicious and pretty aperitif. Drop one or two into a glass of sparkling wine such as Prosecco or Champagne.

(Approx. per flower) Energy 17kcal/75kJ; Protein 0.1g; Carbohydrate 4.5g, of which sugars 4.5g; Fat 0g, of which saturates 0g; Cholesterol 0mg; Calcium 2mg; Fibre 0g; Sodium 3mg

Turkish Delight

This fresh version of Turkish delight tastes very different from many of the commercially produced versions, so it is worth trying even if you think you do not like it. The texture is soft and silky, and the ancient combination of perfumed roses with a hint of lemon makes these fragrant treats a real delight.

MAKES ABOUT 1.6KG/3½LB

butter, for greasing

450g/1lb/2¼ cups caster (superfine) sugar

900ml/1½ pints/3¾ cups water

2.5ml/½ tsp cream of tartar

75g/3oz/⅔ cup cornflour (cornstarch)

200g/7oz/generous 1⅔ cups icing (confectioners') sugar, plus extra for dusting

50g/2oz/¼ cup honey

rose water

lemon extract

pink food colouring

1 Grease an 18cm/7in square tin (pan) and set aside.

2 Put the sugar, 150ml/¼ pint/⅔ cup of the water and the cream of tartar into a heavy pan. Stir over low heat to dissolve the sugar, then bring to the boil and boil, without stirring, until it reaches the soft-ball stage (114°C/238°F). Set aside.

3 Combine the cornflour, icing sugar and 50ml/2fl oz/¼ cup of water in a small, heatproof bowl to make a paste.

4 Boil the remaining 700ml/1 pint/3½fl oz/scant 3 cups of the water in another pan and pour over the cornflour paste, whisking to blend. Return to the pan and simmer until clear and thick.

5 Gradually start adding the sugar syrup to the pan, whisking constantly. Boil for 30 minutes. (The timing is important so set a timer.) It should be a pale yellow colour and almost transparent.

6 Add the honey, rose water, and lemon extract to taste. Add the pink food colouring and combine. Pour the mixture into the tin and leave to cool completely.

7 Turn the Turkish delight out on to a board that has been dusted generously with icing sugar. Cut into cubes and toss in more icing sugar. Serve immediately, or pack into an airtight container with plenty of icing sugar to stop it sticking.

Energy 2971kcal/12672kJ; Protein 3.9g; Carbohydrate 786.5g, of which sugars 717.5g; Fat 0.5g, of which saturates 0.1g; Cholesterol 0mg; Calcium 358mg; Fibre 0.1g; Sodium 84mg

ORANGE SLICES

The commercial versions of these brightly coloured orange wedges have long been popular confections. These home-made ones retain the appealing texture and tang of the bought variety, but are made with freshly squeezed orange juice and contain no artificial colourings, flavourings or preservatives.

MAKES ABOUT 350G/12OZ

grapeseed or groundnut (peanut) oil, for greasing (optional)

enough oranges to make 150ml/ ¼ pint/⅔ cup orange juice (about 10–15, depending on their size)

200g/7oz/1 cup preserving or granulated (white) sugar

2.5ml/½ tsp cream of tartar

35g/1¼oz powdered gelatine

caster (superfine) sugar, for dusting

1 Sprinkle a 25cm/10in square cake tin (pan) with water, or lightly grease the tin and line it with clear film (plastic wrap). Set aside.

2 Juice the oranges and strain the juice. Put the orange juice, sugar, and cream of tartar into a heavy pan and heat over low heat to dissolve the sugar.

3 Once dissolved, add the gelatine and heat gently until it has dissolved as well, stirring constantly.

4 Strain the mixture through a fine sieve (strainer), then pour it into the prepared tin. Leave to set for about 1 hour.

5 When it is firm, turn the jelly out on to a work surface. If you have trouble removing the jelly, dunk the base of the tin briefly into warm water. This should loosen the jelly just slightly, allowing it to release from the tin with ease.

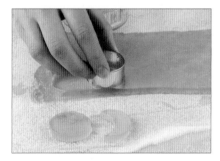

6 Cut the jelly into crescent shapes, using a small round cookie cutter. Start on the right-hand end, cutting a circle. With the second cut, overlap slightly to cut a crescent. Continue this way until you have used all of the jelly.

7 Toss the crescents in the caster sugar to coat and serve immediately. Store in an airtight container for up to 2 weeks.

Energy 911kcal/3882kJ; Protein 30g; Carbohydrate 210g, of which sugars 210g; Fat 0g, of which saturates 0g; Cholesterol 0mg; Calcium 108mg; Fibre 0g; Sodium 126mg

GRAPE JUJUBES

Jujubes used to be common in cinemas in the US, but are seen less often today. They can be made with almost any berry or citrus flavour and it would look lovely to make a few batches using different fruits to create different colours. The preserving sugar helps to set the jujubes and keep them from melting the sugar coating.

4 Add the lemon juice, gelatine, sugar and water to the pan and heat gently until the sugar and gelatine have dissolved.

5 Once everything has dissolved, bring to the boil and boil for 5 minutes.

6 Pour the mixture into the prepared tin and leave to set for 5 hours or until firm.

7 Turn the jelly out on to a chopping board. Cut out little circles with the smallest round pastry (cookie) cutter you can find. Roll in caster sugar. Leave to dry out on a wire rack for 1–2 hours, then roll once more in caster sugar and serve. Store in an airtight container.

MAKES ABOUT 675G/1½LB

400g/14oz Concord or Muscatel grapes

30ml/2 tbsp lemon juice

25g/1oz powdered gelatine

100g/4oz/8 tbsp preserving sugar (or granulated (white) sugar with 15ml/1 tbsp of pectin added)

150ml/¼ pint/⅔ cup water

caster (superfine) sugar, for coating

1 Dampen a square 15cm/6in tin (pan) with water and set aside.

2 Remove the grapes from the stem and place in a heavy pan. Cook over medium heat for 5–10 minutes, or until they burst open and release their juices.

3 Transfer the grapes and juice to a food processor or blender and blend until smooth. Wash the pan, then strain the purée through a sieve (strainer) into it.

Energy 721kcal/3076kJ; Protein 23g; Carbohydrate 167g, of which sugars 167g; Fat 0g, of which saturates 0g; Cholesterol 0mg; Calcium 127mg; Fibre 3g; Sodium 96mg

Ginger Gumdrops

Gumdrops are dense and chewy. They can be made in an assortment of colours and flavours. These are made with spicy candied ginger, which creates a gumdrop that packs more of a punch than store-bought varieties. The texture of the ginger contrasts well with the gummy sweet, and together they form a delicious treat.

MAKES ABOUT 800G/1¾LB

grapeseed or groundnut (peanut) oil, for greasing (optional)

20g/¾oz powdered gelatine

100ml/3½fl oz/scant ½ cup cold water

400g/14oz/2 cups caster (superfine) sugar

100ml/3½fl oz/scant ½ cup hot water

15m/1 tbsp lemon juice

100g/3¾oz candied ginger (see page 157), chopped

50g/2oz/½ cup cornflour (cornstarch)

50g/2oz/½ cup icing (confectioners') sugar

1 Sprinkle a 20cm/8in square cake tin (pan) with water or lightly grease the tin and line it with clear film (plastic wrap). Set aside.

2 Dissolve the gelatine in the cold water in a small bowl.

3 Combine the caster sugar and the hot water in a pan and heat until the sugar has dissolved. Bring to the boil and boil, without stirring, for 10 minutes.

4 Add the soaked gelatine and boil for a further 15 minutes.

5 Add the lemon juice and ginger, remove from the heat and leave to cool slightly. Pour the mixture into the tin and leave to set for 24 hours.

6 Turn the mixture out on to a chopping board dusted with the cornflour and icing sugar. Cut into small rounds with a tiny cookie cutter.

7 Transfer to a cooling rack and allow to dry. This will take about 2 hours. Dust again with the mixture of cornflour and icing sugar, then serve immediately or store in an airtight container at room temperature.

Cook's Tip
It is useful to have a dish of hot water to hand into which you can dip the cutter occasionally. This will help prevent the cutter from sticking and give a cleaner finish.

Energy 2269kcal/9675kJ; Protein 19.8g; Carbohydrate 582.6g, of which sugars 536.6g; Fat 0.3g, of which saturates 0.1g; Cholesterol 0mg; Calcium 302mg; Fibre 1g; Sodium 80mg

RASPBERRY JELLIES

Jellies in the form of dense little fruit sweets such as these are different from the wobbly jellies that are served as dessert. These have just a little bite and, because of the additional gelatine, they maintain their shape. They dissolve in your mouth, releasing their fresh fruit flavour. You could make them with a variety of different fruit purées, if you like, and serve them together for an array of colour and flavour.

MAKES ABOUT 900G/2LB

500g/1¼lb raspberries

25g/1oz powdered gelatine

60ml/4 tbsp cold water

200g/7oz/1 cup preserving sugar or granulated (white) sugar

150ml/¼ pint/⅔ cup water

20ml/4 tsp fresh lemon juice, strained

caster (superfine) sugar, for rolling (optional)

1 Put the raspberries in a heavy pan and heat gently until the fruits soften and the juices run. Do not stir. Strain through a sieve (strainer) placed over a large bowl to catch the juices, pushing the pulp through with the back of a spoon. You should have about 300ml/½ pint/1¼ cups raspberry purée.

2 Sprinkle a 20cm/8in square cake tin (pan) with a little water.

3 Put the gelatine in a small bowl with 60ml/4 tbsp cold water. Set aside.

4 Put the sugar and 150ml/¼ pint/⅔ cup water in a pan. Cook over a low heat, stirring, until the sugar has dissolved. Then bring to the boil and cook until it reaches the soft-ball stage (114°C/238°F).

5 Add the softened gelatine, the raspberry purée and the lemon juice to the reduced sugar syrup.

6 Pour into the dampened tin through a sieve (strainer). Leave to set for 5 hours.

7 Once set, run a small knife around the edge of the tin and turn the jelly out on to a marble slab or a cool solid surface, dusted with caster sugar. If the jelly sticks in the tin, run a warm damp cloth over the bottom of the tin.

8 Cut into shapes with an oiled cookie cutter or a knife. Serve immediately, rolled in caster sugar, if you like. If you are not serving them on the day, dust with caster sugar and store in a cool place in an airtight container for 1–2 days. Roll in sugar again before serving.

Energy 999kcal/4270kJ; Protein 28g; Carbohydrate 233g, of which sugars 233g; Fat 2g, of which saturates 1g; Cholesterol 0mg; Calcium 209mg; Fibre 34g; Sodium 108mg

APPLE PASTE

You can use apples such as Bramley or Granny Smith for a more tart paste, but this simple recipe is also a great way to use up any windfall or floury (mealy) apples. These are intended to be made in little shapes for serving as a sweet, but you could also spread the paste out a bit thinner over two sheets to dry. The thinner paste can be cut into strips and wrapped in baking parchment for children's lunches.

MAKES ABOUT 60

butter, for greasing

4 or 5 apples, washed

100ml/3½fl oz/scant ½ cup water

about 1.2kg/2½lb/6 cups granulated (white) or preserving sugar

15ml/1 tbsp fresh lemon juice, strained

finely grated rind of ½ lemon

caster (superfine) sugar, for rolling

1 Grease a Swiss roll tin (jelly roll pan) and line with baking parchment.

2 Quarter and core the apples, but leave the peel on. Place the fruit in a large, heavy pan. Add the water, cover and simmer over a low heat for 30 minutes, stirring occasionally, until the fruit is soft and tender. Add more water if necessary.

3 Remove from the heat and pass the fruit through a food mill or sieve (strainer).

4 Weigh the fruit pulp and transfer it back into the pan. Measure an equal weight of sugar and stir it into the puréed apple.

5 Place the pan over a very low heat and, stirring occasionally, cook for about one hour until the paste is a dark colour.

6 Test the mixture by putting a spoonful on a plate. It should firm up and, when it cools, it should be matte and not sticky. Stir in the lemon juice and rind.

7 Spread the mixture in the prepared Swiss roll tin, and leave to cool.

8 Once cooled, cut into shapes and roll in caster sugar. Store in an airtight container in the refrigerator. They will keep for up to three weeks.

Energy 83kcal/353kJ; Protein 0g; Carbohydrate 22g, of which sugars 22g; Fat 0g, of which saturates 0g; Cholesterol 0mg; Calcium 2mg; Fibre 0g; Sodium 1 mg

Two-Tone Fruit Jellies

This stunning two-toned treat is made from two differently flavoured layers of silky, springy jelly. Half tangy apricot, half sweet strawberry, these jellies taste as good as they look. This recipe is also a great way of using up overripe fruit. Once you have made these jellies, you can try experimenting with other fruits.

MAKES 30–40

350g/12oz strawberries

350g/12oz apricots

butter, for greasing

500g/1¼lb/2½ cups preserving sugar

75ml/5 tbsp glucose syrup or golden (light corn) syrup

150ml/¼ pint/⅔ cup water

0.75ml/⅛ tsp cream of tartar

15g/½oz powdered pectin or 65g/2½oz liquid pectin

10ml/2 tsp lemon juice

100g/3¾oz/½ cup granulated (white) sugar, for coating

1 Put the fruit in two separate pans, each with 30ml/2 tbsp water, and cook for about 10 minutes until soft and releasing their juices. Purée each mixture separately in a blender or food processor. Put in separate bowls and set aside.

2 Lightly grease a 15cm/6in square tin (pan). Line with clear film (plastic wrap), making the film as smooth as possible.

3 Stir 25g/1oz/2 tbsp of the preserving sugar into the strawberry purée, and another 25g/1oz/2 tbsp of the preserving sugar into the apricot purée. Set aside.

4 In a large, heavy pan, mix the remaining sugar with the glucose or golden syrup, water and cream of tartar. Place over a low heat, stirring until the sugar dissolves.

5 Stop stirring, turn the heat up to medium and bring to the boil. When it reaches a rolling boil, turn the heat up to high. Boil, without stirring, until the syrup reaches 130°C/266°F.

6 Mix half the pectin into the strawberry purée mixture and the other half into the apricot mixture. Put the apricot mixture into a clean heavy pan and pour half of the boiled syrup over it.

7 Add the strawberry mixture to the pan containing the remaining boiled syrup. Gently stir each to combine, but then stop stirring. Boil, without stirring, until the temperature goes back up to 103°C/217°F.

8 Add 5ml/1 tsp lemon juice to each pan and continue boiling until they have both reached 106°C/223°F. Remove from the heat.

9 Give the strawberry mixture a stir, then pour it into the prepared tin. Leave to cool for 10 minutes.

10 Now pour the apricot mixture over the top. Use the tip of a knife to swirl the mixtures together a little. Leave the jelly to set overnight at room temperature, uncovered.

11 Once it has set, lift the jelly out of the tin by taking hold of the edges of the clear film and transferring the jelly to a chopping board.

12 Cut into little squares using a sharp knife, or use tiny cookie cutters to cut it into shapes. Toss the jellies in granulated sugar. Lay them out on baking parchment to dry for about 1 hour. Store them in an airtight container for 1 week. Do not refrigerate.

Variation
You can have fun playing around with flavour combinations. Orange and strawberry or elderflower and rhubarb are good. Substitute equal parts of juices, cordials or purées to create your perfect two-tone jellies.

Energy 70kcal/298kJ; Protein 0.2g; Carbohydrate 18.3g, of which sugars 18.3g; Fat 0g, of which saturates 0g; Cholesterol 0mg; Calcium 11mg; Fibre 0.2g; Sodium 7mg

BLACKBERRY PASTE

A fruit paste has a more jammy consistency and tastes more concentrated than a fruit jelly. They are a wonderful confection for capturing the flavours of the best seasonal fruits. This recipe is for fruits that contain little natural pectin, such as berries and plums.

4 In a large, heavy pan, mix the rest of the preserving sugar with the glucose syrup, water and cream of tartar. Stir over a low heat until the sugar dissolves.

5 Stop stirring, turn the heat up to medium and bring to the boil. When it reaches a rolling boil, turn the heat up to high. Boil, without stirring, until the syrup reaches 130°C/266°F.

6 Mix the pectin into the blackberry purée mixture. Add to the boiling syrup and stir gently to combine. Boil, without stirring, until the temperature goes back up to 103°C/217°F.

7 Add the lemon juice and continue boiling until it reaches 106°C/223°F. Remove the thermometer and place it in a jar of warm water.

MAKES 30–40

800g/1¾lb blackberries

butter, for greasing

500g/1¼lb/2½ cups preserving sugar

75ml/5 tbsp glucose syrup or golden (light corn) syrup

150ml/¼ pint/⅔ cup water

0.75ml/⅛ tsp cream of tartar

15g/½oz powdered pectin or 65g/2½oz liquid pectin

10ml/2 tsp lemon juice

100g/3¾oz/½ cup granulated (white) sugar, for coating

1 Put the blackberries in a heavy pan and heat gently over a low heat until the fruits soften and the juices run. Do not stir. Strain through a sieve (strainer) placed over a large bowl to catch the juices, pushing the pulp through with the back of a spoon. You should have about 500ml/17fl oz/ generous 2 cups blackberry purée.

2 Lightly grease a 15cm/6in square tin (pan). Line with clear film (plastic wrap), making the film as smooth as possible.

3 Transfer the blackberry purée to a bowl and add 50g/2oz/¼ cup of the preserving sugar. Stir together and set aside.

8 Give the syrup a stir at this point, then pour it into the prepared tin. Leave to set overnight at room temperature, uncovered.

9 Lift the paste out of the tin by taking hold of the edges of the clear film and transferring the paste to a chopping board. Peel off the clear film.

10 Cut into shapes using a cookie cutter of your choice (or into squares using a knife) and coat the jellies in granulated sugar. Leave to dry for 1 hour.

11 Serve immediately, or store in an airtight container for up to 1 week. Do not refrigerate.

Energy 70kcal/297kJ; Protein 0.3g; Carbohydrate 18.2g, of which sugars 18.2g; Fat 0g, of which saturates 0g; Cholesterol 0mg; Calcium 17mg; Fibre 0.6g; Sodium 6mg

RASPBERRY PASTE

This delectable paste captures the essence of summer and is a great way to use up slightly overripe berries. The jewel-like shapes make an interesting alternative to chocolates at the end of a special meal, or they can be enjoyed as a fruity treat at any time of the day. They make an attractive present when packaged in a gift box.

MAKES 30–40

700g/1lb 9oz raspberries

butter, for greasing

500g/1¼lb/2½ cups preserving sugar

75ml/5 tbsp glucose syrup or golden (light corn) syrup

150ml/¼ pint/⅔ cup water

0.75ml/⅛ tsp cream of tartar

15g/½oz powdered pectin or 65g/2½oz liquid pectin

10ml/2 tsp lemon juice

100g/3¾oz/½ cup granulated (white) sugar, for coating

7 Add the lemon juice and continue boiling until it reaches 106°C/223°F.

8 Give the syrup a stir at this point, then pour it into the prepared tin. Leave to set overnight at room temperature, uncovered.

9 Lift the paste out of the tin using the edges of the clear film. Place it on a chopping board. Cut into squares using a sharp knife and coat in granulated sugar. Leave to dry for 1 hour. Serve immediately, or store in an airtight container for 1 week. Do not refrigerate.

1 Put the raspberries in a heavy pan and heat gently over a low heat until the fruits soften and the juices run. Do not stir. Strain through a sieve (strainer) placed over a large bowl to catch the juices, pushing the pulp through with the back of a spoon. You should have about 500g/1¼lb raspberry purée.

2 Lightly grease a 15cm/6in square tin (pan). Line with clear film (plastic wrap), making the film as smooth as possible.

3 Stir 50g/2oz/¼ cup of the preserving sugar into the raspberry purée. Set aside.

4 In a large, heavy pan, mix the rest of the preserving sugar with the glucose syrup, water and cream of tartar. Stir over a low heat until the sugar dissolves.

5 Stop stirring, turn the heat up to medium and bring to the boil. When it reaches a rolling boil, turn the heat up to high. Boil, without stirring, until the syrup reaches 130°C/266°F.

6 Mix the pectin into the blackberry purée mixture. Add to the boiling syrup and stir gently to combine. Boil, without stirring, until the temperature goes back up to 103°C/217°F.

Energy 70kcal/297kJ; Protein 0g; Carbohydrate 18g, of which sugars 17g; Fat 0g, of which saturates 0g; Cholesterol 0mg; Calcium 6mg; Fibre 1g; Sodium 4mg

QUINCE PASTE

Quince must be cooked in order to bring out its delicious flavour and deep jewel colouring. It is most often served in the form of a paste. The Spanish call it *membrillo* and serve it with sheep's milk cheese. It is also presented at French and Mexican tables. It is delicious eaten after dinner with a little Manchego or Stilton cheese.

MAKES ABOUT 60

butter, for greasing

4 or 5 large quinces

100ml/3½fl oz/scant ½ cup water

about 1.2kg/2½lb/6 cups granulated (white) or preserving sugar

45ml/3 tbsp lemon juice, strained

caster (superfine) sugar, for coating

1 Grease a Swiss roll tin (jelly roll pan) and line with baking parchment.

2 Wash the quinces well to remove any fuzz. Quarter and core the fruit, but leave the peel on. Cut into smaller chunks and place the fruit in a large, heavy pan.

3 Add the water, cover and simmer over a low heat for about 1 hour, or until the fruit is soft and tender. Stir occasionally. Add more water if necessary.

4 Remove the pan from the heat and pass the fruit through a food mill or sieve (strainer).

5 Weigh the fruit pulp and place it back into the pan. Measure an equal weight of sugar and stir it into the puréed quince.

6 Place the pan over a very low heat and, stirring occasionally, cook for 1½–2 hours until the paste is a dark garnet colour.

7 To test the mixture, put a spoonful on a plate. It should firm up and, when it cools, it should be matte and not sticky.

8 Stir in the lemon juice. Spread the paste out in the tin. Leave to cool. Once cooled, cut into squares using a knife (or into shapes using a cutter) and coat in caster sugar. Store in an airtight container in the refrigerator for 3 weeks.

Energy 86kcal/369kJ; Protein 0.2g; Carbohydrate 22.8g, of which sugars 22.8g; Fat 0g, of which saturates 0g; Cholesterol 0mg; Calcium 11mg; Fibre 0.3g; Sodium 2mg

BAKED PEAR CRISPS

Lightly poaching slices of pear in sugar syrup then drying them out in the oven transforms the delicate texture of a fresh pear into a crisp, sweet treat. They become slightly translucent in the process, making them look a little like stained glass. These are also wonderful dipped in melted dark chocolate.

MAKES ABOUT 20

2 under-ripe pears, such as Comice

juice of 2 limes or lemons

400g/14oz/2 cups caster (superfine) sugar

200ml/7fl oz/scant 1 cup water

1 Line a baking sheet with baking parchment. Preheat the oven to 110°C/225°F/Gas ¼.

2 Slice the pears into paper-thin slices with a very sharp thin-bladed knife or a mandolin. Immediately squeeze lime or lemon juice over them to prevent them from turning brown and to add flavour.

3 Combine the sugar and water in a heavy pan and warm over a medium heat to dissolve. Once the sugar has fully dissolved, turn up the heat and bring to the boil. Cook until the syrup reaches the thread stage (111°C/233°F).

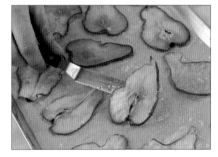

4 Place the pear slices in the reduced syrup (you can do this in two batches) and cook for 2 minutes.

5 Lift the slices from the syrup with a slotted spoon, draining off as much of the syrup as possible. Lay the slices out on the baking sheet in a single layer.

6 Bake in the preheated oven for 2 hours then, using a spatula, flip the slices over and bake for a further 20 minutes, until completely dry.

7 Leave to cool, then serve immediately, or store in an airtight container for up to 2 weeks.

Energy 85kcal/362kJ; Protein 0.1g; Carbohydrate 22.4g, of which sugars 22.4g; Fat 0g, of which saturates 0g; Cholesterol 0mg; Calcium 12mg; Fibre 0.3g; Sodium 2mg

MARZIPAN AND LIQUORICE

NUTS ARE A KEY INGREDIENT IN SWEET-MAKING. WITH THEIR MANY TYPES AND FLAVOURS, THEY ADD NUANCE AND TEXTURE TO RECIPES. SIMPLE NUT PASTES CAN BE COOKED AND MOULDED BY HAND, AS WELL AS BEING MIXED WITH ORANGE RIND AND COATED WITH MELTED CHOCOLATE, SANDWICHED BETWEEN HAZELNUTS OR STUFFED INTO DATES. LIQUORICE ROOT AND ANISEED ARE KEY TO INTENSELY FLAVOURED DROPS, BRITTLE SHARDS AND CHEWY STICKS, AND THE RANGE ON OFFER WILL PLEASE EVEN THE MOST ARDENT LIQUORICE-LOVER.

STUFFED DATES

Originating in North Africa, dates stuffed with nut paste have long been a festive treat in the Middle East and the Mediterranean. Pistachios and dates have a natural affinity, since they grow in the same areas, and the combination is further enhanced in this delectable recipe by the inclusion of marzipan, orange rind and candied peel.

MAKES 12

12 dates, preferably Barhi or Medjool

115g/4oz Boiled Marzipan (*see* page 53)

15ml/1 tbsp Kirsch

finely grated rind of 1 orange

15–20 pistachios

candied orange peel (optional)

1 Prepare the dates by slitting them down one side and removing the stones (pits) with the tip of a knife, leaving a cavity for the stuffing.

2 Combine the marzipan, Kirsch and orange rind in a bowl and mix well using clean hands. Divide the flavoured marzipan into 12 pieces and roll into little balls.

3 Wash your hands. Press a marzipan ball into the centre of each date and gently squeeze the date around the filling to create an even shape.

4 Chop the pistachios finely and sprinkle over the dates. Add a piece of candied peel, if you like. Place each date in a little sweet case.

5 Serve immediately or store, covered, for up to 2 weeks in the refrigerator.

Energy 92kcal/388kJ; Protein 1.3g; Carbohydrate 15g, of which sugars 14.9g; Fat 2.8g, of which saturates 0.3g; Cholesterol 0mg; Calcium 15mg; Fibre 0.7g; Sodium 13mg

MARZIPAN-STUFFED HAZELNUTS

These adorable little bites of toasted hazelnuts sandwiched around orange-flavoured marzipan make a sweet
end to any meal. They take a little time to assemble, but it is a very simple recipe, so making these is a perfect
activity to involve children in, if they are keen to help out.

MAKES ABOUT 40

150g/5oz large, whole hazelnuts, with skins (the largest you can find)

200g/7oz Boiled Marzipan (*see* page 53)

juice and finely grated rind of 1 orange or clementine

cocoa powder and icing (confectioners') sugar, for dusting

1 Line a baking sheet with baking parchment and preheat the oven to 160°C/325°F/Gas 3.

2 Spread out the hazelnuts in an even layer and place in the middle of the oven to bake for 7 minutes. Check the nuts periodically as they can burn quickly. They should be golden brown.

3 Meanwhile, put the boiled marzipan and orange or clementine juice and rind in a small bowl, and knead together with your hands or the back of a spoon.

VARIATION
If you cannot find large hazelnuts, you could use whole almonds or walnut halves instead; they also work well. Just remember to adjust the toasting time for the nuts. Walnuts need only show the slightest tinge of yellow-gold, whereas the hazelnuts should be golden brown.

4 When the nuts are sufficiently toasted, transfer them to a clean dish towel and remove the skins by rubbing them together in the towel.

5 Shake off any excess skin and, using a paring knife, split the nuts in half along their seam. Leave to cool completely.

6 Roll the marzipan filling into about 40 tiny balls, and use each ball to sandwich two hazelnut halves together.

7 Serve immediately, dusted with cocoa powder and icing sugar, or store in an airtight container in a cool place for up to 2 weeks.

Energy 45kcal/186kJ: Protein 0.8g: Carbohydrate 3.6g, of which sugars 3.5g: Fat 3g, of which saturates 0.2g: Cholesterol 0mg: Calcium 9mg: Fibre 0.3g: Sodium 1mg

Espresso and Hazelnut Balls

Marzipan is a wonderful vehicle for other flavours. The bitterness of good fresh coffee or espresso grounds together with the warmth of toasted hazelnuts is always a good combination. Adding a little alcohol can also help to cut the sweetness, making these the perfect accompaniment to coffee after a special dinner.

2 Divide the mixture into 24 pieces and roll into balls.

3 Pour some caster sugar on to a plate and, in batches, roll the balls around in it to coat them completely.

4 Serve immediately, or store, covered, for up to 2 weeks in the refrigerator.

Cook's Tip
The easiest way to gather the ingredients for this recipe is to save a little black coffee from a morning drink and put it in a container in the refrigerator. Toast the hazelnuts in the morning too, so they have plenty of time to cool.

MAKES 24

200g/7oz Boiled Marzipan (*see* page 53)

50g/2oz/⅓ cup hazelnuts, toasted and chopped

25ml/1½ tbsp cold espresso or strong coffee

5ml/1 tsp fresh espresso grounds

2.5ml/½ tsp Cognac or Grand Marnier

caster (superfine) sugar, for coating

1 Put all the ingredients except the sugar into a bowl. Mix together with your hands.

Energy 52kcal/219kJ; Protein 1.2g; Carbohydrate 4.3g, of which sugars 4.2g; Fat 3.5g, of which saturates 0.3g; Cholesterol 2mg; Calcium 12mg; Fibre 0.4g; Sodium 1mg

Mexican Marzipan

This delicious nut paste from Mexico combines almonds and peanuts, which lend a distinctive flavour to the confection. Peanuts are very oily, so the marzipan requires the addition of almonds to give it a good texture. Cutting the paste with a tiny fluted pastry cutter is an elegant way of presenting these sweets.

MAKES ABOUT 675G/1½LB

100g/3¾oz/⅔ cup raw peanuts

300g/11oz/1½ cups caster (superfine) sugar

150ml/¼ pint/⅔ cup water

100g/3¾oz/scant 1 cup ground almonds

1 egg white, slightly beaten

2.5ml/½ tsp vanilla extract

icing (confectioners') sugar, for dusting

1 Prepare an ice-water bath and set it aside. Either chop the peanuts very finely by hand, or grind them briefly, in short bursts, in a food processor. Be very careful that you do not over-process them as it will turn them into peanut butter.

2 Put the sugar and water in a heavy pan and warm over a medium heat until the sugar has dissolved. Increase the heat and bring the mixture to the soft-ball stage (114°C/238°F).

3 As soon as the soft-ball stage has been reached, dip the base of the pan into the ice-water bath to arrest the cooking. Add the ground peanuts and almonds and stir to combine. Stir in the egg white and return to the heat.

4 Stir for a short while over a low heat, until the marzipan thickens slightly. Remove from the heat and leave to cool slightly.

5 Dust a chopping board with icing sugar and turn the almond mixture out on to it. Knead gently for 5–6 minutes, until the marzipan is smooth and holds together.

6 Roll out the marzipan out to a thickness of about 1cm/½in.

7 Use a small fluted pastry (cookie) cutter to stamp out rounds. You could also use any other shape you like.

8 Serve immediately or wrap individually in waxed paper and store in an airtight container for 3 weeks in the refrigerator or 6 months in the freezer.

Energy 2369kcal/9960kJ; Protein 50g; Carbohydrate 334g, of which sugars 325g; Fat 102g, of which saturates 13g; Cholesterol 0mg; Calcium 332mg; Fibre 20g; Sodium 92mg

MARZIPAN BUMBLE BEES

These cute little bees will be a hit with children, and are the perfect decoration for cupcakes or a birthday cake. Make the marzipan a day in advance and leave it to ripen overnight at room temperature, before colouring and shaping it into bumble bees. This will make it easier to work with and it will hold its shape better.

MAKES ABOUT 10

150g/5oz Boiled Marzipan (*see* page 53)

a few drops of yellow food colouring

a few drops of black food colouring

hundreds and thousands (sprinkles)

flaked (sliced) almonds

1 Divide the marzipan into two pieces and colour half yellow and half black.

2 Divide each colour into four pieces. Roll these out into logs about 5mm/¼in in diameter. You will end up with four yellow logs and four black logs. Use clear film (plastic wrap) to cover any with which you are not working.

3 Cut each log into 5mm/¼in pieces.

4 Alternating the colours, sandwich together two yellow pieces and one black, to make the body of a bee.

5 To make the heads, roll a black piece into a ball and press it into the body.

6 To make the eyes, push two yellow, black or white hundreds and thousands into the head.

7 To make the wings, choose two perfect almond flakes and push them gently into the body to create two wings.

8 Serve immediately, or store at room temperature, covered with clear film or in an airtight container. Do not refrigerate, or the flaked almonds will soften and the colour of the hundreds and thousands will bleed.

Energy 67kcal/281kJ; Protein 1g; Carbohydrate 10.2g, of which sugars 10.2g; Fat 2.5g, of which saturates 0.2g; Cholesterol 0mg; Calcium 12mg; Fibre 0.4g; Sodium 3mg

ORANGE-ALMOND MORSELS

These sweet little marzipan balls draped in chocolate are the perfect treat for lovers of chocolate and orange. Because they are small, and covered in chocolate sprinkles, these will appeal to children, though they may prefer milk chocolate. You could make a mixture of milk and dark chocolate ones, to cater for all tastes.

MAKES 24

200g/7oz Boiled Marzipan (*see* page 53)

grated rind of 1 orange

100g/3¾oz dark (bittersweet) chocolate

coloured or chocolate sprinkles

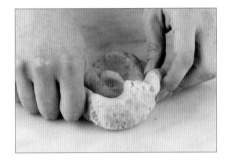

1 Place the marzipan on a board, place the orange rind on top and knead until the rind is evenly incorporated.

2 Roll the marzipan between your hands into a log about 2cm/¾in thick. Cut the log into 24 2cm/¾in pieces and roll each piece into a ball.

3 Melt the dark chocolate in a heatproof bowl set over a pan of barely simmering water.

4 Leave the chocolate to cool for a few minutes. Put the sprinkles in a small bowl. Lay individual doilies out ready for the finished confections.

5 Dip one end of a ball of marzipan into the melted chocolate.

6 Dip the ball into the sprinkles and place it on one of the prepared doilies. Repeat with the remaining balls. Allow the chocolate to set before serving.

7 Uncoated orange-almond balls will keep for 2 weeks in an airtight container in the refrigerator. Once dipped in chocolate, they should be eaten within a few days.

Energy 56kcal/234kJ; Protein 0.6g; Carbohydrate 8.3g, of which sugars 8.1g; Fat 2.3g, of which saturates 0.8g; Cholesterol 0mg; Calcium 7mg; Fibre 0.2g; Sodium 2mg

PISTACHIO-KIRSCH LUCKY CHARMS

This recipe is based on a combination of the two main types of Indian sweets: 'juicy' and 'dry'. The 'juicy' ones are soaked in sugar syrups, while the 'dry' ones are usually semolina- and nut-based. They often include plenty of pistachios and clarified butter. This essentially 'dry' sweet is very simple, made with ground nuts, sugar and a dash of salt, moistened with a little Kirsch for flavour.

4 Slip the nuts out of their skins. Chop the nuts to a fine powder.

5 Add the pistachios and almonds to the sugar syrup and cook, without stirring, over a low heat for a couple of minutes, until the mixture looks like it is drying out. Leave to cool, then stir in the Kirsch.

MAKES ABOUT 400G/14OZ

150g/5oz/¾ cup caster (superfine) sugar, plus extra for dusting

2.5ml/½ tsp salt

15ml/1 tbsp water

125g/4¼oz/¾ cup shelled, raw pistachios

100g/3¾oz/scant 1 cup ground almonds

15ml/1 tbsp Kirsch

1 Prepare an ice-water bath and set it aside. Put the sugar, salt and water in a heavy pan and heat over a medium heat until the sugar has dissolved. Increase the heat and bring the mixture to the soft-ball stage (114°C/238°F).

2 Dip the base of the pan into the ice-water bath momentarily to arrest the cooking, then set the pan aside.

3 Blanch the pistachios in boiling water for 1 minute, then drain and leave to cool slightly.

6 Sprinkle a work surface with sugar. Turn the paste out on to it, press it into a disc and roll it out to a thickness of 1cm/½in. Using tiny cutters, cut the paste into little 'lucky charms'. Roll in more sugar. Serve immediately or store in an airtight container in the refrigerator for 3 weeks.

Energy 1993kcal/8321kJ; Protein 43g; Carbohydrate 180g, of which sugars 174g; Fat 125g, of which saturates 14g; Cholesterol 0mg; Calcium 393mg; Fibre 13g; Sodium 1667mg

MEALIE CANDY

An old Scottish recipe from the countryside, this delicious treat bears a slightly strange name, but the flavour and texture are delightful. In the old sweetshops of Scotland, the 'sweetie wives', as the shopkeepers were called, would have made these with ground ginger. If you can obtain whole liquorice root and a spice grinder for this recipe, the resulting taste is wonderful.

MAKES ABOUT 750G/1LB 11OZ

butter, for greasing

75g/3oz oatmeal or jumbo oats ground in a food processor

400g/14oz/2 cups caster (superfine) sugar

200ml/7fl oz/scant 1 cup water

100g/3¾oz black treacle (molasses)

2.5ml/½ tsp ground liquorice root or ground ginger

1 Preheat the oven to 180°C/350°C/Gas 4. Line a baking tray with baking parchment and grease with a little butter. Set aside.

2 Spread the oatmeal out on another baking tray and toast for 10 minutes, until it is golden. Keep a close eye on it.

3 Put the sugar, water and treacle in a heavy pan, heat gently until the sugar dissolves, then boil for 10 minutes. Gently stir in the toasted oatmeal and liquorice or ginger.

COOK'S TIP
The combination of nutritious oatmeal, iron-rich black treacle and a hint of liquorice or ginger, means this confection actually has some health benefits.

4 Pour the mixture into the prepared baking tray. Leave to cool completely.

5 Turn out on to a board and cut into circles or squares.

6 Serve immediately, or wrap the sweets individually in greaseproof (waxed) paper and store in an airtight container at room temperature for up to 3 weeks.

Energy 2134kcal/9090kJ; Protein 11g; Carbohydrate 542g, of which sugars 487g; Fat 7g, of which saturates 0g; Cholesterol 0mg; Calcium 640mg; Fibre 5g; Sodium 225mg

Baked Marzipan Wafer Sandwiches

Baked marzipan is wonderful because it becomes soft and chewy with a crispy edge. The baking time must be very brief and at a high temperature in order to achieve this. If you prefer a crunchy wafer, you could lower the oven temperature and cook them for a little longer. The sweet jam filling is divine!

MAKES ABOUT 750G/1LB 11OZ

100g/4oz/1 cup icing (confectioners') sugar, plus extra for dusting

500g/1¼lb Boiled Marzipan (*see* page 53)

15ml/1 tbsp lemon juice

150g/5oz/½ cup strawberry jam

1 Preheat the oven to 200°C/400°F/Gas 6. Line a baking sheet with baking parchment.

2 Dust a work surface lightly with icing sugar and roll out the marzipan to a thickness of about 5mm/¼in.

3 Stamp out rounds using a plain round pastry (cookie) cutter and place them on the prepared baking sheet.

4 Bake the marzipan for 5 minutes, then remove from the oven and leave to rest on the baking sheet for 10 minutes.

5 Using an offset spatula, turn the wafers over and prick them with a skewer.

6 Combine the icing sugar and lemon juice in a small bowl and brush the icing over the tops of the marzipan wafers. Leave to set.

7 Spread half of the wafers with strawberry jam (over the top of the icing). Top with the other half of the wafers, with the iced sides on top.

8 Serve these on the same day that you make them.

Energy 3096kcal/13024kJ; Protein 53g; Carbohydrate 459g, of which sugars 451g; Fat 129g, of which saturates 11g; Cholesterol 146mg; Calcium 596mg; Fibre 31g; Sodium 161mg

CHERRY-ALMOND STARS

Amarena cherries are a wild Italian variety of the fruit. They are very sour straight from the tree, but they are stoned (pitted) and packed in sugar in jars. The sugar macerates the cherries and extracts their natural juices, creating a delicious syrup. They can be found in speciality delicatessens and Italian stores, and are worth seeking out.

MAKES 30–35

100g/3¾oz/scant 1 cup ground almonds

100g/3¾oz/generous ½ cup granulated (white) sugar

1 egg white

10ml/2 tsp Kirsch

15–18 Amarena cherries, halved

1 Preheat the oven to 180°C/350°F/ Gas 4. Line a baking sheet with baking parchment.

2 Combine the ground almonds, sugar, egg white and Kirsch together in a large mixing bowl with a wooden spoon.

3 Fit a piping (pastry) bag with a star-shaped nozzle, and fill it with the mixture.

4 Pipe the mixture into little bitesize stars and top each one with half of an Amarena cherry, cut side up.

5 Place the stars into the oven and bake for about 7 minutes, until golden.

6 Leave to cool completely and serve immediately. These will keep for a couple of days in an airtight container at room temperature.

COOK'S TIP
Halve the cherries through the hole where they have been stoned (pitted) rather than halving them through the stem. This will give you a more attractive cherry half to place on top of your almond stars.

Energy 30kcal/126kJ; Protein 0.7g; Carbohydrate 3.3g, of which sugars 3.2g; Fat 1.6g, of which saturates 0.1g; Cholesterol 0mg; Calcium 8mg; Fibre 0.2g; Sodium 2mg

Liquorice Shards

This is a hard version of liquorice, to suck on rather than chew. The bicarbonate of soda lightens the texture a little, so the shards are slightly brittle. Liquorice roots are available in most health food stores and in some traditional sweet shops as well. If you cannot find them, you could use a star anise pod instead, which are easier to obtain.

MAKES ABOUT 550G/1LB 4OZ

butter, for greasing

200g/7oz/1 cup caster (superfine) sugar

100g/3¾oz golden (light corn) syrup

100g/3¾oz black treacle (molasses)

100ml/3½fl oz/scant ½ cup water

2.5ml/½ tsp cream of tartar

1 liquorice root, pounded

65g/2½oz liquid fruit pectin or 12g/¼oz powdered fruit pectin

2.5ml/½ tsp bicarbonate of soda (baking soda)

2.5ml/½ tsp salt

5ml/1 tsp anise extract

1 Grease a 23cm/9in square cake tin (pan) and line with clear film (plastic wrap) as smoothly as possible.

2 Combine the sugar, golden syrup, black treacle, water and cream of tartar in a heavy pan. Stir over a low heat until the sugar has dissolved. Add the liquorice root and boil, without stirring, until it reaches 120°C/265°F.

3 In a separate bowl, combine the pectin (add 60ml/4 tbsp water if using powdered pectin), bicarbonate of soda and salt.

4 Pour the pectin mixture into the syrup and stir to combine. Boil again until the syrup reaches 103°C/217°F, then stir in the anise extract.

5 Pour the syrup into the prepared tin, discarding the liquorice root, and leave to set for about 4 hours. Turn out on to a chopping board and break into shapes. Serve immediately, or store in an airtight container for up to 3 weeks.

Energy 1343kcal/5727kJ; Protein 2.5g; Carbohydrate 355.2g, of which sugars 355.2g; Fat 0g, of which saturates 0g; Cholesterol 0mg; Calcium 632mg; Fibre 0g; Sodium 1361mg

PONTEFRACT CAKES

These soft and intense liquorice cakes are from Pontefract, England, and date back to the 17th century. Originally, a seal with a depiction of Pontefract Castle was applied to the top of each cake. If you have some little madeleine, tartlet or jelly moulds, try using the bottom of those. Or, if you have a wax seal stamp, that would look appealing.

MAKES ABOUT 550G/1LB 4OZ

100g/3¾oz butter, plus extra for greasing

200g/7oz/1 cup caster (superfine) sugar

75ml/5 tbsp golden (light corn) syrup

45ml/3 tbsp black treacle (molasses)

120ml/8 tbsp sweetened condensed milk

2.5ml/½ tsp salt

7.5ml/1½ tsp anise extract

a few drops of black food colouring

5ml/1 tsp bicarbonate of soda (baking soda)

1 Grease a 23 x 33cm/9 x 13in baking tray and line with baking parchment.

2 Place all of the ingredients in a heavy pan. Heat gently, stirring, until dissolved.

3 Turn up the heat and bring the syrup up to 112°C/233°F, stirring constantly, without scraping down the sides of pan.

4 Pour the mixture into the prepared tray. Leave to cool, then chill for 10 minutes.

5 Remove from the refrigerator and stamp out small rounds with a small plain pastry (cookie) cutter. Transfer the rounds to a sheet of baking parchment.

6 Press the tops of the cakes with a stamp or mould. Serve immediately, or wrap in waxed paper and store in an airtight container for 1 month.

Energy 1668kcal/7114kJ; Protein 3.1g; Carbohydrate 441.2g, of which sugars 441.2g; Fat 0g, of which saturates 0g; Cholesterol 0mg; Calcium 785mg; Fibre 0g; Sodium 1690mg

Liquorice Sticks

A favourite with children and adults alike all over the world, liquorice sticks are delectable eaten on their own, or you could dip them in sherbet. You can make these the traditional way with anise oil and some black food colouring, or you can make red liquorice sticks and omit the anise.

MAKES ABOUT 20

125g/4¼oz/generous ½ cup butter, plus extra for greasing

400g/14oz/2 cups caster (superfine) sugar

400g/14oz sweetened condensed milk

250ml/8fl oz/1 cup golden (light corn) syrup

0.75ml/⅛ tsp salt

5ml/1 tsp anise extract (omit this for red liquorice sticks)

2.5ml/½ tsp black food colouring paste (or red for red liquorice sticks)

1 Line a 23cm/9in square baking tin (pan) with foil. Extend the foil over the edges of the tin. Grease the foil.

2 Melt the butter in a large, heavy pan. Add the sugar, sweetened condensed milk, golden syrup and salt. Stir well until the sugar dissolves.

3 Boil the mixture at a steady, moderate rate over a medium heat, stirring frequently, until it reaches the firm-ball stage (120°C/248°F). This should take 15–20 minutes. The mixture scorches easily so scrape the bottom of the pan well when you stir it to prevent the mixture from sticking.

4 Remove from the heat. Add the anise extract (if using) and the food colouring to the pan.

5 Quickly pour the mixture, without scraping, into the prepared tin. Cool for several hours or until firm. Use the foil to lift the liquorice out of the tin and on to a chopping board. Peel away and discard the foil.

6 Using a buttered sharp knife, cut the mixture into 1cm/½in wide strips.

7 Serve immediately, wrap the sticks individually in waxed paper or line a pretty box with paper and place them inside it. Store for up to 1 month.

Energy 229kcal/965kJ; Protein 1.9g; Carbohydrate 41.9g, of which sugars 41.9g; Fat 7.1g, of which saturates 4.6g; Cholesterol 22mg; Calcium 73mg; Fibre 0g; Sodium 125mg

LIQUORICE-STAR ANISE DROPS

These little liquorice drops are intensified by the addition of two types of anise: the oil from the anise seed and the seeds and seed-pod of the star anise. The combination creates a punchy old-fashioned black liquorice flavour. The salt is inspired by Danish salt liquorice, though this version contains less salt as it can be rather overpowering.

MAKES ABOUT 24

butter, for greasing

200g/7oz/1 cup caster (superfine) sugar

100g/3¾oz golden (light corn) syrup

100g/3¾oz black treacle (molasses)

100ml/3½fl oz/scant ½ cup water

2.5ml/½ tsp cream of tartar

3 star anise

65g/2½oz liquid fruit pectin or 15g/½oz powdered fruit pectin

2.5ml/½ tsp salt

5ml/1 tsp anise extract

sea salt, to sprinkle on top

1 Grease a baking sheet and line with baking parchment or clear film (plastic wrap), ensuring it is as smooth as possible.

2 Combine the sugar, golden syrup, black treacle, water and cream of tartar in a heavy pan. Stir over low heat to dissolve the sugar, then add the star anise and bring to the boil. Boil until it reaches hard-ball stage (130°C/266°F).

3 In a separate bowl, combine the pectin (add 60ml/4 tbsp water if using powdered pectin) and salt.

4 Pour the pectin into the syrup and stir to combine. Continue to stir to avoid the possibility of the syrup boiling over.

5 Bring to the boil again until the syrup reaches the firm-ball stage (120°C/248°F). Immediately remove from the heat. Stir in the anise extract. Remove and discard the star anise.

6 Pour the syrup on to the prepared sheet in drops. Sprinkle with sea salt. Leave them to set for 4 hours. Serve immediately or store in an airtight container for up to 3 weeks.

Energy 56kcal/239kJ; Protein 0.1g; Carbohydrate 14.8g, of which sugars 14.8g; Fat 0g, of which saturates 0g; Cholesterol 0mg; Calcium 26mg; Fibre 0g; Sodium 57mg

MARZIPAN FRUITS AND VEGETABLES

These marzipan fruits are fun and easy to make for the novice marzipan-modeller, and are a good introduction to marzipan for children. Here we make carrots, strawberries and peaches, but there are many other fruits and vegetables you could make. Use fronds from the tops of real carrots as decoration, or little pieces of dill. The peaches are beautiful with coloured dust brushed on to look like a 'blush'. To create the texture on the strawberries you can use a miniature box grater as used for nutmeg and carefully press it to the surface.

MAKES 175G/6OZ

175g/6oz marzipan (either use store-bought marzipan or make your own Boiled Marzipan, *see* page 53)

yellow, orange, red and green food colouring

peach or pale pink edible powder

greens from carrot tops or fresh dill leaves

1 Cut off 25g/1oz of marzipan, then divide the remainder into thirds.

2 Colour one of the large pieces of marzipan a pale yellow for the peaches. Knead the colouring in until it is an even shade.

3 Colour another one of the large pieces of marzipan orange for the carrots. Knead the colouring in until it is an even shade.

4 Colour the last large piece a bright red for the strawberries. Knead until it is an even shade.

5 Colour the remaining small piece green for the strawberry stems and peach leaves. Knead until it is an even shade.

6 Take the yellow marzipan and shape it into small balls.

7 Create a slit along one side of each peach using a cocktail stick (toothpick) to give a peach shape. Use a small, soft, dry and clean brush to apply the edible powder to one area of each peach to create a 'blush'.

8 Take the orange marzipan and roll it out into thin logs.

9 Cut the logs into short sections and shape each of these into a carrot, with one end narrower than the other. Press the side of the cocktail stick into the marzipan crossways to make little lines.

10 Roll the red marzipan into small balls, then pinch one end and shape each ball into a strawberry shape.

11 Gently press the strawberries on a small grater to give a textured effect.

12 Roll out most of the green marzipan. Cut long, thin leaves for the peaches, then use a small flower cutter to stamp out shapes for the strawberry leaves. Roll the remaining green marzipan into very thin lengths to make stems for the peaches and strawberries.

13 Position the leaves on the peaches and strawberries, then use a cocktail stick to affix the stems in the middle of the leaves. For the carrots, use the cocktail stick to press little bits of greenery on top of each carrot.

14 Serve immediately in petit four cases or store at room temperature, covered with clear film (plastic wrap) or in an airtight container. Do not refrigerate.

Energy 681kcal/2874kJ; Protein 9g; Carbohydrate 118g, of which sugars 118g; Fat 22g, of which saturates 2g; Cholesterol 0mg; Calcium 116mg; Fibre 6g; Sodium 35mg

CHOCOLATE TRUFFLES, MOULDED CHOCOLATES AND HAND-DIPPED CHOCOLATES

THINK VALENTINE'S DAY. THINK EASTER. THINK CHRISTMAS. THINK CHOCOLATE. WHAT BETTER WAY TO CELEBRATE THESE HOLIDAYS THAN WITH A SELECTION OF HOME-MADE TRUFFLES AND MOULDED CHOCOLATE CONFECTIONS? GANACHE-FILLED TRUFFLES ARE SIMPLE TO MAKE AND LEND THEMSELVES TO FLAVOURFUL PARTNERSHIPS. EVEN EASIER IS A NUTTY BARK THAT CAN BE BROKEN INTO BITESIZE PIECES. TEMPERED PROPERLY, THESE CANDIES WILL LOOK LIKE TINY JEWELS GLISTENING WITH A DARK AND PROFESSIONAL-LOOKING GLAZE.

DARK CHOCOLATE TRUFFLES

Smooth, creamy and intensely chocolatey, these classic truffles are a truly decadent, grown-up treat. Use the best-quality chocolate you can, as this will really give the truffles an extra-special edge. These are perfect for gifts and look very attractive piled up in a box, or served in a pretty glass bowl.

MAKES ABOUT 100

120ml/4fl oz/½ cup double (heavy) cream

100g/3¾oz golden (light corn) syrup

1 vanilla pod (bean), split in half

350g/12oz dark (bittersweet) chocolate (66–70% cocoa solids), chopped

50g/2oz/4 tbsp unsalted butter, softened (it needs to be very soft)

unsweetened cocoa powder, for rolling

1 Stir the cream and golden syrup together in a heavy pan, then scrape the vanilla seeds out of the pod and add to the pan along with the pod.

2 Warm over low heat and bring to just below the boil (a foamy layer of milk should just be starting to form).

3 Remove from the heat, transfer to a large heatproof mixing bowl and cover with clear film (plastic wrap). Allow to cool, then chill overnight for optimum vanilla flavour.

4 Grease a 20cm/8in square baking tin (pan) and line with clear film.

COOK'S TIP
Here, the truffles are made into rough, rustic shapes. If you prefer, you can roll them into neat balls.

5 Place the chocolate in a heatproof bowl and set it over a pan of barely simmering water. Using a chocolate thermometer, heat the chocolate to just below 46°C/115°F. Remove from the heat.

6 Meanwhile, place the bowl containing the cream and golden syrup mixture over a pan of simmering water, remove and discard the vanilla pod, then heat the cream mixture to just below 46°C/115°F.

7 Once they have both reached the desired temperature, pour the melted chocolate and the heated cream into a blender, and blend until it is thick and creamy. Alternatively, pour the liquids into a jug (pitcher) and blend with an immersion blender. Add the very soft butter, bit by bit, blending well between each addition so it is completely incorporated.

8 Pour the ganache into the prepared baking tin and smooth the surface with an offset spatula. Leave to cool for a few hours until it has set. You can then place it into the refrigerator until you are ready to form the truffles.

9 To form the truffles, turn the ganache block out on to a marble slab or other cold, hard surface. Remove the clear film. Dip a clean, sharp knife in hot water, wipe it dry, then slice the block of ganache into 2cm/¾in squares.

10 Dust your palms and fingers with cocoa powder and roll the squares into rustic balls. Roll these in more cocoa powder.

11 Serve immediately, or place the truffles in a bag or container with extra cocoa powder (to keep them from sticking together) and store in the refrigerator. Remove from the refrigerator at least 30 minutes before serving, as chocolate is best eaten at room temperature.

Energy 62kcal/256kJ; Protein 0.4g; Carbohydrate 3.6g, of which sugars 3.6g; Fat 5g, of which saturates 3.1g; Cholesterol 9mg; Calcium 4mg; Fibre 0.1g; Sodium 6mg

GRAND MARNIER CHOCOLATE TRUFFLES

These adult treats contain the classic combination of Grand Marnier and dark chocolate. Made with wild, tropical oranges, the brandy pairs especially well with a fruity chocolate such as Valrhona's 64% single-estate chocolate from Madagascar. Finishing the truffles by rolling them in chopped candied orange peel adds both texture and additional flavour, as well as making them even prettier.

MAKES ABOUT 100

120ml/4fl oz/½ cup double (heavy) cream

100g/3¾oz golden (light corn) syrup

1 vanilla pod (bean), split in half

350g/12oz dark (bittersweet) chocolate (66–70% cocoa solids), chopped

50g/2oz/4 tbsp unsalted butter, softened (it needs to be very soft)

10ml/2 tsp Grand Marnier

100g/3¾oz/⅔ cup candied orange peel, chopped and tossed in caster (superfine) sugar

1 Stir the cream and golden syrup together in a heavy pan, then scrape the vanilla seeds out of the pod and add to the pan along with the pod.

2 Warm over a low heat and bring to just below the boil (a foamy layer of milk should just be starting to form).

3 Remove from the heat, transfer to a large heatproof mixing bowl and cover with clear film (plastic wrap). Chill overnight for optimum vanilla flavour.

4 Grease a 20cm/8in square baking tin (pan) and line with clear film (plastic wrap).

5 Place the chocolate in a heatproof bowl and set it over a pan of barely simmering water. Using a chocolate thermometer, heat the chocolate to just below 46°C/115°F. Remove from the heat.

6 Meanwhile, place the bowl containing the cream and golden syrup mixture over a pan of simmering water, remove and discard the vanilla pod, then heat the cream mixture to just below 46°C/115°F.

7 Once they have both reached the desired temperature, pour the melted chocolate and the heated cream into a blender, and blend until it is thick and creamy. Alternatively, pour the liquids into a jug (pitcher) and blend with an immersion blender. Add the very soft butter, bit by bit, blending well between each addition.

8 Add the Grand Marnier and blend.

9 Pour the ganache into the prepared baking tin and smooth the surface with an offset spatula.

10 Leave the ganache to cool for a few hours until it has set. You can then place it into the refrigerator until you are ready to form the truffles.

11 To form the truffles, turn the block of ganache out on to a marble slab or other cold, hard surface. Remove the clear film.

12 Dip a clean, sharp knife in hot water, wipe it dry, then slice the block of ganache into 2cm/¾in squares. There should be abut 100.

13 Roll the squares of ganache in the palms of your hands to create smooth balls.

14 Roll each ball in the chopped candied orange peel and caster sugar mixture so that it is fully coated.

15 Serve immediately, or place the truffles in a bag or container and store them in the refrigerator. This can cause the sugar on the candied peel to dissolve, so you will need to toss them in caster sugar again before serving. Remove the truffles from the refrigerator at least 30 minutes before serving, as chocolate tastes at its best when consumed at room temperature.

Energy 66kcal/277kJ; Protein 0.4g; Carbohydrate 7.4g, of which sugars 7g; Fat 4.2g, of which saturates 2.5g; Cholesterol 6mg; Calcium 7mg; Fibre 0.1g; Sodium 20mg

CHAMPAGNE TRUFFLES

A version of this traditional classic is made by almost every good chocolatier. You could make them with any sparkling wine that you like to drink, such as prosecco or cava, instead of Champagne. Rosé Champagne makes an especially delicious truffle. Here real gold dust has been used for an extra-special feel, but you could just finish them with an extra roll in icing sugar, if you like.

MAKES ABOUT 100

250g/9oz dark (bittersweet) chocolate (70% cocoa solids), chopped

200g/7oz milk chocolate (40% cocoa solids), chopped

150ml/¼ pint/⅔ cup double (heavy) cream

50g/2oz/¼ cup unsalted butter, plus extra for greasing

100ml/3½fl oz/scant ½ cup Champagne or other sparkling wine

15ml/1 tbsp brandy

700g/1lb 10oz dark chocolate (70% cocoa solids), tempered (*see* pages 56–57)

unsweetened cocoa powder and icing (confectioners') sugar, for rolling

edible gold dust (optional)

1 Grease a 20cm/8in square baking tin (pan) and line with clear film (plastic wrap). Line a baking sheet with baking parchment. Put the chopped dark and milk chocolate in a heatproof bowl. Set aside.

2 Put the cream and butter in a small, heavy pan and heat to just under a boil over moderate heat. Swirl the cream around occasionally so that it does not burn around the edges of the pan.

3 Pour the heated cream over the chopped chocolate and let it sit for about 1 minute before adding the Champagne and brandy.

4 Whisk by hand until all the chocolate is melted and you have a smooth ganache. Alternatively, use a hand-held immersion blender or blend the cream and chocolate in a food processor.

5 Pour the mixture into the prepared tin and leave until the mixture begins to firm up.

6 To form the truffles, scrape the ganache up into a piping (pastry) bag fitted with a 1cm/½in plain nozzle. Pipe small, even blobs on to the parchment-lined baking sheet. Place in the refrigerator for about 20 minutes or until firm.

7 Dust your palms with cocoa powder and roll the ganache blobs into balls. Return these to the refrigerator for 10 minutes, until firm.

8 For the next stage, you will need your tempered chocolate, so you can prepare it while the ganache is chilling.

9 Place a wire rack on the work surface with a sheet of baking parchment underneath to catch the drips. Using a dipping fork, dip each ball of ganache into the tempered dark chocolate and then place on a wire rack.

10 Place the icing sugar in a small bowl and roll the truffles in it to coat.

11 Roll the truffles in edible gold dust, if using. Alternatively, dip a clean, dry pastry brush into the gold dust, hold it over the truffles and tap the handle of the pastry brush. Leave to set for about 30 minutes.

12 Serve immediately or store the truffles in the refrigerator in an airtight container, spaced well apart. Remove from the refrigerator at least 30 minutes before serving, as chocolate should be eaten at room temperature.

Energy 144kcal/601kJ; Protein 1.3g; Carbohydrate 14.8g, of which sugars 13.7g; Fat 9.2g, of which saturates 5.4g; Cholesterol 9mg; Calcium 18mg; Fibre 0g; Sodium 16mg

BURNT CARAMEL TRUFFLES

The key to getting the sumptuous burnt caramel flavour of these truffles is in the careful cooking of the caramel. It needs to be boiled until dark and rich, but just removed from the heat before it actually burns. These confections make a lovely gift, if you can find a little gift box and some mini paper or foil cases.

MAKES ABOUT 100

50ml/2fl oz/¼ cup cold water

200g/7oz/1 cup caster (superfine) sugar

2.5ml/½ tsp cream of tartar

225ml/7½fl oz/scant 1 cup double (heavy) cream

50g/2oz/¼ cup unsalted butter, plus extra for greasing

2.5ml/½ tsp sea salt

425g/15oz dark (bittersweet) chocolate (70% cocoa solids), finely chopped

unsweetened cocoa powder, for dusting

1 Grease a 20cm/8in square baking tin (pan) and line with clear film (plastic wrap).

2 Place the water in a heavy pan and add the sugar. Add the cream of tartar and heat gently, stirring occasionally, until the sugar has dissolved.

3 Turn the heat up to high and bring to the boil. Boil until a dark caramel forms, taking care not to let it burn, although it should be nearing that stage.

4 Slowly add the cream to the caramel (it will spatter so use caution). Use a whisk to incorporate it fully. Add the butter and salt, and whisk until smooth.

5 Put the chopped chocolate in a large heatproof bowl. Pour over the caramel. Whisk gently until smooth and melted.

6 Pour into the prepared tin. Leave the mixture to set for a couple of hours at room temperature, then chill until firm.

7 To form the truffles, turn the ganache block out on to a marble slab or other cold, hard surface. Remove the clear film. Dip a clean, sharp knife in hot water, wipe it dry, then slice the block of ganache into 2cm/¾in squares.

8 Dust your palms and fingers with cocoa powder and roll the squares into rustic balls. Roll these in more cocoa powder.

9 Serve immediately in mini paper or foil cases, if you like. Alternatively, place the truffles in a bag or container with extra cocoa powder (to keep them from sticking together) and store in the refrigerator. Remove from the refrigerator at least 30 minutes before serving, as chocolate should be eaten at room temperature.

Energy 89kcal/372kJ; Protein 1g; Carbohydrate 10g, of which sugars 10g; Fat 6g, of which saturates 3g; Cholesterol 9mg; Calcium 6mg; Fibre 0g; Sodium 21mg

White Chocolate Espresso Truffles

The combination of white and dark chocolate, and silky coffee-flavoured truffle is absolutely delicious in these treats. The dark chocolate will show through the final white chocolate layer of the truffle, but that is intentional and looks fabulous when you bite or cut into them. These are perfect after a special meal, served with coffee.

MAKES ABOUT 100

250ml/8fl oz/1 cup double (heavy) cream

50g/2oz whole espresso beans

400g/14oz white chocolate, chopped

15ml/1 tbsp brandy

300g/11oz dark (bittersweet) chocolate (70% cocoa solids), tempered (see pages 56–57)

550g/1lb 4oz white chocolate, tempered (see pages 56–57)

10g/¼oz espresso beans, very finely ground

1 Line a baking sheet with baking parchment and set aside.

2 Place the cream and espresso beans in a small pan over moderate heat and bring to just under the boil. Remove from the heat and allow the beans to steep for 10 minutes, then heat the mixture to just under the boil again.

3 Place the chopped white chocolate in a heatproof bowl and, holding a fine-mesh sieve (strainer) above it to catch the espresso beans, pour in the hot cream. Discard the espresso beans.

4 Add the brandy and leave to cool. When the mixture is cool and the chocolate looks melted, whisk to form a smooth, creamy ganache. Take care not to overmix it, as the white chocolate can seize up. Leave for 15 minutes to begin to firm.

5 Scrape the ganache into a piping (pastry) bag fitted with a 5mm/¼in plain nozzle. If the ganache is still too soft, it will run out of the piping bag, so fill the bag over a bowl to catch any drips.

6 Pipe even blobs on to the parchment-lined baking sheet, then chill in the refrigerator for 20 minutes, or until firm.

7 Roll the ganache blobs into balls. Return these to the refrigerator for 10 minutes, until firm.

8 For the next stage, you will need the tempered dark chocolate, so you can prepare it while the ganache is chilling.

9 Dip each ball of ganache into the tempered dark chocolate using a dipping fork or regular fork, and place it back on the baking sheet.

10 Leave them to set for 15 minutes while you temper the white chocolate. Dip each truffle into the tempered white chocolate. Place back on the baking sheet and leave to set for 30 minutes.

11 Sprinkle each truffle with ground espresso beans. Serve immediately or store in an airtight container, spaced well apart, in the refrigerator. Remove 30 minutes before serving, as chocolate should be eaten at room temperature.

Energy 155kcal/647kJ; Protein 1.9g; Carbohydrate 15.1g, of which sugars 14.8g; Fat 10.3g, of which saturates 6g; Cholesterol 7mg; Calcium 56mg; Fibre 0g; Sodium 23mg

CEYLON CINNAMON TRUFFLES

In Mexico the combination of chocolate and cinnamon is common, and the union is delicious. The delicate flavour of Ceylon cinnamon is more appropriate for these truffles than the more bitter Cassia bark, which is usually used for ground cinnamons. Ceylon cinnamon is readily available, but you will need to grind it yourself in a coffee grinder or with a mortar and pestle. The flavour will also be much fresher if you do this.

MAKES ABOUT 100

200ml/7fl oz/scant 1 cup double (heavy) cream

100ml/3½fl oz/scant ½ cup liquid glucose

2 Ceylon cinnamon sticks

300g/11oz dark (bittersweet) chocolate (70% cocoa solids), chopped

100g/3¾oz/scant ½ cup unsalted butter, softened

400g/14oz dark (bittersweet) chocolate (70% cocoa solids), tempered (*see* pages 56–57)

400g/14oz milk chocolate (40% cocoa solids), tempered (*see* pages 56–57)

freshly ground Ceylon cinnamon, for sprinkling

1 Line a baking sheet with baking parchment and set aside.

2 Place the cream and liquid glucose in a small pan. Snap the cinnamon sticks in half and add them to the pan. Bring to just under the boil and stir to blend in the glucose, then remove from the heat. Cover with a lid and leave to steep for 15 minutes.

3 Place the pan containing the cream mixture back over the heat, remove the lid and bring it to just under the boil again.

4 Place the chopped dark chocolate in a large heatproof bowl and, holding a fine-mesh sieve (strainer) above it to catch the cinnamon sticks, pour in the hot cream mixture. Discard the cinnamon sticks. Leave to stand for 10 minutes.

5 Using a whisk or an immersion blender, combine the chocolate and cream mixture to form a smooth, creamy ganache. Gradually add the softened butter, stirring well between each addition, until thoroughly combined.

6 Scoop the ganache into a piping (pastry) bag fitted with a 1cm/½in plain nozzle. Pipe out even blobs on to the lined baking sheet. Chill in the refrigerator for 20 minutes, or until firm.

7 Roll the ganache blobs into balls. Return these to the refrigerator for 10 minutes, until firm.

8 For the next stage, you will need your tempered dark chocolate, so you can prepare it while the ganache is chilling.

9 Dip each ball of ganache into the tempered dark chocolate with a dipping fork or regular fork and place it back on the lined baking sheet.

10 Leave them to set for 15 minutes while you temper the milk chocolate. Using a clean dipping fork or regular fork, dip each truffle into the tempered milk chocolate. Place it back on the lined baking sheet and leave to set for about 30 minutes.

11 Sprinkle each truffle with ground cinnamon. Serve immediately, or store in an airtight container, spaced apart, in the refrigerator. Remove 30 minutes before serving, as chocolate should be eaten at room temperature.

Energy 155kcal/647kJ; Protein 1g; Carbohydrate 15g, of which sugars 14g; Fat 10g, of which saturates 6g; Cholesterol 11mg; Calcium 29mg; Fibre 0g; Sodium 14mg

Lavender-Milk Chocolate Truffles

A plant with endless uses, lavender looks beautiful, smells wonderful and has relaxing and soothing properties. Its delicate taste is especially suited to sweet honey and creamy milk chocolate. An edible shimmery dust provides the perfect finishing touch to these truffles, but you can always omit it for a simpler treat.

6 To form the truffles, scrape the ganache up into a piping bag fitted with a 1cm/½in plain nozzle. Pipe small, even blobs on to the parchment-lined baking sheet and chill in the refrigerator for 20 minutes, or until firm.

7 For the next stage, you will need your tempered milk chocolate, so you can prepare it while the ganache is chilling.

8 Roll each blob of chilled ganache into a ball between your hands. Then, using forks, dip each ball into the tempered milk chocolate. Place on a wire rack.

9 Dip a clean, dry pastry brush into the pot of purple or silver dust and then carefully hold it over the truffles. With the other hand, tap the handle of the pastry brush. This will release the dust and allow it to fall freely and evenly over the truffles. Leave to set for 30 minutes.

10 Serve immediately, or store in an airtight container, spaced apart, in the refrigerator. Remove them 30 minutes before serving, as chocolate is best eaten at room temperature.

MAKES ABOUT 100

butter, for greasing

200ml/7fl oz/scant 1 cup double (heavy) cream

80ml/5 tbsp liquid glucose

20ml/4 tsp honey

20ml/4 tsp dried edible lavender buds

300g/11oz dark (bittersweet) chocolate (64% cocoa solids), chopped

400g/14oz milk chocolate (40% cocoa solids), tempered (*see* pages 56–57)

purple and silver edible shimmery dust

1 Grease a 20cm/8in square baking tin (pan) and line with clear film (plastic wrap).

2 Place the cream, liquid glucose and honey in a small pan. Bring to just under the boil and stir to blend in the glucose and honey. Add the lavender buds and remove from the heat. Cover and leave to steep for 15 minutes, then heat to just under the boil again.

3 Place the chopped dark chocolate in a heatproof bowl and, holding a fine-mesh sieve (strainer) above it to catch the lavender, pour in the hot cream. Discard the lavender. Leave for 10 minutes.

4 Using a whisk or immersion blender, combine the chocolate and cream to form a smooth, creamy ganache.

5 Pour the ganache into the prepared tin and leave it for about 15 minutes to begin to firm up.

Energy 98kcal/411kJ; Protein 1g; Carbohydrate 10g, of which sugars 9g; Fat 6g, of which saturates 4g; Cholesterol 8mg; Calcium 22mg; Fibre 0g; Sodium 10mg

WHITE AND DARK CHOCOLATE BARK

Chocolate barks are essentially sophisticated chocolate bars: the best way to enjoy a good quality chocolate with a little extra embellishment. This recipe is very easy to make and takes hardly any time at all to prepare. The addition of crunchy sea salt is reminiscent of chocolate-covered pretzels.

MAKES ABOUT 550G/1LB 4OZ

50g/2oz dark (bittersweet) chocolate (70% cocoa solids)

500g/1¼lb white chocolate, finely chopped

5ml/1 tsp flaky sea salt, such as Maldon

1 Line a baking tray with baking parchment and set aside.

2 Chop the dark chocolate into fine shards.

3 Place the white chocolate in a heatproof bowl positioned over a pan of barely simmering water. Do not let the water touch the bottom of the bowl or the chocolate will burn. Stir occasionally to assist the melting.

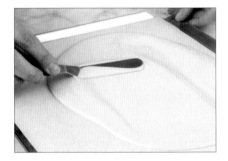

4 Pour two-thirds of the melted white chocolate into the prepared baking tray and spread it evenly using an offset metal spatula. Sprinkle with the salt, then sprinkle with the finely chopped dark chocolate.

COOK'S TIP
Bark makes a great gift. Simply break the sheet up into big pieces and wrap them individually in baking parchment or waxed paper to stop any cocoa butter seeping through, then finish them with wrapping paper and a ribbon.

5 Pour the remaining white chocolate on the top. Smooth it with an offset spatula and leave to set for 12–15 minutes.

6 Remove the chocolate from the baking tray by sliding the baking parchment on to a worktop. Place a cutting board on top of it and invert the bark. Pull off the parchment paper. Cut the bark into irregular pieces with a sharp knife.

7 Serve immediately or store the pieces of bark in an airtight container, spaced well apart, in the refrigerator. Remove the bark 30 minutes before serving, as chocolate should be eaten at room temperature.

Energy 2908kcal/12159kJ; Protein 42.4g; Carbohydrate 323.9g, of which sugars 321.3g; Fat 169.1g, of which saturates 99.5g; Cholesterol 5mg; Calcium 1370mg; Fibre 0g; Sodium 2521mg

MILK CHOCOLATE AND MACADAMIA NUT BARK

You could use any of your favourite nuts here, but the macadamia works very well, especially with the buttery crunchy coating they have once caramelized. A sprinkling of salt adds an extra dimension to the chocolate and nut flavour combination. Use a good quality sea salt, such as Maldon, for the best taste.

MAKES ABOUT 1KG/2¼LB

200g/7oz/1 cup caster (superfine) sugar

100g/3¾oz/scant ½ cup unsalted butter

250g/9oz macadamia nuts, chopped

500g/1¼lb milk chocolate
(40% cocoa solids)

5ml/1 tsp flaky sea salt,
such as Maldon

1 Line two baking trays with baking parchment and set aside.

2 Put the sugar and half of the butter in a small pan and warm over a medium heat until the butter starts to bubble.

3 Add the chopped macadamia nuts and, using a wooden spoon, stir constantly until coated. Stir in the remaining butter, then remove from the heat.

4 Spread the nuts out on one of the baking trays and leave to cool.

5 Place the milk chocolate in a heatproof bowl and set over a pan of barely simmering water. Do not let the water touch the bottom of the bowl.

6 Pour the melted chocolate into the other prepared baking tray. Spread the chocolate evenly with an offset spatula to about 5mm/¼in thick.

7 Sprinkle over the salt, then sprinkle the caramelized nuts on top. Leave to set for 12–15 minutes.

8 Remove the chocolate from the tray by sliding the baking parchment on to a chopping board. Slide an offset spatula between the chocolate and the paper and pull the paper away. Cut the bark into irregular pieces with a sharp knife.

9 Serve immediately or store in an airtight container, spaced well apart, in the refrigerator. Remove 30 minutes before serving, as chocolate is best eaten at room temperature.

Energy 5378kcal/22437kJ; Protein 60g; Carbohydrate 514g, of which sugars 512g; Fat 357g, of which saturates 125g; Cholesterol 23mg; Calcium 1490mg; Fibre 0g; Sodium 3228mg

FLAKED ALMOND BARK

This is one of the easiest and most delicious chocolate treats you can make, and it is extremely versatile. This recipe is for a bark made with flaked almonds suspended in dark chocolate and topped with pistachios, but you could use whichever combination of chocolate type and nuts you prefer.

MAKES ABOUT 450G/1LB

200g/7oz/scant 2 cups flaked (sliced) almonds

200g/7oz dark (bittersweet) chocolate (55%–64% cocoa solids)

50g/2oz/½ cup chopped pistachio nuts

1 Line a baking tray with clear film (plastic wrap) and set aside. Preheat the oven to 160°C/325°F/Gas 3.

2 Spread the nuts out on another baking sheet and place in the heated oven until just toasted. This should take about 7 minutes, depending on your oven. Watch them closely so they do not burn and go bitter.

3 Melt the dark chocolate in a heatproof bowl set over a pan of barely simmering water. Stir it occasionally to help it melt.

4 Add the warm, toasted almonds to the chocolate and stir to combine. Quickly scrape the mixture into the lined baking tray and smooth the surface with an offset spatula. Tap the tray on the surface a few times to release any air bubbles.

COOK'S TIP
If you chill the chocolate to help it set, it may shatter slightly when you start to cut the pieces of bark. To prevent this, allow the chocolate to warm a little more to room temperature before cutting.

5 Sprinkle the chopped pistachio nuts on top. Leave for 12–15 minutes to set. Alternatively, chill it in the refrigerator.

6 Lift the bark up by the edges of the clear film, gently lean the pistachio side against your fingertips and peel away the clear film with the other hand. Place the bark on to a chopping board.

7 Cut the bark into irregular pieces using a sharp knife.

8 Serve immediately, or store in an airtight container, spaced apart, in the refrigerator. Remove 30 minutes before serving, as chocolate is best eaten at room temperature.

Energy 2575kcal/10705kJ; Protein 60.6g; Carbohydrate 147.5g, of which sugars 130.3g; Fat 197.7g, of which saturates 46.9g; Cholesterol 18mg; Calcium 611mg; Fibre 17.9g; Sodium 315mg

ROSE AND VIOLET CREAMS

Old-fashioned and classic, chocolate creams made with sweet, delicate floral essences are becoming popular once again. You can make the dainty crystallized rose petals and violets, or they can be found at speciality supermarkets and delicatessens. You could also omit them, leaving the filling as a surprise, as these look very sophisticated and sleek without the petals.

MAKES ABOUT 50

300g/11oz Fondant (*see* page 38)

2–3 drops rose syrup

2–3 drops violet syrup

400g/14oz dark (bittersweet) chocolate (at least 70% cocoa solids), tempered (*see* pages 56–57)

Crystallized Rose Petals (*see* page 162)

Crystallized Violets (*see* page 163)

1 Place a sheet of baking parchment underneath a wire rack.

2 Divide the fondant in half. Knead the violet syrup into one half of the fondant and knead the rose syrup into the other half. Roll them both into long, thin logs.

3 Cut each log into 25 bitesize pieces and roll them into balls.

4 Dip each ball of fondant into the tempered chocolate, using a dipping fork, then place on the wire rack.

5 Decorate the rose creams with the rose petals and the violet creams with the violets. Leave to set for 30 minutes.

6 Serve immediately, or store in an airtight container, spaced apart, in the refrigerator. Remove 30 minutes before serving, as chocolate is best eaten at room temperature.

Energy 66kcal/278kJ; Protein 0.5g; Carbohydrate 10.5g, of which sugars 9.9g; Fat 2.8g, of which saturates 1.6g; Cholesterol 1mg; Calcium 6mg; Fibre 0g; Sodium 2mg

CHOCOLATE PEPPERMINT CREAMS

Junior Mints, Peppermint Patties and After Eight Mints are all inspirations for these little chocolate treats. They are very easy to make and delicious to eat. The darker the chocolate the better, as this provides the best contrast to the strong peppermint fondant.

MAKES ABOUT 80

2–3 drops peppermint oil

300g/11oz Fondant (*see* page 38)

400g/14oz dark (bittersweet) chocolate (at least 70% cocoa solids), tempered (*see* pages 56–57)

1 Line a baking sheet with baking parchment or place a sheet of baking parchment under a wire rack.

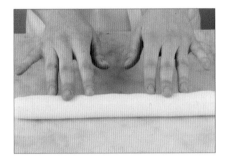

2 Knead the peppermint oil into the fondant and divide the mixture into 4 pieces. Roll into 4 logs.

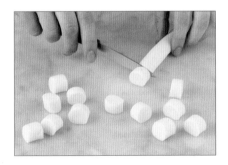

3 Cut each log into about 20 bitesize pieces and either flatten them into discs using the flat edge of a knife or roll into balls and then flatten them with your hands.

VARIATION
If you do not have much time, you can use a good store-bought fondant instead of making it.

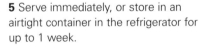

4 Dip each disc of peppermint fondant into the tempered chocolate using a dipping fork. Place on the baking parchment or cooling rack and leave for about 30 minutes, until completely set.

5 Serve immediately, or store in an airtight container in the refrigerator for up to 1 week.

Energy 26kcal/107kJ; Protein 0g; Carbohydrate 3g, of which sugars 3g; Fat 1g, of which saturates 1g; Cholesterol 0mg; Calcium 2mg; Fibre 0g; Sodium 0mg

PEANUT BUTTER CUPS

Despite its association with children, peanut butter can be used to make a very sophisticated chocolate. The silky texture of the peanut butter ganache inside a crisp milk chocolate shell is truly scrumptious. Although tempering chocolate will give the best results, you could just melt the chocolate and not temper it if you want to make these with children or you are short of time.

MAKES 18

250g/9oz milk chocolate, tempered (*see* pages 56–57)

115g/4oz milk chocolate, finely chopped

100g/3¾oz/scant ½ cup smooth peanut butter

sea salt, such as Maldon or fleur de sel

1 Set out 18 mini cupcake liners, then put another 18 inside them so they are double thickness.

2 Using a clean brush, paint the insides with a generous layer of tempered milk chocolate, reserving about 100g/3¾oz for the tops. Set them aside to set for 20 minutes.

3 Put the chopped chocolate in a heatproof bowl over a pan of barely simmering water and leave to melt. Stir in the peanut butter.

4 Remove from the heat and leave the mixture to cool to 29°C/85°F. (It needs to be this cool or it will melt the cups when you fill them.)

5 Transfer the ganache to a squeeze bottle and three-quarter fill the chocolate cups with it. Chill them in the refrigerator for 20 minutes to set the filling.

6 Meanwhile, check that the rest of the tempered chocolate is still at the right temperature, or temper a little more milk chocolate. Remove the cups from the refrigerator and top with the rest of the tempered chocolate. It is easiest to do this using a squeeze bottle.

7 Sprinkle the tops with a little salt. Leave to set for 20 minutes.

8 Serve immediately, or store in an airtight container, spaced apart, in the refrigerator. Remove 30 minutes before serving, as chocolate should be eaten at room temperature.

COOK'S TIP
It is well worth paying a little extra to buy an organic peanut butter, as the flavour will be much better.

Energy 138kcal/575kJ; Protein 2g; Carbohydrate 13g, of which sugars 13g; Fat 9g, of which saturates 4g; Cholesterol 2mg; Calcium 21mg; Fibre 0g; Sodium 47mg

SALTED CARAMEL CHOCOLATES

These elegant chocolates consist of a dark caramel and sea salt ganache, coated with a layer of yet more dark chocolate. Salt and caramel make a wonderful combination, and they have been used together in confectionery for many years. Today, it has become very fashionable to use this combination in all sorts of sweet treats. Use a good quality sea salt, such as Hawaiian pink salt, for the best flavour.

MAKES ABOUT 100

50ml/2fl oz/¼ cup cold water

200g/7oz/1 cup caster (superfine) sugar

2.5ml/½ tsp cream of tartar

225ml/8fl oz/scant 1 cup double (heavy) cream

50g/2oz/¼ cup unsalted butter, plus extra for greasing

2.5ml/½ tsp sea salt, crushed, plus extra to decorate

425g/15oz dark (bittersweet) chocolate (70% cocoa solids), finely chopped

400g/14oz dark chocolate (61–64% cocoa solids), tempered (*see* pages 56–57)

1 Grease a 20cm/8in square cake tin (pan), then line with clear film (plastic wrap). Line a baking sheet with baking parchment.

2 Place the water in a heavy pan, add the sugar and cream of tartar and heat gently to dissolve, stirring occasionally.

3 Once the sugar has dissolved, bring it to the boil and boil until the syrup caramelizes. It can be as light or as dark as you like, but do not allow it to burn.

4 Slowly and very carefully add the cream (it will spatter, so use caution and wear oven gloves). Use a whisk to incorporate it fully. Add the butter and salt, and whisk until smooth.

5 Put the chopped dark chocolate in a large, heatproof bowl. Pour in the caramel mixture and, using a whisk, combine the caramel and chocolate into a smooth, creamy ganache.

6 Pour the ganache into the lined cake tin and smooth the top with an offset spatula. Leave to set for a couple of hours, then place in the refrigerator and chill for about 30 minutes.

7 When the ganache is set, turn the chocolate out on to a marble slab or other cold, hard surface. Remove the clear film. Dip a large knife in hot water, wipe it dry and use it to slice the block into 2cm/¾in squares.

8 Return to the refrigerator to chill for a further 30 minutes. Meanwhile, temper the remaining dark chocolate.

9 Dip the chilled squares in the melted chocolate and transfer them to the baking sheet. Sprinkle with sea salt. Leave to set for about 30 minutes.

10 Serve as they are or in individual paper or foil cups. Store in an airtight container, spaced apart, in the refrigerator. Remove 30 minutes before serving, as chocolate should be eaten at room temperature.

Energy 130kcal/543kJ; Protein 0.9g; Carbohydrate 15g, of which sugars 14.1g; Fat 8.1g, of which saturates 4.7g; Cholesterol 10mg; Calcium 11mg; Fibre 0g; Sodium 11mg

Hazelnut Praline Truffles

Chocolate and hazelnuts are a match made in heaven, and these decadent chocolates are the perfect showcase for this taste sensation. Toasting the nuts not only brings out the flavour, but it also makes them more crunchy. In this recipe they are then mixed with a light, subtly flavoured caramel and coated in milk chocolate.

MAKES ABOUT 100

150g/5oz/generous ¾ cup hazelnuts

50ml/2fl oz/¼ cup cold water

200g/7oz/1 cup sugar

2.5ml/½ tsp cream of tartar

225ml/8fl oz/1 cup double (heavy) cream

50g/2oz/¼ cup unsalted butter, plus extra for greasing

425g/15oz dark (bittersweet) chocolate, finely chopped

400g/14oz milk chocolate, tempered (*see* pages 56–57)

1 Grease a 20cm/8in square baking tin (pan) and line it with clear film (plastic wrap), making the film as smooth as possible. Preheat the oven to 180°C/350°F/Gas 4.

2 Spread the hazelnuts out on a baking sheet lined with baking parchment so that they are all in one layer. Place in the oven. Set a timer for 7 minutes and then check them. They should be golden and have a firm texture. Toast for a little longer if necessary. Allow to cool slightly, then rub the nuts in a dish towel to remove the skins.

3 Place the water in a heavy pan and add the sugar. Add the cream of tartar, then heat gently to dissolve, stirring occasionally.

4 Once the sugar has dissolved, do not stir the mixture. Turn the heat up to high and bring the mixture to the boil. Boil the syrup, without stirring, until it caramelizes slightly and is a light golden colour.

5 Carefully pour the caramel over the toasted hazelnuts on the baking sheet. Leave it to set.

6 Once the caramel has set, break the slab into pieces, then blitz to a fine powder in a food processor.

7 Gently heat the cream in a pan until it is just below boiling. Meanwhile, place the chopped chocolate in a large heatproof bowl.

8 Pour the cream over the chocolate and whisk gently until it is smooth and the chocolate has melted. Fold in the ground hazelnut powder.

9 Pour the mixture into the prepared tin and chill in the refrigerator for about 1 hour, until set.

10 Turn the chocolate out on to a marble slab or other cold, hard surface. Remove the clear film. Dip a large knife in hot water, wipe it dry and use it to slice the block into 2cm/¾in squares.

11 Place the squares of chocolate back in the refrigerator to chill for a further 30 minutes. The next step requires your tempered milk chocolate, so you should prepare it at this stage, while the ganache is chilling. Line a baking sheet with baking parchment.

12 Dip the squares of ganache into the tempered milk chocolate using a dipping fork, and place on the baking parchment. Leave to set for about 30 minutes, or until completely set.

13 Serve immediately or store in an airtight container, spaced apart, in the refrigerator. Remove 30 minutes before serving, as chocolate should be eaten at room temperature.

Energy 75kcal/315kJ; Protein 1g; Carbohydrate 7g, of which sugars 7g; Fat 5g, of which saturates 3g; Cholesterol 4mg; Calcium 16mg; Fibre 0g; Sodium 5mg

CRYSTALLIZED GINGER CHOCOLATES

Ginger and dark chocolate complement each other very well, creating a grown-up flavour combination that is deep and complex. Fresh root ginger is added to the ganache in this recipe, giving it a fiery taste, while candied ginger adds a sweet yet peppery note and a contrast in texture.

MAKES ABOUT 50

200ml/7fl oz/scant 1 cup double (heavy) cream

100ml/3½fl oz/scant ½ cup liquid glucose or golden (light corn) syrup

50g/2oz fresh root ginger, chopped

300g/11oz dark (bittersweet) chocolate (70% cocoa solids), chopped

100g/3¾oz/scant ½ cup unsalted butter, softened, plus extra for greasing

50g/2oz candied ginger

400g/14oz dark chocolate (61–64% cocoa solids), tempered (*see* pages 56–57)

1 Grease a 20cm/8in square cake tin (pan), then line with clear film (plastic wrap). Line a baking sheet with baking parchment.

2 Place the cream, liquid glucose or golden syrup and fresh ginger in a small pan. Heat gently and bring to just under the boil, stirring well, then remove from the heat. Cover and leave to steep for 15 minutes.

3 Put the chopped dark chocolate in a large, heatproof bowl.

4 Heat the cream once again to just under the boil. Hold a fine-mesh sieve (strainer) over the bowl containing the chocolate, and pour the steeped and heated cream through it. Leave it to stand for about 10 minutes.

5 With a whisk or immersion blender, combine the chocolate and cream to form a smooth, creamy ganache. Add the butter and whisk or blend to combine.

6 Pour the ganache into the lined cake tin and smooth the top with an offset spatula. Put in the refrigerator and leave for about 30 minutes, or until firm.

7 Meanwhile, chop the candied ginger into 5mm/¼in pieces. Set aside.

8 When the ganache is set, turn it out on to a marble slab or other cold, hard surface. Remove the clear film. Dip a large knife in hot water, wipe it dry and use it to slice the block into 4cm/1½in squares. Cut each square in half diagonally to make triangles.

9 Chill for a further 30 minutes. The next step requires the tempered dark chocolate, so you should prepare it at this stage, while the ganache is chilling.

10 Dip the triangles of ganache into the tempered chocolate using a dipping fork, and place on the baking sheet.

11 Place a piece of candied ginger on each. Leave for about 30 minutes, until completely set.

12 Serve immediately, or store in an airtight container, spaced apart, in the refrigerator. Remove 30 minutes before serving, as chocolate should be eaten at room temperature.

COOK'S TIP
The best candied ginger comes from Australia. It certainly has a bite, but it is not too strong in flavour. The texture of ginger root is transformed by being boiled in sugar syrup during the crystallization process.

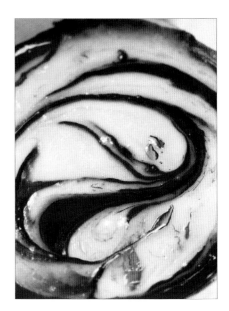

Energy 57kcal/240kJ; Protein 1g; Carbohydrate 6g, of which sugars 5g; Fat 4g, of which saturates 2g; Cholesterol 5mg; Calcium 4mg; Fibre 0g; Sodium 5mg

CANDIED GRAPEFRUIT AND PINK PEPPER TRUFFLES

Although fresh grapefruit can be sour, it will be very popular when it is served in combination with luscious chocolate. The bitterness of the dark chocolate emphasizes the sweet notes of the fruit, bringing out its fresh flavour, while infusing the cream with pink peppercorns adds a subtle spicy note. Finished with a sprinkle of crushed pink peppercorns and a sliver of candied peel, these make very sophisticated after-dinner treats.

MAKES ABOUT 100

200ml/7fl oz/scant 1 cup double (heavy) cream

100ml/3½fl oz/scant ½ cup liquid glucose or golden (light corn) syrup

grated rind of 2 grapefruits

5ml/1 tsp whole pink peppercorns, plus extra crushed peppercorns for decoration

300g/11oz dark (bittersweet) chocolate (70% cocoa solids), chopped

100g/3¾oz/scant ½ cup unsalted butter, softened, plus extra for greasing

50g/2oz/⅓ cup candied grapefruit or citron peel, finely chopped

400g/14oz dark chocolate (61–64% cocoa solids), tempered (*see* pages 56–57)

1 Grease a 20cm/8in square cake tin (pan), then line with clear film (plastic wrap). Line a baking sheet with baking parchment.

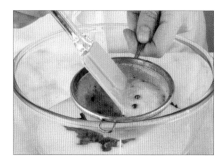

4 Heat the cream once again to just under the boil. Holding a fine-mesh sieve (strainer) over the bowl containing the chocolate, pour the heated cream through it. Leave to stand for 10 minutes.

5 With a whisk or immersion blender, combine the chocolate and cream to form a smooth, creamy ganache. Add the butter and whisk or blend to combine thoroughly.

6 Pour the ganache into the lined tin and smooth the top with a spatula. Chill in the refrigerator for 30 minutes, or until firm.

9 Dip the squares of ganache into the tempered chocolate using a dipping fork and place them on the prepared baking sheet.

10 Decorate with crushed pink peppercorns and candied grapefruit peel. Leave for about 30 minutes to set completely.

11 Serve immediately, or store the truffles in an airtight container, spaced apart, in the refrigerator. Remove them 30 minutes before serving, as chocolate should be eaten at room temperature.

2 Place the cream, liquid glucose or golden syrup, and grapefruit rind in a small pan. Heat gently and bring to just under the boil, stirring well, then stir in the whole pink peppercorns. Remove from the heat. Cover and leave to steep for 15 minutes.

3 Put the chopped dark chocolate in a large, heatproof bowl.

7 When set, turn the ganache out on to a marble slab, cold chopping board or other cold, hard surface. Remove the clear film. Dip a large knife in hot water, wipe it dry and use it to first trim any rough edges, then to slice the block into 2cm/¾in squares.

8 Return to the refrigerator to chill for a further 30 minutes. Meanwhile, temper the dark chocolate.

Energy 57kcal/239kJ; Protein 0g; Carbohydrate 6g, of which sugars 6g; Fat 4g, of which saturates 2g; Cholesterol 5mg; Calcium 4mg; Fibre 0g; Sodium 5mg

Hand-painted Jasmine Green Tea Chocolates

These impressive-looking twice-dipped chocolates are as delicious as they are beautiful. Using acetate sheets to transfer a thin film of coloured cocoa butter to the surface is fairly simple and the result looks professional. Working with teas in ganaches is also very interesting. Use a high-quality tea leaf, such as silver-tip jasmine, so that the delicate flavour of the green tea leaves comes through as well as the perfumed jasmine flowers.

MAKES ABOUT 100

200ml/7fl oz/scant 1 cup double (heavy) cream

100ml/3½fl oz/scant ½ cup liquid glucose or golden (light corn) syrup

15g/½oz jasmine green tea leaves

300g/11oz dark (bittersweet) chocolate (70% cocoa solids), chopped

100g/3¾oz/scant ½ cup unsalted butter, softened, plus extra for greasing

450g/1lb white chocolate

50g/2oz cocoa butter

a few drops of food colouring

1 Grease a 20cm/8in square cake tin (pan), then line with clear film. Line a baking sheet with baking parchment.

2 Place the cream and liquid glucose in a small pan. Heat gently and bring to just under the boil, stirring well, then remove from the heat. Add the tea leaves, cover and leave to steep for 10 minutes.

3 Put the chopped dark chocolate in a large, heatproof bowl.

4 Heat the cream once again to just under the boil. Holding a fine-mesh sieve (strainer) over the bowl containing the chocolate, pour the steeped and heated cream through it. Leave to stand for about 10 minutes.

5 With a whisk or immersion blender, combine the chocolate and cream to form a smooth, creamy ganache. Add the butter and whisk or blend to combine.

6 Pour the ganache into the lined cake tin and smooth the top with an offset spatula. Put in the refrigerator and leave for about 30 minutes, or until firm.

7 When the ganache is set, turn it out on to a marble slab or other cold, hard surface. Remove the clear film. Dip a large knife in hot water, wipe it dry and use it to slice the block into 2cm/¾in squares.

8 Return to the refrigerator to chill for a further 30 minutes. Meanwhile, temper 200g/7oz of the white chocolate (*see* pages 56–57).

9 Dip each square of ganache into the tempered white chocolate and place on the prepared baking sheet to set. Place in the refrigerator and leave to set for 30–60 minutes.

10 Meanwhile, prepare the acetate transfers. Take a sheet of acetate and lay it flat. If it has been rolled up, press it between some baking parchment, and lay something heavy on top of it.

11 Melt the cocoa butter in a heatproof bowl set over a pan of simmering water. When it is just melted, stir in a few drops of the food colouring of your choice.

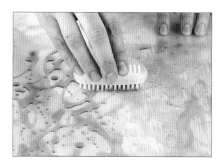

12 Pour this into a squeeze bottle for easy distribution. Shake well to combine the colour, then apply the coloured cocoa butter to the acetate in any design you like. Splatter it or smooth it out, depending on the effect you want to choose. You can also use a clean nail brush to create brush strokes in the layer. Leave to set for about 15 minutes.

13 When the pattern is set, cut the acetate into squares slightly larger than the truffles. Now temper the remaining white chocolate (*see* pages 56–57).

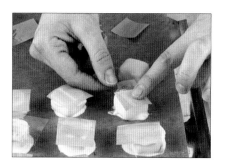

14 Dip the chocolates into the tempered chocolate in batches. Place the dipped chocolates back on to the baking sheet and, while the chocolate is wet, gently press a transfer sheet on to each one. Press the acetate down slightly and rub with the back of a fork or your finger.

15 Leave the acetates for 30 minutes, until the chocolates have set, then carefully peel them off. Serve immediately, or store in an airtight container, spaced apart, in the refrigerator. Remove them 30 minutes before serving, as chocolate should be eaten at room temperature.

Variation
Mylar works just as well as acetate sheets for transferring the designs to the chocolates.

Energy 65kcal/370kJ; Protein 1g; Carbohydrate 5g, of which sugars 5g; Fat 5g, of which saturates 3g; Cholesterol 5mg; Calcium 15mg; Fibre 0g; Sodium 70mg

MINT MELTAWAYS

A meltaway centre is different from a ganache one, because it uses coconut oil or cocoa butter instead of cream. This creates a silky texture that melts in your mouth very quickly. Once mixed with chocolate, the flavour of coconut oil is undetectable. Do not overheat the oil as it can burn the chocolate, resulting in a grainy texture.

3 Whisk in the chopped chocolate until smooth. Stir in the peppermint extract. Pour the mixture into the prepared tin and chill in the refrigerator for 30 minutes, until set.

4 Turn the set mixture out on to a marble slab or other cold, hard surface. Dip a large knife in hot water, wipe it dry and use it to slice the block into 2cm/¾in squares. Chill the pieces again for about 10 minutes.

5 Meanwhile, temper the remaining dark chocolate.

6 Dip the peppermint pieces into the tempered chocolate and transfer to a clean sheet of baking parchment.

7 Decorate with a drizzle of tempered chocolate and add a green or silver ball immediately. Leave to set for 30 minutes.

8 Serve immediately, or store in an airtight container, spaced apart, in the refrigerator. Remove 30 minutes before serving, as chocolate should be eaten at room temperature.

MAKES 50–100

115g/4oz coconut oil

450g/1lb dark (bittersweet) chocolate (at least 60% cocoa solids), chopped

2.5ml/½ tsp peppermint extract

250g/9oz dark chocolate (at least 60% cocoa solids), tempered (*see* pages 56–57)

green or silver sugar balls

1 Line a 15cm/6in or 20cm/8in square cake tin (pan) with baking parchment. The size of tin you choose depends on how thick or thin you want the meltaways to be – a smaller tin will create a thicker confection.

2 Melt the coconut oil very gently in a large heatproof bowl set over a pan of simmering water. Use a sugar thermometer to ensure it does not rise above 24°C/74°F.

Energy 46kcal/192kJ; Protein 0g; Carbohydrate 4g, of which sugars 4g; Fat 3g, of which saturates 2g; Cholesterol 0mg; Calcium 2mg; Fibre 0g; Sodium 0mg

CHOCOLATE RASPBERRY MELTAWAYS

These soft, velvety meltaways are made with a fruity, fresh raspberry purée that brings out the flavour of the dark chocolate. Drizzled with milk chocolate and dusted with edible pink dust, these chocolates are extremely attractive and would make an ideal gift, presented in a pretty box or bag and tied with a ribbon.

MAKES 50–100

115g/4oz coconut oil

400g/14oz dark (bittersweet) chocolate (at least 60% cocoa solids), chopped

100g/3¾oz/1¼ cups puréed raspberries, strained (made from 200g/7oz whole berries – *see* Cook's Tip page 134)

250g/9oz dark chocolate (at least 60% cocoa solids), tempered (*see* pages 56–57)

100g/3¾oz milk chocolate, tempered (*see* pages 56–57)

edible pink dust or silver balls

1 Line a 15cm/6in or 20cm/8in square cake tin (pan) with baking parchment, depending on how thick or thin you want the meltaways to be – a smaller tin will give a thicker confection.

2 Melt the coconut oil very gently in a large heatproof bowl positioned over a pan of simmering water. Use a sugar thermometer to ensure that it does not rise above 24°C/74°F.

3 Whisk in the chopped chocolate until smooth. Stir in the raspberry purée. Pour the mixture into the tin. Chill in the refrigerator for 30 minutes, until set.

4 Turn the set mixture out on to a marble slab or other cold, hard surface. Dip a knife in hot water, wipe it dry and use it to slice the block into 2cm/¾in squares. Chill the pieces again for 10 minutes.

5 Temper the remaining dark chocolate.

6 Dip the raspberry pieces into the tempered dark chocolate and transfer to a clean sheet of baking parchment.

7 Decorate with a drizzle of tempered milk chocolate and use a clean, dry pastry brush to sprinkle the tops with edible pink dust, or add silver balls.

8 Serve immediately or store in an airtight container, spaced apart, in the refrigerator. Remove 30 minutes before serving, as chocolate should be eaten at room temperature.

COOK'S TIP
Coconut oil is solid at room temperature, but it is very soft.

Energy 49kcal/204kJ; Protein 0g; Carbohydrate 5g, of which sugars 5g; Fat 3g, of which saturates 2g; Cholesterol 1mg; Calcium 5mg; Fibre 0g; Sodium 1mg

GOLD AND SILVER CHOCOLATE EASTER EGGS

A simple but elegant Easter egg, these can be made in your choice of milk, dark or white chocolate. A mixture of all three would be beautiful. For a special Easter egg hunt, dust one egg with gold dust and the other with silver dust and include jelly beans, chocolate coins or any other confection inside the eggs.

MAKES 1 LARGE EGG OR 2 SMALL EGGS

500g/1¼lb milk chocolate, tempered (*see* pages 56–57)

500g/1¼lb white chocolate, tempered (*see* pages 56–57)

jelly beans or any other confections

edible gold and silver dust or liquid

1 Polish the inside of your egg moulds with a muslin cloth. Line a baking tray with baking parchment and set aside.

2 Temper the milk chocolate and keep it warm by placing the bowl over a pan of hot water, wrapping a heating pad around it, or standing it on a hot water bottle.

3 Ladle tempered chocolate into one half of the mould. Working quickly, swirl the chocolate around the sides, then pour any excess chocolate back into the bowl. Repeat with the other mould half.

4 Invert the moulds on to the baking parchment. Leave to set for 30 minutes, then repeat the process.

5 If you plan to put heavy chocolates or sweets inside, you may wish to coat it with a third layer of chocolate. After you have applied the final layer, leave the moulds to set for about 3 hours. As it cools, the chocolate will shrink slightly, making it easier for the chocolate to be released from the moulds.

6 Temper a small amount of the remaining milk chocolate. Cut two squares of baking parchment and place them near the moulds on a clean area of work surface. These will protect the egg from being marked by your fingers.

7 Gather together the fillings. It is a good idea to wrap the jelly beans or other sweets in coloured foil or little pieces of wrapping paper so that they do not taint the chocolate. It also muffles the sound and protects the egg if they are shaken.

8 Remove the chocolate egg halves from the moulds and place them rounded-side down on the baking parchment. Do not touch the outside of the chocolate egg with your fingers as it will leave marks.

9 Using an offset spatula, spread a little tempered chocolate along the edges of the eggs. This will act like glue.

10 Fill one side of the egg with the filling. Press the two sides together, using the parchment squares to avoid fingerprints.

11 To finish the eggs, pipe a design around the seam with tempered white chocolate. Leave to set for about 2 hours. Paint the eggs with the edible gold dust or liquid and the seam with the silver.

12 Either wrap the eggs in pretty foil or present them on a dish. You could also box them up, or encase them in cellophane and tie with a bow.

COOK'S TIP

Do not be tempted to unmould the eggs before waiting 3 hours. If they are three layers thick, wait until the next day to unmould them. Early unmoulding can result in the chocolate peeling away from the shell, destroying the perfect finish.

Energy 5245kcal/21945kJ; Protein 79g; Carbohydrate 576g, of which sugars 576g; Fat 308g, of which saturates 184g; Cholesterol 115mg; Calcium 2450mg; Fibre 0g; Sodium 975mg

CHERRY-KIRSCH TRUFFLES

Some people are not keen on commercial cherry-flavoured chocolates, but even if you are one of those people it is well worth trying these home-made ones, as they taste completely different. Store-bought types often contain a sweet, squidgy, slightly synthetic-tasting cherry rather than a sour, firm-textured one. This classic recipe consists of a perfect cherry nestled in a Kirsch-spiked ganache, enrobed in intense dark chocolate.

MAKES 30

500g/1¼lb dark (bittersweet) chocolate (61–64% cocoa solids), tempered (*see* pages 56–57)

40g/1½oz Amarena or other good quality sour cherries in syrup

15ml/1 tbsp Kirsch

90ml/6 tbsp double (heavy) cream

75g/3oz/¼ cup golden (light corn) syrup

100g/3¾oz dark (bittersweet) chocolate (70% cocoa solids), chopped

1 Line a baking sheet with baking parchment and set aside.

2 Coat the cups of a chocolate mould with most of the tempered dark chocolate. Hold the mould at an angle over a clean bowl so that the chocolate runs down, coating the cups, and any excess drizzles out into the bowl.

3 Tap on a work surface to release any bubbles. Lay the mould upside down on the baking sheet. After a few minutes, check the mould to see if the chocolate has begun to set on the sides.

4 Using a large palette knife or the back of a sharp knife, scrape away any excess chocolate from the flat plastic surrounding the cups.

5 Return the mould to the baking sheet to allow the chocolate to set fully before adding the filling. This will take 1 hour.

6 Meanwhile, strain the cherries and reserve the syrup. Put 60ml/4 tbsp of the syrup in a small bowl and stir in the Kirsch. Set aside.

7 Make the ganache. Place the cream and golden syrup in a small pan and bring to the boil.

8 Melt the chopped chocolate in a heatproof bowl set over a pan of barely simmering water. Pour the cream over the chocolate and, using an immersion blender, blend into a ganache.

9 Add the reserved cherry syrup and mix again. Leave it to cool to 29°C/85°F on a sugar thermometer.

10 Transfer the ganache to a squeeze bottle and half-fill each chocolate cup with the ganache.

11 Push a cherry into the centre of the ganache in each cup.

12 Fill the cups almost to the top with more ganache, leaving just enough space for a final layer of tempered chocolate on top.

13 Cover the ganache with a layer of tempered chocolate. Scrape any excess chocolate off the top (which will become the bottom of the chocolates) with an offset spatula, and leave to set for 1 hour.

14 Invert the mould and tap lightly to remove the chocolates. Serve immediately, or store in an airtight container, spaced apart, in the refrigerator. Remove 30 minutes before serving, as chocolate should be eaten at room temperature.

COOK'S TIP
If the cherries are too large to fit in your chocolate mould, slice them in half and have just half a cherry in each one.

Energy 136kcal/569kJ; Protein 1g; Carbohydrate 15g, of which sugars 15g; Fat 8g, of which saturates 5g; Cholesterol 6mg; Calcium 9mg; Fibre 0g; Sodium 2mg

CHOCOLATE LIPS AND HEARTS

Lips and hearts are appropriate shapes for these rich, intense chocolates, which are perfect for a romantic dinner or Valentine's gift. They are quite fiddly to make but the results are impressive – the trick is to make the chocolate shell just thick enough to contain the runny caramel, as a too-thick shell ruins the delicacy of the truffle.

MAKES ABOUT 25

300g/11oz/1½ cups caster (superfine) sugar

50ml/2fl oz/¼ cup water

1 vanilla pod (bean), split and seeds scraped

175ml/6fl oz/¾ cup double (heavy) cream

45ml/3 tbsp golden (light corn) syrup

90g/3½oz/7 tbsp unsalted butter, softened

a pinch of salt

edible gold leaf (optional)

white chocolate, tempered (*see* pages 56–57), for drizzling (optional)

500g/1¼lb dark (bittersweet) chocolate (at least 64% cocoa solids), tempered (*see* pages 56–57)

1 Line a shallow baking tray with baking parchment and set it aside.

2 Put the sugar and water into a large, heavy pan and heat gently, stirring, until the sugar has dissolved. Once it has dissolved, stop stirring. Add the scraped vanilla seeds and the pod.

3 Continue to cook until the sugar syrup is a dark caramel colour, but be careful not to let it burn. (As soon as you see the first wisp of smoke, it is done.)

4 Meanwhile, while the caramel is cooking, pour the cream and golden syrup into a small pan and bring to the boil. Keep your eye on the caramel too.

5 When the caramel is ready, remove it from the heat. Slowly pour the cream mixture into it, taking great care that you do not burn your hand from the spattering of the caramel or the steam. Use a whisk to mix and release more of the steam and dissipate the bubbles.

6 Stir in the butter and salt, and remove the vanilla pod.

7 Insert a sugar thermometer and let the caramel cool to 27°C/80°F. This can take a couple of hours. When it has cooled, pour it into a squeeze bottle and set aside.

8 If you want to decorate the outside of the chocolates, place small pieces of gold leaf inside the cups of a chocolate heart mould and drizzle tempered white chocolate in lip-shaped ones. Let the white chocolate set a little, then scrape away any excess on the mould.

9 Coat the cups with most of the tempered dark chocolate. Hold the mould at an angle over a clean bowl so that the chocolate runs down, coating the inside of the cups, and any excess drizzles out into the bowl.

10 Tap on a work surface to release any bubbles. Lay the mould upside down on the baking sheet. After a few minutes check the mould to see if the chocolate has begun to set on the sides.

11 Using a large palette knife or the back of a sharp knife, scrape away any excess chocolate from the flat plastic surrounding the lip and heart cups.

12 Return the moulds to the baking sheet and allow the chocolate to set completely. This will take about 1 hour.

13 When the filling is cool enough and the chocolate has set, fill the cups with the caramel, using the squeeze bottle. Tap on a surface to release any bubbles and leave them, uncovered, overnight.

14 The next day, temper a little more dark chocolate and pour over the set caramel filling. Scrape any excess chocolate off the top (which will be the bottom of the chocolates) with a spatula. Leave to set for 1–1½ hours.

15 Invert the moulds and tap lightly to remove the chocolates. Serve immediately, or store in an airtight container in the refrigerator for up to 1 week. Remove 30 minutes before serving, as chocolate should be eaten at room temperature.

Energy 83kcal/349kJ; Protein 0.2g; Carbohydrate 13.8g, of which sugars 13.8g; Fat 3.8g, of which saturates 2.1g; Cholesterol 9mg; Calcium 10mg; Fibre 0g; Sodium 7mg

CHOCOLATE CONFECTIONS

CHOCOLATE CAN BE USED FOR MANY MORE TREATS THAN TRUFFLES OR FILLED CHOCOLATES. IT LENDS ITS RICH FLAVOUR TO GOOEY BROWNIES, ITS ELEGANCE TO PRETTY PETITS FOURS, AND ITS TEMPERED SHINE TO DAINTY BOXES. THERE IS SOMETHING TO TEMPT EVERY PALATE IN THIS CHAPTER, AS CHOCOLATE IS PAIRED WITH NUTS, CANDIED FRUITS, SPONGE CAKE, MARSHMALLOWS, COCONUT AND MANY OTHER DELICIOUS INGREDIENTS.

CHOCOLATE BOATS

Buttery sweet shortcrust pastry boats are the perfect vehicle for rich, dark chocolate ganache. You can prepare the pastry shells in advance, then simply create the ganache at the last minute, making these easy and elegant petits fours for a special occasion. You will need some small boat moulds.

MAKES ABOUT 24

FOR THE PASTRY

115g/4oz/½ cup unsalted butter, softened

50g/2oz/¼ cup caster (superfine) sugar

175g/6oz/1½ cups plain (all-purpose) flour

a pinch of salt

½ egg yolk

FOR THE FILLING

60ml/4 tbsp double (heavy) cream

50ml/2fl oz/¼ cup golden (light corn) syrup or liquid glucose

175g/6oz dark (bittersweet) chocolate (64–70% cocoa solids), finely chopped

1 To make the pastry, cream the butter and sugar together until light but not too fluffy (you do not need to incorporate too much air into the butter).

2 Add the flour and salt, and mix until just combined. Add the egg yolk and bring together into a ball.

3 Wrap the ball in clear film (plastic wrap) and press into a disc. Chill in the refrigerator for about 30 minutes, until it is firm but not hard.

4 Lightly dust a worktop and the dough with flour. Roll out the dough to about 3mm/⅛in thickness. The pastry boats need to be strong enough to stand on their own, but not so thick that they dominate the chocolate.

5 Cut teardrop shapes that are slightly larger than the moulds. Use a knife to lift them gently off the worktop and into the moulds. Press them into place and trim off any excess. Place them on a baking sheet. Chill for 15 minutes. Meanwhile, preheat the oven to 180°C/350°F/Gas 4.

6 Bake the pastry shells for 7 minutes, or until they are just golden at the edges and are baked through.

7 Leave to cool, then remove from the moulds and transfer to a serving tray.

8 To make the filling, place the cream and golden syrup or glucose in a small pan and bring to the boil.

9 Put the chopped chocolate in a large, heatproof bowl and pour the hot cream over it. Stir every few minutes until the chocolate is melted.

10 Spoon the ganache into the pastry shells. Serve immediately or store in an airtight container in the refrigerator for up to 3 days. Allow to come to room temperature before serving.

Energy 126kcal/526kJ; Protein 1.2g; Carbohydrate 14.4g, of which sugars 7.5g; Fat 7.6g, of which saturates 4.6g; Cholesterol 19mg; Calcium 17mg; Fibre 0.2g; Sodium 41mg

CHOCOLATE AND APRICOT BOATS

Chocolate and apricot may seem a surprising pairing, but the tangy sweet fruit comes to life in an entirely new way when combined with delicious dark chocolate. Raspberry jam would work here too, but apricot will surprise and excite the palates of your friends and make these little boats irresistible.

MAKES ABOUT 24

FOR THE PASTRY

115g/4oz/½ cup unsalted butter, softened

50g/2oz/¼ cup caster (superfine) sugar

175g/6oz/1½ cups plain (all-purpose) flour, plus extra for dusting

a pinch of salt

½ egg yolk

FOR THE APRICOT FILLING

4 apricots, halved, stones (pits) removed

200g/7oz/1 cup caster (superfine) sugar

FOR THE CHOCOLATE FILLING

4 tbsp/60ml double (heavy) cream

50g/2oz golden (light corn) syrup or liquid glucose

175g/6oz dark (bittersweet) chocolate (64–70% cocoa solids), chopped into small pieces

100g/3¾oz white chocolate

1 To make the pastry, cream the butter and sugar until light but not too fluffy (you do not need to incorporate too much air into the butter).

2 Add the flour and salt, and stir until just combined. Add the egg yolk and bring together into a ball. Wrap the ball in clear film (plastic wrap) and press into a disc. Place in the refrigerator to chill and rest for about 30 minutes, until it is firm but not hard.

3 Lightly dust a worktop and the dough with flour. Roll out the dough to about 3mm/⅛in thickness. The pastry boats need to be strong enough to stand on their own, but not so thick that they dominate the chocolate.

4 Cut the pastry into teardrop shapes that are slightly larger than the moulds.

5 Use a knife to lift them gently off the worktop and into the moulds. Press them into place and trim off any excess. Place them on a baking sheet. Chill for 15 minutes. Meanwhile, preheat the oven to 180°C/350°F/Gas 4.

6 Bake the pastry shells for 7 minutes, or until they are just golden at the edges and are baked through. Leave to cool, then remove from their moulds and transfer to a serving tray.

7 To make the apricot filling, cut the apricot halves into quarters, place in a small, heavy pan and cover with the sugar. Stir, then allow to macerate off the heat for about 30 minutes.

8 Place the fruit and sugar over a medium heat, bring to the boil, then cook for 10 minutes until the fruit starts to break down.

9 Purée the cooked fruit in a food processor or blender. Leave to cool.

10 Meanwhile, make the chocolate filling. Put the cream and syrup or glucose in a small pan and bring to the boil.

11 Place the chopped chocolate in a heatproof bowl and pour the hot cream mixture over it. Stir every few minutes until the mixture is smooth.

12 Put the white chocolate in a separate heatproof bowl set over a pan of barely simmering water. Melt very slowly.

13 To assemble the boats, spoon a little of the puréed apricot into each pastry boat. Spoon the ganache over the top and leave to set for 10 minutes. Drizzle white chocolate over the top and leave to set for 30 minutes. Serve immediately, or store in an airtight container for 2 days.

Energy 183kcal/770kJ; Protein 2g; Carbohydrate 26g, of which sugars 20g; Fat 9g, of which saturates 5g; Cholesterol 19mg; Calcium 29mg; Fibre 0g; Sodium 13mg

MINI CHOCOLATE BROWNIES

There are countless recipes for brownies and as many reasons why each particular recipe is best. This is a recipe for those who like a combination of cake and moist, gooey texture. The pieces of chocolate that melt into it give pockets of pure chocolate flavour. For hungrier guests, cut it into 9 larger squares.

MAKES 16

300g/11oz dark (bittersweet) chocolate (70% cocoa solids), chopped

125g/4¼oz/generous ½ cup unsalted butter, plus extra for greasing

3 eggs

175g/6oz/¾ cup soft light brown sugar

2.5ml/½ tsp salt

2.5ml/½ tsp vanilla extract

100g/3¾oz/scant 1 cup plain (all-purpose) flour

150g/5oz dark chocolate (55–64% cocoa solids), chopped into 1cm/½in pieces

1 Preheat the oven to 160°C/325°F/ Gas 3. Grease a 20cm/8in square cake tin (pan) and line with baking parchment so that it comes up the sides of the tin.

2 Place the chopped chocolate (70% cocoa solids) and butter in a heatproof bowl set over a pan of barely simmering water. Allow it to melt gently, stirring every few minutes until smooth. When melted, remove from the pan of water and leave to cool slightly.

3 In a clean bowl, whisk the eggs, soft light brown sugar, salt and vanilla extract until frothy and light.

4 Mix the frothy egg mixture into the melted chocolate.

5 Fold in the flour and chocolate pieces. Transfer the mixture to the prepared tin.

6 Bake for exactly 27 minutes, until the top is just set but the insides are gooey. All ovens differ, but it is important not to let them overcook. If you think your oven is a little cool, then give it a minute more, but they will seem a little soft when they are done. Remember, they continue to firm up as they cool.

7 Once cool, remove from the tin and cut into 16 squares. Serve immediately, or store in an airtight container for 4 days.

Energy 228kcal/955kJ; Protein 2.7g; Carbohydrate 27.6g, of which sugars 22.6g; Fat 12.7g, of which saturates 7.5g; Cholesterol 49mg; Calcium 26mg; Fibre 0.2g; Sodium 62mg

MINI CHOCOLATE-SWIRL BROWNIES

Chocolate brownies with cream cheese are an all-time favourite luxury. In this version, the cream cheese is swirled together with a little brown sugar and the seeds from a vanilla pod for extra flavour and texture. The brown sugar is added to the chocolate mixture as well, which gives a richer, stickier brownie.

MAKES 16

125g/4¼oz/generous ½ cup unsalted butter, plus extra for greasing

300g/11oz dark (bittersweet) chocolate (minimum 64% cocoa solids)

5 eggs

225g/8oz/1 cup soft light brown sugar

2.5ml/½ tsp salt

2.5ml/½ tsp vanilla extract

100g/3¾oz/scant 1 cup plain (all-purpose) flour, sifted

275g/10oz/1¼ cups cream cheese

½ vanilla pod, scraped

1 Preheat the oven to 160°C/325°F/Gas 3. Grease a 20cm/8in square cake tin (pan) and line with baking parchment so that it comes up the sides of the tin.

2 Place the butter and chocolate in a heatproof bowl set over a pan of barely simmering water. Allow it to melt gently, stirring every few minutes until smooth. When melted, remove from the pan of water and leave to cool slightly.

3 In another bowl, whisk three of the eggs with 175g/6oz/¾ cup of the soft light brown sugar, the salt and the vanilla extract until frothy and light.

4 Fold the cooled melted chocolate into the frothy egg mixture. Fold in the sifted flour and transfer the mixture to the prepared tin.

5 Whisk the cream cheese, remaining two eggs, remaining sugar and vanilla seeds in another bowl. Drop blobs of the cream cheese mixture on top of the brownie mixture and swirl with a knife.

6 Bake for exactly 30 minutes, until just set on top. All ovens differ a little, but it is very important not to overcook them. If you think your oven is a little cool then give it a minute more, but they will seem a little soft when they are done. Remember, they continue to firm up as they cool.

7 Remove from the oven and leave to cool in the tin. When cool, remove from the tin and cut into 16 squares. (You could also cut it into 9 larger squares, if you do not want them to be mini.) Serve immediately, or store in an airtight container for up to 5 days.

Energy 330kcal/1380kJ; Protein 5g; Carbohydrate 31g, of which sugars 26g; Fat 22g, of which saturates 13g; Cholesterol 108mg; Calcium 52mg; Fibre 0g; Sodium 85mg

CHOCOLATE DRAGÉES

Covered in layers of caramel, milk chocolate and dark chocolate, and finished with icing sugar, these little morsels are a balance of sweet, bitter, salty, crunchy and smooth. Almonds are the classic base for these confections, but if you want to vary the recipe, they are delicious made with hazelnuts or cashews instead.

MAKES ABOUT 1.7KG/3¾LB

500g/1¼lb/3⅓ cup whole almonds

400g/14oz/2 cups caster (superfine) sugar

2.5ml/½ tsp salt

50g/2oz/¼ cup unsalted butter

350g/12oz milk chocolate (minimum 40% cocoa solids)

400g/14oz dark (bittersweet) chocolate (minimum 55% cocoa solids)

icing (confectioners') sugar, for dusting

1 Preheat the oven to 180°C/350°F/Gas 4.

2 Spread the almonds out in a single layer on a baking sheet lined with baking parchment, and place in the oven to toast for 7 minutes. They should have a little colour and may begin to just crack open a little. Remove from the oven and keep in a warm place.

3 Put the sugar in a large, heavy pan with just enough water to moisten the sugar. Heat over a medium heat, swirling the pan around occasionally, until the sugar melts and starts to colour. Do not stir.

4 When all the sugar has melted, add the salt and butter. Let it all melt together and swirl the pan again. When the mixture is a caramel colour, drop in the hot, toasted nuts. Using a wooden spoon, stir constantly to coat them in the caramel. When completely coated, pour the nuts back on to the baking sheet they were toasted on. When cool enough to touch, break them apart a bit with your fingers.

5 Melt the milk chocolate in a heatproof bowl set over a pan of barely simmering water, stirring occasionally. Remove the bowl from the heat. Leave to cool slightly.

6 Prepare an ice-water bath and position the bowl containing the chocolate over it. Drop in the caramelized almonds. Stir until the nuts are coated in chocolate. Transfer the nuts to the baking sheet. Leave until the chocolate is set.

7 Meanwhile, melt the dark chocolate in a clean heatproof bowl set over a pan of barely simmering water, stirring occasionally. Remove the bowl from the heat and leave to cool slightly.

8 Position the bowl of dark chocolate over the ice-water bath, add the coated nuts and stir until they are well coated. Transfer the nuts to the baking sheet. Leave until the chocolate is set.

9 Finally, put the icing sugar in a bowl and toss the almonds in it until coated. Shake off any excess sugar and serve immediately, or store in a cool, dry place in an airtight container.

Energy 8869kcal/37120kJ; Protein 153g; Carbohydrate 908g, of which sugars 891g; Fat 540g, of which saturates 540g; Cholesterol 220mg; Calcium 2150mg; Fibre 65g; Sodium 1400mg

CHOCOLATE LACE WITH WHITE PEARL DUST

Tempered chocolate can be used to make a multitude of shapes. Piping perfectly tempered chocolate into lacy shapes creates intricate forms that allow the chocolate to maintain its delicate texture while being stable enough to wrap up in cellophane and give as a gift. You can omit the edible white pearl dust, if you like.

MAKES 6

200g/7oz dark (bittersweet) chocolate (minimum 64% cocoa solids), tempered (*see* pages 56–57)

edible white pearl dust

1 Lay out 6 medium-sized paper doilies to use as templates. Place a sheet of baking parchment on top of the doilies, checking you can see the pattern through the parchment.

2 Fill a plastic piping bag with tempered chocolate and cut a tiny hole in the tip. If you are using a cloth or reusable piping bag, fit it with a tiny round nozzle.

3 Pipe the chocolate on to the baking parchment immediately, following the lines of the doilies in a lacy pattern.

COOK'S TIP
If you have very warm hands, wear disposable latex gloves and hold an ice pack before touching the lace.

4 Allow the chocolate to set, and sprinkle with white pearl dust. The best way to do this is to dip a clean pastry or paintbrush into the powder, position it over the lace and tap it. Repeat until the shapes are all covered.

5 Carefully peel the paper from the chocolate with the aid of a palette knife, taking care not to melt the chocolate with your hands. Serve immediately, or store in an airtight container in the refrigerator for up to 1 week.

Energy 170kcal/712kJ; Protein 2g; Carbohydrate 21g, of which sugars 21g; Fat 9g, of which saturates 6g; Cholesterol 2mg; Calcium 11mg; Fibre 0g; Sodium 2mg

CHOCOLATE BOXES

These stunning little boxes are actually little individual sponge petits fours. They take some time to assemble, but they are completely delicious. The soft sponge, crisp chocolate and creamy filling offer all the texture of a sophisticated gateau, but you do not need to be a trained pastry chef to make them; you just need a little patience.

MAKES 4

FOR THE SPONGE

15g/½oz/1 tbsp butter, melted, plus extra for greasing

3 eggs

100g/3¾oz/generous ½ cup caster (superfine) sugar

100g/3¾oz/scant 1 cup self-raising (self-rising) flour

40g/1½oz/⅓ cup cornflour (cornstarch)

45ml/3 tbsp hot water

FOR THE CHOCOLATE BOXES

200g/7oz dark (bittersweet) chocolate

30–45ml/2–3 tbsp apricot jam, warmed

FOR THE FILLING

200ml/7fl oz/scant 1 cup double (heavy) cream

15ml/1 tbsp brandy or cognac

15ml/1 tbsp caster (superfine) sugar

100g/3¾oz milk chocolate, for grating

1 Preheat the oven to 160°C/325°F/ Gas 3. Grease a 20 x 30cm/8 x 12in cake tin (pan) and line with baking parchment.

2 Beat the eggs in a large bowl until they begin to froth, then add the sugar. Beat together for about 5 minutes until light and fluffy.

3 Sift in the flour and cornflour, and fold together very gently with a spatula.

4 Combine the melted butter and hot water in a jug (pitcher) and fold into the cake mixture.

5 Pour the mixture into the prepared tin and bake for about 25–30 minutes until set and coming away from the sides of the tin but not too coloured. Leave to cool in the tin for 10 minutes, then transfer to a wire rack to cool completely.

6 Temper the dark chocolate (*see* pages 56–57). Pour it on to a baking sheet lined with acetate. Spread it into a thin layer and leave to set for 30 minutes.

7 Invert the chocolate on to a chopping board lined with baking parchment. Peel off the acetate. Dip a long sharp knife in hot water, wipe it dry, then use it to cut the chocolate into 16 4cm/1½in squares. Set aside.

8 Cut the cake into 4 4cm/1½in squares. You can use any leftover cake for a trifle, or temper more chocolate and use to create more chocolate boxes.

9 Place the cake squares on the plate, cake stand or platter you intend to serve the boxes on as they are hard to move once assembled.

10 Melt the apricot jam in a small pan and brush it on the sides of the cake squares. Press 4 squares of chocolate on to the glazed sides of each sponge square. Use a very sharp knife with a thin blade to trim any excess chocolate from the corners of the boxes.

11 Whip the cream in a large bowl with the brandy and sugar. Spoon into the chocolate boxes. Grate milk chocolate over the top and serve immediately.

Energy 924kcal/3864kJ; Protein 11g; Carbohydrate 97g, of which sugars 87g; Fat 57g, of which saturates 33g; Cholesterol 259mg; Calcium 130mg; Fibre 0g; Sodium 136mg

CHOCOLATE BERRY CUPS

These lovely little chocolate cases are so easy to make and look fantastically cute. Dark chocolate and delicious berries are the perfect way to end a meal. You could also fill the chocolate cups with whipped cream or home-made chocolate mousse, if you like.

MAKES 12

600g/1lb 6oz dark (bittersweet) chocolate (64–70% cocoa solids), tempered (*see* pages 56–57)

1.2kg/2¼lb/9 cups berries, such as raspberries, mulberries or blackberries

1 Lay 12 paper cupcake cases out in a baking tray, then double them up for extra support.

2 Pour a little chocolate into each case, then using a clean, dry pastry brush or small, clean paintbrush, paint the insides of the cups with the chocolate. Leave them to set for about 2 minutes.

VARIATIONS
• For a more indulgent treat, add whipped cream to the chocolate cups, before adding the berries. Whisk 200ml/7fl oz/scant 1 cup double (heavy) cream.
• If the berries are tart, sprinkle over some caster (superfine) sugar.

3 Paint on another layer of chocolate.

4 Allow the chocolate cups to set completely. This could take up to 5 hours. Peel away the cupcake cases and place the chocolate cups on serving plates.

5 Fill the cups with berries, then serve immediately. You can store the cases in an airtight container in the refrigerator for up to a week, but once you have filled them they need to be served within a few hours.

Energy 73kcal/304kJ; Protein 0.7g; Carbohydrate 6.3g, of which sugars 5.9g; Fat 5.5g, of which saturates 3.1g; Cholesterol 8mg; Calcium 11mg; Fibre 0.4g; Sodium 4mg

Chocolate-coated Marshmallows on Biscuits

The inspiration for this recipe came from the all-American summertime treat, 'S'mores'. These are traditionally made around a campfire, in which marshmallow is toasted until it is nearly black and bubbly before being carefully slid on to a biscuit with a piece of chocolate on it. Another biscuit is used to sandwich it all together and the treat is ready. This recipe does not require the marshmallow to be burnt, only uses one biscuit and aims for a more attractive finish, but the ingredients, flavours and essential idea are the same.

MAKES ABOUT 24

75g/3oz/6 tbsp unsalted butter, softened

90g/3½oz/½ cup soft light brown sugar

15ml/1 tbsp honey

15ml/1 tbsp golden (light corn) syrup

50ml/2fl oz/¼ cup milk

10ml/2 tsp vanilla extract

75g/3oz/¾ cup plain (all-purpose) flour, plus extra for dusting

75g/3oz/¾ cup wholemeal (whole-wheat) flour

2.5ml/½ tsp baking powder

a pinch of salt

about 24 large marshmallows (to make your own, *see* Vanilla Marshmallows, page 132)

200g/7oz dark (bittersweet) chocolate (about 64–70% cocoa solids), tempered (*see* pages 56–57)

1 Cream the butter, soft light brown sugar, honey and golden syrup in a large bowl or in an electric stand mixer for about 1 minute until smooth and creamy, but not pale and fluffy. You do not want to work too much air into the dough.

2 Add the milk and vanilla extract, and mix to combine.

3 Measure the plain flour, wholemeal flour, baking powder and salt into a small bowl. Use a whisk to mix them together well, before adding them to the butter mixture. Mix briefly, until just combined.

4 Transfer the dough to a sheet of clear film (plastic wrap) and press the dough into a disc. Wrap in the clear film and chill in the refrigerator for about 1 hour.

5 Preheat the oven to 180°C/350°F/ Gas 4, and line a baking sheet with baking parchment.

6 Lightly flour a work surface and roll the dough out to about 5mm/¼in in thickness. Cut it into 3cm/1¼in squares (use a ruler if you like them perfect) and lay them on the prepared baking sheet.

7 Bake the biscuits (cookies) in the oven for 8–10 minutes until they are light golden in colour. Transfer to a wire rack to cool completely.

8 Place the cooled biscuits on a baking sheet lined with baking parchment. Using an offset spatula, dot each biscuit with a drop of tempered chocolate to hold the marshmallows in place.

9 Place a marshmallow on each biscuit.

10 Drizzle the top of the marshmallows with more tempered chocolate. This can be messy, or neat, depending on your preference.

11 Serve immediately, or store in an airtight container for up to 3 days.

Energy 122kcal/515kJ; Protein 1g; Carbohydrate 19g, of which sugars 14g; Fat 5g, of which saturates 3g; Cholesterol 8mg; Calcium 15mg; Fibre 0g; Sodium 17mg

FLOURLESS CHOCOLATE PETIT FOUR CUPCAKES

A deliciously light flourless chocolate cake, this recipe is great for those who cannot eat wheat, and for everyone else too! The cakes will rise up quite high like a soufflé, and then sink down again as they cool. The crackly appearance lends to their charm. The cupcakes are adorable topped with little piped blobs of chocolate buttercream, but you could omit the icing and dust with cocoa powder or icing sugar instead, if you like.

MAKES ABOUT 40

FOR THE CAKES

100g/3¾oz/scant ½ cup unsalted butter

115g/4oz dark (bittersweet) chocolate, chopped into smallish chunks, plus extra chunks for decoration

3 eggs, separated

100g/3¾oz/½ cup caster (superfine) sugar

a pinch of salt

FOR THE ICING

25g/1oz/¼ cup unsweetened cocoa powder

40ml/8 tsp boiling water

125g/4¼oz dark (bittersweet) chocolate (60–70% cocoa solids), melted

185g/6½oz/generous ¾ cup unsalted butter, softened (it needs to be very soft)

400g/14oz/3½ cups icing (confectioners') sugar, sifted

2.5ml/½ tsp vanilla extract

sprinkles or sugar flowers, to decorate

1 Preheat the oven to 180°C/350°F/ Gas 4. Line four 10-hole mini cupcake tins (pans) with mini paper cases.

2 Melt the butter and chocolate in a large heatproof bowl set over a pan of just-simmering water, making sure the water does not touch the bottom of the bowl. Leave until just melted, then remove from the heat and set aside.

3 Meanwhile, place the egg yolks in a large mixing bowl or in the bowl of an electric stand mixer. Whisk on medium speed for 1 minute, then add half of the caster sugar (reserving the other half for the egg whites) and beat until light and fluffy. This will take a few minutes.

4 Scrape the yolk and sugar mixture into the chocolate and fold together gently. It should appear marbled. Do not be tempted to over-mix at this stage.

5 In a clean, dry bowl, whisk the egg whites until frothy. Add the remaining sugar and the salt, and whisk until almost-stiff peaks form. This will take a few minutes. Fold the egg whites into the chocolate mixture until just combined, and pour into the cupcake cases.

6 Bake for 10 minutes, or until the top of the cakes rise up, crack slightly, and feel firm to the touch but retain a wobble. Transfer to a wire rack to cool.

7 Meanwhile, prepare the icing. Whisk together the cocoa powder and boiling water, and set aside.

8 Beat the very soft butter at low speed for 2 minutes, then add 300g/11oz/ 2¾ cups of the icing sugar and the vanilla extract and beat to combine.

9 Add the cocoa powder and water mixture and combine, then add the melted chocolate. Cream for another 2–3 minutes on low speed. If the icing seems too soft to pipe, add the remaining icing sugar.

10 Using a piping (pastry) bag fitted with a small round nozzle, pipe a blob of icing on to each cake. Decorate with sprinkles or sugar flowers.

11 Serve immediately. These can be stored in an airtight container for up to 2 days, but they are at their best on the day they are made.

Energy 142kcal/597kJ; Protein 1g; Carbohydrate 17g, of which sugars 17g; Fat 8g, of which saturates 5g; Cholesterol 34mg; Calcium 8mg; Fibre 0g; Sodium 14mg

HAZELNUT ROCHES

Roches are essentially nut clusters held together with chocolate. What makes them so special is the texture and finish imparted by the use of cocoa butter. You will need to work quickly so that the chocolate and cocoa butter do not set before you finish forming the roches. You could experiment with other nuts and different types of chocolate, such as almond and milk chocolate, or macadamia and white chocolate.

MAKES ABOUT 24

250g/9oz hazelnuts, roughly chopped

7.5ml/1½ tsp brandy

50g/2oz/½ cup icing (confectioners') sugar

50g/2oz cocoa butter

250g/9oz dark (bittersweet) chocolate, tempered (*see* pages 56–57)

1 Preheat the oven to 180°C/350°F/ Gas 4. Line a baking tray with baking parchment and set aside.

2 Place the chopped hazelnuts in a bowl and toss with the brandy and icing sugar. Transfer the nuts to the baking parchment in a single layer, then bake for 10 minutes, tossing occasionally.

3 Melt the cocoa butter in a heatproof bowl set over a pan of barely simmering water. Temper the chocolate.

4 Put a spoonful of nuts into the empty bowl, then add 5ml/1 tsp of the cocoa butter and stir to coat the nuts. Gradually, add more nuts and more cocoa butter, and stir until about half the nuts are in the bowl and are completely coated.

5 Add a couple of tablespoons of tempered chocolate and stir to combine.

6 Place small clusters on to the prepared baking tray. Repeat the process with the remaining nuts, cocoa butter and chocolate.

7 Leave the roches to set for about 1 hour, then serve immediately or store in an airtight container for up to 1 week.

Energy 148kcal/617kJ; Protein 2g; Carbohydrate 9g, of which sugars 9g; Fat 12g, of which saturates 3g; Cholesterol 1mg; Calcium 18mg; Fibre 1g; Sodium 2mg

CHOCOLATE FRUIT AND NUT CLUSTERS

Inspired by fruit and nut chocolate bars, these fruit and nut clusters are like a little energy boost. Tossing the nuts in the brandy and icing sugar before toasting gives them a crunchy shell underneath the cocoa butter and milk chocolate. This, combined with the squidginess of the raisins, makes for a treat with a delightful texture.

4 Allow the nuts to cool slightly, then toss with the raisins.

5 Put a spoonful of the nuts and raisins into a bowl, then add 5ml/1 tsp of the cocoa butter and stir to coat. Gradually, add more nuts and raisins, and more cocoa butter, and stir until about half the nuts and raisins are in the bowl and completely coated.

6 Add a couple of tablespoons of tempered chocolate and stir to combine.

7 Place small clusters on to the prepared baking tray. Repeat the process with the remaining nuts and raisins, cocoa butter and chocolate.

8 Leave to set for about 1 hour, then serve immediately or store in an airtight container for up to 1 week.

MAKES ABOUT 24

100g/3¾oz hazelnuts, roughly chopped

75g/3oz almonds, roughly chopped

10ml/2 tsp brandy

50g/2oz/½ cup icing (confectioners') sugar

50g/2oz cocoa butter

75g/3oz/⅔ cup raisins

250g/9oz milk chocolate, tempered (*see* pages 56–57)

1 Preheat the oven to 180°C/350°F/ Gas 4. Line a baking tray with baking parchment and set it aside.

2 Place the chopped hazelnuts and almonds in a bowl and toss with the brandy and icing sugar. Transfer the nuts to the baking parchment in a single layer, then bake for 10 minutes, tossing occasionally.

3 Meanwhile, melt the cocoa butter in a heatproof bowl set over a pan of barely simmering water.

VARIATION
You could use dried cranberries in place of the raisins for a tart burst of fruity flavour.

Energy 137kcal/570kJ; Protein 2g; Carbohydrate 11g, of which sugars 11g; Fat 10g, of which saturates 3g; Cholesterol 2mg; Calcium 38mg; Fibre 1g; Sodium 12mg

CHOCOLATE COINS WITH CANDIED FRUIT

These chocolate discs are studded with little gems of cut candied fruits, and make an infinitely more sophisticated and thoughtful present than store-bought ones. They are also a great way to use up any candied fruits left over from Christmas, and can be done without tempering the chocolate, if you want to make them quickly.

MAKES ABOUT 24

50g/2oz candied fruit

200g/7oz dark (bittersweet) chocolate (64–70% cocoa solids), tempered (*see* pages 56–57)

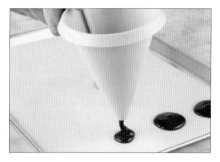

3 Put the tempered chocolate in a funnel with a catch and drop little round coins of chocolate on to the baking parchment. Alternatively, use a spoon.

4 Quickly decorate the tops with the slices of candied fruit. It may best to do this in batches, or enlist the help of someone else to add the fruit.

5 Allow the chocolate to set completely for about 1 hour, then peel the discs away from the paper, being careful not to mark them with your fingers, and place on a pretty serving dish.

6 Store in an airtight container in a cool place for up to 1 week. The candied fruit may bleed if they are refrigerated, so it is best to avoid doing this.

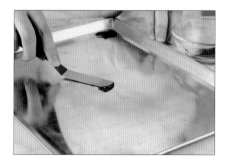

1 Line a baking sheet with baking parchment. If you smear little blobs of melted chocolate on the baking sheet the paper will stick better so you get a wrinkle-free surface.

2 Slice the candied fruit into small, attractively-shaped pieces.

Energy 49kcal/204kJ; Protein 0.4g; Carbohydrate 6.6g, of which sugars 6.2g; Fat 2.5g, of which saturates 1.4g; Cholesterol 1mg; Calcium 6mg; Fibre 0.1g; Sodium 7mg

CHOCOLATE JAZZIES

These classics are simply tempered chocolate with hundreds and thousands embedded in them. Make them in different shapes and sizes – children really love the animal shapes. Look out for fun moulds on-line or from cake decorating stores. Kids usually prefer white and milk chocolate to dark chocolate, but it's good to have an assortment.

MAKES 250G/9OZ

250g/9oz white, milk or dark (bittersweet) chocolate, tempered (*see* pages 56–57), or a mixture of all 3 types

hundreds and thousands (rainbow sprinkles)

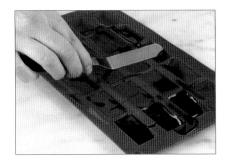

1 Pour the tempered chocolate into clean, dry moulds. Use a different mould for each type of chocolate, if you are using more than one.

2 Use an offset spatula to scrape any excess chocolate off the top to give a neat finish.

3 Tap the moulds on a work surface to release any air that may be trapped in the chocolate.

4 Generously sprinkle the moulds with the hundreds and thousands and leave them to set for a few hours.

5 Tap to release the chocolates, then turn out and serve immediately, or store in an airtight container in a cool place for up to 1 week.

Energy 1300kcal/5443kJ; Protein 19g; Carbohydrate 142g, of which sugars 142g; Fat 77g, of which saturates 46g; Cholesterol 58mg; Calcium 550mg; Fibre 0g; Sodium 213mg

CHOCOLATE TUILES

Light and crisp, these make the perfect accompaniment to ice cream or chocolate mousse. You can pipe them into shapes or bend them while they are still hot, or leave them in long flat strips. You could also form them into the first letters of people's names to add a personal touch to a special dessert.

MAKES 20–30

125g/4¼oz/generous ½ cup butter, softened, plus extra for greasing

100g/3¾oz/scant 1 cup plain (all-purpose) flour, plus extra for dusting

125g/4¼oz/scant ¾ cup caster (superfine) sugar

3 egg whites

25g/1oz/¼ cup unsweetened cocoa powder

icing (confectioners') sugar, for dusting

1 Grease a baking sheet and dust it with flour. Preheat the oven to 180°C/350°F/Gas 4.

2 Cream the butter and sugar until light and fluffy. Add the egg whites and whisk until fully incorporated.

3 Sift the flour and cocoa powder into the mixture and fold in with a rubber spatula or metal spoon. Try not to over-mix the batter or it will become tough.

4 Using a piping (pastry) bag fitted with a large round nozzle, pipe the mixture into shapes (or use moulds to create shapes). Bake for 6–8 minutes, until they are just golden.

5 To shape them, immediately wrap them around the handle of a wooden spoon, then slide them off on to a wire rack. Be quick – they start to set as soon as you remove them from the oven.

6 Serve immediately, dusted with icing sugar, or store in an airtight container for up to 3 days.

VARIATION
You can make these without cocoa powder by using more plain (all-purpose) flour instead of the cocoa.

Energy 62kcal/260kJ; Protein 0.8g; Carbohydrate 7g, of which sugars 4.4g; Fat 3.6g, of which saturates 2.4g; Cholesterol 10mg; Calcium 9mg; Fibre 0.2g; Sodium 46mg

CHOCOLATE ICE CREAM CONES

There is something magical about the smell of ice cream cones cooking on a hot pan. It is easy to whip up this batter and have it in the refrigerator to pull out after supper or on a hot summer's day. If you need to make these ahead of time, be sure to store them in an airtight container. They are best eaten when they are fresh, and the theatre of making them is fun for friends to watch.

MAKES 6 STANDARD CONES
OR 10 SMALL CONES

2 eggs, at room temperature

90g/3½oz/½ cup caster (superfine) sugar

60g/2½oz/5 tbsp unsalted butter, melted and cooled

45ml/3 tbsp milk

2.5ml/½ tsp vanilla extract

40g/1½oz/⅓ cup plain (all-purpose) flour, sifted

10g/½oz/2 tbsp unsweetened cocoa powder

a pinch of salt

vegetable oil, for greasing

1 Whisk the eggs and sugar in a large bowl for 5 minutes, until pale and frothy.

2 Add the melted butter, milk and vanilla and whisk briefly to combine. Sift in the flour, cocoa powder and salt, and whisk until smooth. Transfer the batter to a jug (pitcher). Leave to rest for about 1 hour.

3 Heat a special ice cream cone iron or a heavy frying pan and brush the surface with oil.

4 Ladle a little batter (less than you think) on to it to form a circle, and heat for 1–2 minutes, or until just beginning to steam.

5 Flip the circle with a spatula and cook the other side for 1 minute.

6 Immediately remove the circle using the spatula and wrap it around a conical mould, or form the circle into a cone shape using your hands.

7 Pinch the end to seal securely and set aside on a wire rack to cool completely.

8 Repeat the process with the rest of the batter. Fill the cones with ice cream and serve immediately. If the cones go soft, place them in a hot oven for a few minutes and re-shape them.

VARIATIONS
• For a fun twist, dip the edge of the cones in melted chocolate, then dip the chocolate into hundreds and thousands (rainbow sprinkles).
• For a more decadent version, spread the circle with melted chocolate before forming the circle into a cone shape, with the chocolate layer on the inside.
• For plain cones, omit the unsweetened cocoa powder and use 50g/2oz/½ cup flour instead.

Energy 118kcal/497kJ; Protein 2g; Carbohydrate 13g, of which sugars 10g; Fat 7g, of which saturates 4g; Cholesterol 61mg; Calcium 21mg; Fibre 0g; Sodium 30mg

DOUBLE CHOCOLATE-COATED STRAWBERRIES

Classic and classy, these elegant treats are extremely simple to make but look very impressive for a special occasion. Try to use the best quality strawberries when they are in season. They should be ripe but quite firm – if they are too moist they will not work as well. You could make this recipe with other fruits, such as raspberries, cherries or wedges of peach or nectarine.

MAKES ABOUT 300G/11OZ

200g/7oz fresh, ripe strawberries

50g/2oz white chocolate, tempered (*see* pages 56–57)

50g/2oz dark chocolate, tempered (*see* pages 56–57)

1 Line a baking sheet with baking parchment and set it aside.

2 Wash the strawberries by dipping them briefly in a bowl of cold water. Do not soak them or they will absorb too much water.

3 Lay the berries out on a few layers of kitchen paper or a clean dish towel to dry. Dab them with additional towels to remove all water. Using a small sharp pair of scissors, trim away any brown stems or leaves, but leave pretty leaves on.

4 Place the tempered chocolates in two separate bowls. Dip the berries in dark chocolate, holding them by the stem.

5 Drag the berries gently along the side of the bowl to remove any excess chocolate before placing the dipped berries on the lined baking sheet.

6 Once the chocolate has set, dip the tips of the berries into the white chocolate. Place on the baking sheet to set.

7 Allow the chocolate to set completely before serving. The berries will start to weep moisture as they sit, so they should be used within a few hours.

VARIATION
If you need to take a shortcut, you do not have to temper the chocolate. Tempering gives the chocolate its beautiful finish and smooth texture, but it is not essential here. If you want to make these quickly, simply melt the chocolate over a pan of barely simmering water and continue with the recipe.

Energy 574kcal/2401kJ; Protein 8g; Carbohydrate 73g, of which sugars 72g; Fat 30g, of which saturates 18g; Cholesterol 3mg; Calcium 184mg; Fibre 4g; Sodium 70mg

Mini Lamingtons

These delicious cakes are a favourite treat in Australia, and are quickly gaining popularity in the UK. The test of a true lamington is in the texture of the sponge. It must be moist and fluffy, but incredibly light. The chocolate glaze is also very important. Many recipes call for cocoa, but the flavour is immeasurably better when real dark chocolate is used. The furry coconut coating brings it all together.

MAKES 12–15

butter, for greasing

3 eggs

100g/3¾oz/generous ½ cup caster (superfine) sugar

100g/3¾oz/scant 1 cup self-raising (self-rising) flour

35g/1½oz/⅓ cup cornflour (cornstarch)

15g/½oz/1 tbsp butter, melted

45ml/3 tbsp hot water

300g/11oz/scant 3 cups desiccated (dry unsweetened shredded) coconut

FOR THE ICING:

15g/½oz/1 tbsp butter

375g/13oz/3¼ cups icing (confectioners') sugar, sifted

150g/5oz dark (bittersweet) chocolate (55% cocoa solids), chopped

90ml/6 tbsp milk

1 Preheat the oven to 160°C/325°F/Gas 3. Grease a 20 x 30cm/8 x 12in cake tin (pan) and line with baking parchment.

2 For the cake, use an electric whisk to beat the eggs until they begin to froth. Add the sugar, and beat until light and fluffy.

3 Sift in the flour and cornflour and fold in with a rubber spatula or metal spoon.

4 Combine the melted butter and hot water in a jug (pitcher) and fold into the cake mixture.

5 Pour into the prepared tin and bake for 25–30 minutes, until just set and coming away slightly from the edge of the tin.

6 Allow to cool in the tin for 10 minutes before turning the cake out on to a wire rack to cool completely. Cut the cake into 12–15 pieces.

7 Put the coconut in a wide, shallow dish and set aside.

8 Place all of the icing ingredients in a heatproof bowl set over a pan of barely simmering water. Whisk constantly to make an emulsified icing. Turn off the heat, leaving the bowl over the hot water.

9 Use a dipping fork to dip each cake into the icing. Wipe the bottom of the cake along the edge of the bowl to remove excess icing. Gently place the dipped cake into the coconut and turn to coat.

10 Place on a wire rack and leave to set for 15 minutes. Serve immediately, or store in an airtight container for 3 days.

Energy 365kcal/1530kJ; Protein 4.1g; Carbohydrate 48.7g, of which sugars 40.9g; Fat 18.4g, of which saturates 13.9g; Cholesterol 48mg; Calcium 53mg; Fibre 2.9g; Sodium 46mg

CHOCOLATE CRACK COOKIES

These little cookies are bites of gooey cake with an icing sugar shell. The ground almonds give the flavour more depth, and the rum packs a punch to make these a truly decadent treat. They are great as a gift or as a grown-up snack. The name is given to them because of their cracked appearance, which is caused by baking them with the icing sugar coating, which cracks as the cookie bakes.

MAKES 900G/2LB

525g/1lb 5oz dark (bittersweet) or plain (semisweet) chocolate

90g/4oz/½ cup unsalted butter

4 eggs

150g/5oz/¾ cup caster (superfine) sugar, plus extra for rolling

45ml/3 tbsp rum

185g/6½oz/1⅔ cups ground almonds

130g/4½oz plain/generous 1 cup (all-purpose) flour

7.5ml/1½ tsp baking powder

2.5ml/½ tsp salt

icing (confectioners') sugar, for rolling

1 Melt the chocolate and butter in a heatproof bowl set over a pan of barely simmering water, stirring occasionally. Set the bowl aside to cool slightly.

2 In an electric stand mixer or in a mixing bowl using a handheld whisk, beat the eggs and sugar for 5 minutes until thick and foamy. Add the rum, then add the slightly cooled chocolate.

3 In another large bowl, stir the almonds, flour, baking powder and salt together.

4 Pour the chocolate mixture into the dry ingredients and stir to combine. Chill in the refrigerator for at least 2 hours.

5 Scoop teaspoonfuls of the mixture and roll them into balls. Place on a sheet of baking parchment. Line two baking trays with baking parchment.

6 Put the caster sugar and icing sugar in two small bowls. Roll the dough balls first in caster sugar then in icing sugar. Place on the prepared baking trays and chill again for about 30 minutes.

7 Preheat the oven to 180°C/350°F/ Gas 4. Roll the balls once more in icing sugar, then bake for 8–10 minutes until the surface is cracked and they are just set. Take care not to overcook them – the centres should be gooey.

8 Leave to cool slightly before serving. Store in an airtight container for up to 3 days.

Energy 5984kcal/25072kJ; Protein 109g; Carbohydrate 607g, of which sugars 496g; Fat 352g, of which saturates153g; Cholesterol 1166mg; Calcium 1040mg; Fibre 29g; Sodium 2111mg

INDEX

Acknowledgements

The publishers would like to thank the following for permission to reproduce their images (t = top, b = bottom, l = left, r = right and m = middle): 8b and 8t Alinari/Bridgeman Art Library; 9b Bonhams, London, UK/Bridgeman Art Library; 9t The Stapleton Collection/ Bridgeman Art Library; 10l, 10r, 11l, 11r, 13l, 13m, 13r, 16l, 16r and 17 istockphoto; 12 Tom Gardner/Alamy; 14l Museo de America, Madrid, Spain/ Bridgeman Art Library; 14r Archives Charmet/Bridgeman Art Library; 15 Mary Evans Picture Library/Alamy.